# The Journalism of
# MILENA JESENSKÁ

# The Journalism of
# MILENA JESENSKÁ

## A Critical Voice in Interwar Central Europe

Edited and translated from the Czech,
and with an Introduction by
*Kathleen Hayes*

*Berghahn Books*
New York • Oxford

First published in 2003 by **Berghahn Books**
www.BerghahnBooks.com

**Library of Congress Cataloging-in-Publication Data**
Jesenská, Milena, 1896-1944.
  The journalism of Milena Jesenská / edited and translated from
the Czech, and with an introduction by Kathleen Hayes.
    p. cm.
  Contents: Articles from Tribuna, 1920-1922 -- Articles from
Národní listy and Lidové noviny.
  1922-1929 -- Articles from Přítomnost, 1938-1939.
  ISBN 1-57181-560-0 (alk. paper)
    I. Hayes, Kathleen. II. Title.

PN5355.C95 Z7659468 2002
891.8'6452--dc21
                                              2002066600

**British Library Cataloguing in Publication Data**
A catalogue record for this book is available from the British Library
Printed in the United States on acid-free paper
ISBN 1-57181-560-0 hardback

# Contents

## I. Articles from *Tribuna*, 1920–1922

## II. Articles from *Národní listy* and *Lidové noviny*, 1922–1929

# Acknowledgements

My thanks are due, first and foremost, to Marie Jirásková, who kindly put me in touch with Jesenská's relations, offered criticism of the proposal and lent photographs from her archive. The consultations with Dr Jirásková, who has written an account of Jesenská's life during the war and compiled a bibliography of her articles, were invaluable. I would also like to thank the members of staff, in particular Mrs Králová, at the Newspaper Archive of the National Museum in Prague for their assistance over the past few years. A number of people generously gave up hours of their time reading drafts and answering queries: Jan Holub, Radek Honzák, Tomáš Míka and Kristin Olson. Henry Knight provided me with material that I did not have access to in Prague. I am grateful to Robert B. Pynsent, in particular, for his detailed criticism and suggestions. I could not have completed the project without the help of these people and the support of family and friends.

This translation is published with the permission of Jesenská's relations. The photographs are published with the permission of Marie Jirásková, the Jílovská family, the Institute for Art History of the Academy of Sciences of the Czech Republic and the Museum of Czech Literature, Prague.

# A Note on the Text

The texts translated here represent a limited selection of the more than one thousand articles that Milena Jesenská wrote over the course of her career. In making this selection, I tried to choose articles that would be of interest from literary and historical perspectives, as well as those that indicated the diversity of subjects treated by Jesenská. Some of the articles were first published in newspapers and later, slightly altered, in book collections; the translations are based on the earlier versions. The article 'The Curse of Outstanding Qualities', here included in the *Národní listy* and *Lidové noviny* section, was first published in Jesenská's collection *Cesta k jednoduchosti* (The Path to Simplicity, Prague, 1926). All italicised words in the translations, except for foreign-language words, indicate emphasis in the original texts. I was fortunate to have the opportunity to consult the translations, usually of excerpts of articles, that appeared in various English biographies of Jesenská, as well as those that appeared in Philip Boehm's translation of Kafka's *Letters to Milena*.

# Introduction

## *Between the Wars*

The publication of Franz Kafka's letters to Milena Jesenská in 1952 established the myth of Milena, the 'living fire' as Kafka described her, in the imagination of the public.[1] Her letters to him were lost. Biographies and a few collections of Jesenská's newspaper articles gradually filled out the contours of this myth. A portrait of an unusual person emerged, one whose life was emblematic of a generation that came of age at the end of the First World War and saw its ideals destroyed by the Second World War.[2]

Jesenská was born in Prague on 10 August 1896, at a time when the Austro-Hungarian Empire was plagued by nationality conflicts.[3] She studied at the Minerva, the first grammar school for girls in the monarchy, opened in 1890. It was probably largely because of her education that she rejected the traditional role of mother and housewife, which defined the place of women in Czech society at that time. She took it for granted that the world of culture and employment was open to her. Her mother, Milena *née* Hejzlarová, who might have provided a counterbalancing conservative role model, died in 1913 when Jesenská was sixteen.

Jesenská's adolescence was more tumultuous than most, acted out in rebellion against her father, Jan Jesenský (1870–1947), a professor of dentistry. She rejected his Czech nationalism and anti-Semitism, cultivating acquaintances in German and Jewish circles in a city that was divided along ethnic lines. According to various testimonies, she spent her father's money freely and experimented with drugs that she stole from his clinic. It is rumoured that she had an abortion.[4] In June 1917, her father had her committed to the Veleslavín psychiatric clinic. This was probably his last attempt to put an end to his daughter's relationship with the Jew Ernst Pollak (1886–1947). In spite of her father's disapproval, Jesenská married Pollak in March 1918 upon her release from Veleslavín and the couple moved to Vienna.

Her new life in Vienna could hardly have been less idyllic. Pollak's infidelities put a strain on their marriage. Jesenská had no close friends in the city and she felt out of place in Pollak's jaded social circle. She was also isolated by language; to begin with, her command of German was not perfect. As her husband's salary could not support them both in the inflation-ridden city, Jesenská began to submit articles and translations to newspapers and journals in Prague. It was at this time that she became acquainted with Franz Kafka (1883–1924): she wrote to him, probably in the autumn of 1919, asking for permission to translate his work. The daily correspondence with Kafka lasted until the fall of 1920. He ended the relationship when he became convinced that she would not leave her husband. They saw each other several more times, but exchanged only a few more letters before Kafka's death.

Throughout the 1920s, Jesenská continued to contribute regularly to Prague newspapers (*Tribuna*, *Národní listy* and *Lidové noviny*). She was best known for her pieces written for the Women's Page of these newspapers: articles about fashion, interior design and social issues. Two collections of her articles were published, as well as a collection of recipes, which had been sent to her by readers.[5] She also worked as a translator and editor. In 1925, she divorced Pollak and moved back to Prague, where she made friends among the intellectual avant-garde. In April 1927, she married Jaromír Krejcar (1895–1949), 'the most important architect among Czech functionalists of the twenties'.[6] On 14 August 1928, she gave birth to a daughter, whom she called by the male name of Honza (1928–1981).

While still pregnant, Jesenská suffered health problems that left her with a limp for the rest of her life. The history of these problems is not quite clear. She broke her leg skiing in the spring of 1928. She recovered, but later in the summer she became critically ill, diagnosed with septicaemia. According to another account, she had ankylosis of the knee, probably caused by gonorrhoea.[7] She became addicted to the painkiller morphine and continued to suffer from addictions throughout the 1930s. She lost her job as a regular columnist for *Lidové noviny* and earned a meagre living translating and working for left-leaning newspapers and journals (*Tvorba*, *Svět práce*, *Právo lidu*). She joined the Communist Party. In 1933, Krejcar left to work in the Soviet Union; their marriage ended formally in 1934. Jesenská's last partner was Evžen Klinger (1906–1982), a Hungarian Jew from Slovakia and communist functionary whom she later helped to flee the country.

In 1937, Jesenská began to contribute to the respected liberal weekly *Přítomnost*; her articles treated the political crises in Czechoslovakia on the eve of the Second World War. Following the *Anschluss* in March 1938, the Sudeten German Party (*Sudetendeutsche Partei*) of Konrad Henlein (1898–1945) in Czechoslovakia openly declared its Nazi orientation and the German national minority stepped up its demand for union with the Reich. Under pressure from Hitler, Chamberlain and Daladier, the Czechoslovak government ceded a third of the territory and a third of the population of Bohemia and Moravia to Germany, in the Munich Agreement of 30 September 1938. President Edvard Beneš (1884–1948) resigned on 5 October and a new president, Emil Hácha (1872–1945), was appointed. The Second Czecho-Slovak Republic, governed by Prime Minister Rudolf Beran (1887–1954), was short-lived. On 15 March 1939, the Germans occupied the country, creating the Protectorate of Bohemia and Moravia, with Baron von Neurath (1873–1956) appointed Reich Protector.

Although she helped others to emigrate, Jesenská remained in Prague and continued to write for *Přítomnost*. When the editor-in-chief, Ferdinand Peroutka (1895–1978), was arrested, she assumed his editorial duties. The last issue of *Přítomnost* was published on 30 August 1939. Jesenská also worked for the underground resistance group *Obrana národa* (Defence of the Nation), which, among other things, helped people to flee the country, crossing to Poland or Yugoslavia.[8] She helped to distribute and probably also wrote for the underground journal *V boj* (Into the Fight). Arrested on 12 November 1939, she was put on trial in Dresden. The charges against her were dropped for lack of evidence, but the Gestapo nonetheless kept her in custody. She was sent to Ravensbrück concentration camp. There she became close friends with Margarete Buber-Neumann (1901–1989), who later wrote a biography of Jesenská, describing her as 'an unbroken spirit, a free woman in the midst of the insulted and injured.'[9] Jesenská died in the camp on 17 May 1944.

## Post-war Vienna

At first glance, one is struck by the incongruous extremes in Jesenská's life: the rebellious adolescence; the stint in the psychiatric clinic; the arrests for theft;[10] the successful career as a fashion columnist, despite her alleged lack of interest in clothes; the attraction to communism; the rejection of communism; self-sacrifice in resistance to the German occupation. When one looks closely at Jesenská's writing, however, one discovers that these incongruities were only apparent. The themes that she chose to write about and the outlook that she expressed were strongly influenced by her experience of the First World War and remained surprisingly consistent over the twenty years of her career.

The impact of the war is most apparent in the articles that she wrote at the beginning of her career, when she was contributing to

*Tribuna* from Vienna. She was interested in the novelties of the era, including film and advertisements.[11] Many of her articles, however, treat the tangible financial problems of the residents of the city. Criticism of the inequities of the capitalist system recurred in her writing, which was characterised by a certain moralising tone and by empathy for the poor.

In June 1921, she published an article entitled 'A Dream. "Any where – out of the world"', which consisted of an account of a nightmare. While the horror that it expressed was personal, it also reflected her experience of post-war Vienna. She wrote about war breaking out all over the globe:

> I did not hear anything definite about the catastrophe. Only the mad rush and haste and distress drove me too to flee. Where we were fleeing, I did not know. I did not even find out why we were fleeing. Endless trains, one after another, departed from the station, going out into the world, all of them overcrowded. Panic gripped the railway employees; no one wanted to be last. People fought desperately for seats. Endless crowds of people blocked my way to the platform; there was no hope I would ever push through them. I was overwhelmed by despair.[12]

She was given a ticket and told that it would take her over the border. Yet she was disturbed by the thought that she would escape while thousands of others waited: 'But the malice in my heart replied: "But after all, don't you hope to save yourself?"/ "Well yes, perhaps, after all," I thought./ And the heart: "But isn't a person who finds salvation base?"'[13] In the dream, the departure of the train heralded the catastrophe. The earth collapsed into a void and the world was transformed into a network of railroads over which people who had lost their homes travelled. At the border, she was stopped by a customs official. When she took out her ticket and unfolded it, she discovered that it contained the message: 'Condemned to death.'

For Jesenská, trains and technology in general were symbolic of the new era. She wrote: 'The very fact that a person has made a machine, a kind of monster over which, as soon as he has finished it and set it in motion, he loses full control and cannot even prevent it from killing him, that in itself is a heroism requiring as much courage as the crusaders had'.[14] 'Before a machine,' she wrote, 'a locomotive, a viaduct or an airship, I am always oppressed by a mysterious, humble dread; I think that the new century of techni-cal inventions will bring with it new fairytales. [...] I do not know what they will be like.'[15]

References to trains and railway stations recur in her articles about Vienna. In 'Dance over the Abyss', she wrote about the contrast between the rich and poor travellers who alternated on the Vienna train platforms.[16] In 'Children in Vienna', she described the women who took the train several stations out of the city to exchange soap and kerosene for food from the villagers. She also described poor children who travelled by train to other countries in Europe to spend the summer with more privileged families who had agreed to look after them.[17] The lives of these children were marked by the war and post-war poverty: 'They are shameless, insolent, accustomed to using curses in order to get a place in the queue at the grocer's, at the coal-merchant's, at the baker's, on the tram, at the railway station. They are extortionists – like everyone today – and demand a shameless sum for the services they provide: for errands, washing dishes, shopping. They are gloomy and unhappy, mentally stunted and yet as independent as adults. They are creatures deprived by God of their naïvete.'[18] Later in her career, the motif of trains reappeared in her writing, once again as an image of the horror of the times: 'It seems that there is only one route left for Viennese Jews: from the Westbahnhof to Dachau. Every week in the early hours of the morning a train stands on the rails, carrying Viennese Jews to a concentration camp. Eight carriages, one man beside the next. They sit next to one another, shoulder to shoulder, heads resting against the seats, hands motionless in their laps, faces as if they had been carved. They sit thus in numb despair for five, six hours, until the train moves.'[19]

Jesenská came from an affluent family and had not lacked for money in her childhood. In Vienna, however, she found herself scrounging food and fuel.[20] The acquaintances from her intellectual circle also suffered on account of poverty; she wrote of their plight in 'Former Idyll – Present-day Drama'.[21] Because of the extreme inflation, all one's energy, she wrote, was devoted to attending to the basic needs. People succumbed under this pressure, finding relief in alcohol, cocaine and morphine.[22] A note of despair informs her descriptions of everyday life: 'Can one today punish a thief, a drunkard, a murderer or a fanatic by the normal means when there is not a single normal day in the life of that person? And can one wonder at all that everything everywhere is in a state of degeneration and apathy, that there is no interest, effort or enthusiasm anywhere? An empty stomach, shattered nerves and a numb, heavy head absorb all existence and there is no time, strength, desire or even hope left for the mind.'[23]

This environment nourished her enthusiasm for social justice. In December 1920, in addition to articles about the presents readers should buy for Christmas, she also published an article about beggars, urging people to give generously.[24] She stated that she did not know by what means poverty would be eradicated – socialism, communism, charity, or hard work – but for the moment, the only solution was to give blindly, without asking why or how the money would be used. Considering the circumstances in Vienna, the extravagances of the rich and the deals on the black market were immoral. 'Medicine that one cannot buy anywhere in Vienna,' she wrote, 'passes through these hands [in the black-market cafés] and continues on immediately to countries with a stronger currency, medicine for lack of which people in hospitals and sanatoriums are suffering and perhaps even dying.'[25] Elsewhere, she interpreted the drive to accumulate wealth and to make a display of success as the outcome of privation.[26]

Throughout the 1920s, Jesenská used her fashion column to criticise the privileges of the rich. In 'Greenhouses for Live Plants', she described the unreal world of luxury in which rich children grew up. She argued that simplicity and thrift created a healthy environment for children and claimed that it was a good thing there were not many rich and indulgent mothers in the world.[27] The lives of the rich lacked diversity and adventure.[28] She criticised expensive new fashions and stated that they only served the financial goals of the leading firms.[29] She advised readers to refrain from buying expensive dresses that they would wear only a few times and to spend their money instead on practical items for the household.[30] She urged them to remain firm in the struggle against the great French fashion companies, to be satisfied with the clothes they had bought the year before, rather than buy new, showy, expensive and impractical garments.[31]

Jesenská argued that the terrible experiences of the war had given rise to a new culture of thrift, simplicity and health. This new culture found its fashion ideal in the 'democratic' and practical products of America, which enabled every man to look like a gentleman. (It is characteristic that she made reference to men. She believed that liberating fashions for women imitated the designs of clothes for men.) The older generation, she wrote in 'The Trenchcoat, or Ten-in-One', might have difficulty accepting the new ideal:

> But the robust young boys who lived through the war will welcome it. In the war, they learned about a terribly painful simplification, in comparison with which every simplicity of civilisation seems like an enormous luxury. Face to face with the simplicity of war, they sealed in their hearts the humility of those who have once looked upon death and by chance survived. Those who are even younger absorbed this atmosphere of robust humility in the newly liberated world. They

converted it into a kind of sports training, a joyful hardiness and a manly perseverance. They will seize hold of the new American coat with joy and exultation – it's just what they have been waiting for![32]

According to her, the era challenged people to seek simplicity and balance in every aspect of their lives, from clothing to personal relationships. People were obliged to reject outdated styles, in architecture and dress, just as they were obliged to reject outdated concepts and social conventions. 'There is no time for nonsense,' she wrote, in 'Painted Clothes'.[33] In 'Fashion and the Standard Ideal', she wrote: 'The present age, which mocks luxury and all that is extraneous, requires people to think clearly and for their own benefit.'[34] She identified a modern approach with progress, rather than with novelty. Cinema, she claimed, was more modern than theatre because it was accessible to more people.[35] For Jesenská, modernity had a political dimension: it was linked with democracy. For this reason, she almost always praised America in her articles as a land where there was social and political equality, manifest also as a striving for efficiency in dress and management of the household.[36]

## Simplicity: on the Inside and on the Outside

In 'Adolescent Girls', Jesenská wrote: 'It is a coincidence that there are pictures of clothes above and below [this article]. To be honest – and perhaps you will have noticed this already – clothes do not interest me at all. What attracts me is the culture of the individual. That certain human expression – the expression of the culture of the soul that people wear in their faces and leave traces of in everything they do.'[37] Jesenská's articles about clothes, accessories and interior design usually began with a long introduction, explaining the appropriate outlook on the matter at hand, followed by a few brief comments on the items to be purchased. She was an arbiter of taste, but she did not simply want to advise her readers what colours or cuts to buy. Rather, she wanted to explain to them why they should cultivate this kind of taste, why this taste was the only acceptable and modern option. She wanted to convey an outlook to her readers and thus most of her articles have a proselytising tone. In 'For Tennis', she wrote: 'When the slogan "Sport for a healthy body" was taken up, a struggle was declared against the sophistication, the extreme intellectual complexity, the melancholy and gravity, which characterised that generation's outlook on life. Movement in the open air, close contact with nature, open windows and hardy muscles brought a cure for the people of the

post-war years, who all needed to shore up the split within themselves.'[38] Throughout the 1920s, she promoted this cult of health,
hygiene and exercise, the origins of which actually predated the
war. In an article from 1923, for example, Jesenská argued that there
were two kinds of human wisdom: that which originated in the
brain; and that which originated in the body. She stated that only
the second kind of wisdom was 'positive, joyful and useful in life';
a brain that was trained led one to grief, while a body that was
trained brought one joy.[39]

She later modified this view. While she asserted that '[h]ealthy
people are more honourable, upright and vigorous than sick
people', she nonetheless held that the 'nerves of the body and
mind' were linked inextricably.[40] It was a mistake, she claimed, to
cultivate the body exclusively because the greatest delight in life
was the delight of the mind. By 1930, Jesenská had come to believe
that the cult of the body, sport and nature had gone too far. This
change in attitude probably reflected her experience of illness. In
1929, in an article about dressing-gowns, she wrote:

> I think that only a woman who has once fallen seriously ill has a real,
> expensive and luxurious dressing-gown. [...] On the day when the doctor
> gives permission to leave the bed, a member of the family, who has been
> at the invalid's bedside the whole time, arrives with a beautiful new
> dressing-gown. Such a dressing-gown sanctifies the first depression,
> when the person sees that from her waist down she has mysterious
> useless sticks that do not bear their own weight and do not walk, when
> she feels that never in her life will she make the five steps across the
> room to the window.[41]

Jesenská's approach to fashion was determined by her belief in the
importance of a healthy, physically fit body. 'Good clothes' were
those that supported the healthy growth of the body and did not
hinder movement. 'Bad clothes' were those that prevented one
from moving freely and comfortably.[42] Dress and shoes should be
practical, functional. For this reason, she criticised French fashion,
which she regarded as extravagant. In 'French Suits', she wrote: 'I
am not saying that it is not pretty. On the contrary, perhaps very
beautiful. It is only that it is such an illogical, unnecessary and
purely luxurious style of dress that it justifies all the jokes about
and allusions to women's finery. Beautiful attire is a praiseworthy
cultural accomplishment. A measure of social development. An
expression of inner nobility. Fancy attire is an ugly redundance of
indolent, superfluous people.'[43]

One's clothes and appearance were a sign of character. Finery and
ostentation revealed a degenerate character. Jesenská criticised all

manifestations of useless ornamentation. In an article about good and bad designs of book-plates, she argued that the aesthetic aspect of an item should be subordinate to the function and logic of that item. When the decoration did not support the function, but rather concealed or disrupted it, the decoration was bad, 'giving evidence of incorrect thinking, an uneconomical and unbalanced outlook on the world.'[44] In 'The Romanticism of Desks', she attacked elaborate signatures: 'In the offices sit people who, when they sign their names, wave their hands in the air for a long time, working up to the signature. And when they finally get going, they write their names down on paper in tiny, spidery, decorative lines and finish it with a cascade of spidery curves. Such people are probably meticulous and tyrannical, bourgeois pedants, respectful towards their superiors, rude towards their subordinates.'[45]

The description recalls the portrait of the officer in Kafka's 'In the Penal Colony' (*In der Strafkolonie*, 1919) and the description of the execution machine that carved a judgement in elegant swirls onto the body of the condemned man. Mark Anderson, in his *Kafka's Clothes* (1992), has argued that Kafka was influenced by the aesthetic espoused by Adolf Loos (1870–1933), who identified ornament with degeneration. This aesthetic also informed Jesenská's views on style. Most likely she was familiar with the essay by Loos, 'Ornament and Crime' (*Ornament und Verbrechen*); at any rate, a Czech translation of it was published in *Tribuna* when she was still contributing to that newspaper.[46] Loos' architectural work constituted a link between pre-war Vienna and the Czech Purist-Functionalist architecture of the 1920s, the aesthetic of which was promoted by Jesenská in her fashion column.[47] That Jesenská was well acquainted with the tenets of Functionalism is indicated by the four articles she wrote on the *Deutscher Werkbund* housing exhibition, which she visited in Stuttgart in 1927.[48] Jesenská had espoused this aesthetic of simplicity from the beginning of her career. Even in her first fashion article, for example, on underwear, she wrote: 'the simplest is prettiest, as few ribbons as possible and then only where they are functional'.[49] In Functionalism she recognised an aesthetic that appealed to her sensibilities, outlined in hundreds of articles about clothes and items of everyday use.

The simplification of one's attire and the cultivation of a healthy, hardy body, were not, for Jesenská, goals in themselves, but rather external aspects of the striving to improve one's character. The insistence on the need for self-improvement was a more fundamental and lasting aspect of her credo than was the claim that the wisdom of the body was superior to the wisdom of the mind. Jesenská repeatedly stressed in her articles that the contemporary ideal of physical beauty had nothing to do with true beauty. In 'A Beautiful Woman', she wrote: 'Beauty is not something physical. Beauty is not a gift from God. Beauty is a personal merit. The harmonious face of a Madonna can be distinctly unpleasant; and the most unattractive face can be miraculous. There is no division between body and soul. A person is not physically ugly and spiritually beautiful, or vice versa. A person is one, a person is whole.'[50] Likewise, ugliness was not, according to her, a physical quality. Rather, she wrote: 'only awkwardness is ugly, ridiculousness and insatiable vanity'.[51] She believed that people looked ridiculous when they did not recognise their own physical shortcomings.[52] One had to look at oneself critically. Most importantly, one had to strive to be a better person:

> Perhaps everything that is required of an individual and perhaps the highest degree of bravery and self-improvement can be expressed by the phrase: to take one's place among the rest. That means that one has to do exactly the opposite of what nature has done and to refine exactly the opposite of what has been given to one by nature. That means that one has to cultivate in oneself everything that makes one a good companion for all the others and to allow to wither away everything that drives one to pursue one's own good at the expense of the common good.[53]

Style was not only an expression of personality, but also of morality.

## Women and Fashion

Jesenská's fashion column was almost exclusively addressed to women readers; her advice on clothing promoted an image of the new modern woman. For Jesenská, the clearest sign of progress in fashion was the adoption of masculine styles of dress for women. Men's clothes were, according to her, simple, elegant and practical. By dressing like men, women were claiming the freedoms that previously only men had enjoyed. Women's clothes restricted movement; they were awkward and Jesenská had associated awkwardness with ugliness, unnaturalness. In an article from 1920, she gave advice about outfits that women should wear when bicycling:

> For women, riding a bicycle is a rather tasteless affair; the regular movement of the knees and thighs is not the most attractive. But this, too, depends entirely on you! If you are transformed into a boy, if you wear trousers, a shirt and a cap, you will completely lose that dull awkwardness that a skirt gives to the movement of the knees. It is a great error

to think that a skirt is more proper than trousers. Perhaps it is more common (one has to add: among Czechs); perhaps boys will even run after you in some village and shout if you cross the village green wearing trousers and some old woman will be startled and spit at you – but really that is all.[54]

The simplicity of men's clothing also suited a working woman, 'who is always in a hurry and needs something that she can throw on before she rushes off'.[55] 'The independent, boyish woman of our times needs clothes in which she can move freely,' wrote Jesenská.[56]

In an article about hairstyles, she argued that short boyish haircuts were comfortable and more hygienic than the long hair of their mothers. 'Now no one will ever stop this transformation of our lives from closed spaces to rooms with wide-open windows, to fresh air, water, exercise and health.'[57] The inconvenience of long hair, which Jesenská associated with the shy, convent-educated girls of the previous generation, did not suit the active, sporting life of modern women.[58]

Aside from being practical, a masculine style of dress represented a better world for women. She commented that, 'as soon as a person puts on a pair of trousers, the world is twice as beautiful'.[59] Writing about the trench-coat, Jesenská commented that the same article of clothing was appropriate for women as well as for men: 'This coat belongs to you, just as the whole world belongs to you, with all the new and good things that it has invented for you.'[60] A modest, more masculine attire was also appropriate because a modern woman did not want to be decorative. In 'We Won't Give In', she wrote:

> We have known for a long time now that fashion is nonsense. We are not interested in being fashionable, urbane women; we are interested in having good and useful clothing. We have lots of worries and little money. We have a serious relationship to life and we do not exaggerate the importance of outfits at the expense of other pleasures. We have an understanding of exercise and health, hygienic attire and simplicity. We are losing the predilection for useless decorativeness and we have adopted this slogan not only for clothes, but also for all outward forms of life.[61]

She advised women to avoid wearing makeup and to dress modestly for work: shoes with low heels and skirts of a decent length. A woman who wore a short skirt and a low-cut blouse for work behind a typewriter was vulgar, in her opinion.[62] In an article entitled 'Decorative Object?', which was published under a drawing of silk evening-dresses, Jesenská argued that working girls and mothers did not have the time to be decorative. Her rhetorical question reveals her understanding of the duty of the individual to the community: 'Who can solve this difficult riddle? Which woman is more useful: the one who was taken an obligation upon herself and, together with all working people, shoulders a bit of the burden, helping all the rest; or the one who is concerned with "the obligation to be decorative?"'[63] A woman who wore makeup was acting as bait to trap a man. In this article, Jesenská made explicit the connection between the changes in fashion in accordance with the emancipation of women and the rejection of ornament in architecture:

> I do not know what we would look like as the decoration of life. I do not think it would suit us. Certainly, it would bore us terribly. Imagine that we led an existence like that of the stucco cherubs on the Art Nouveau facades; in the winter, in the summer, in the day and at night we would adorn something, always wearing the same smile. And then, when the plaster crumbled off us, we would have no choice but to smile on because we would not know how to do anything else anymore. Thank you very much for such a role in life. It must be very unpleasant.[64]

In her interpretation of a woman's obligation to be decorative, however, Jesenská was not always consistent.

## A Woman's Duty

The change in Jesenská's perspective on women's rights and duties can be traced in the newspaper articles that she wrote during the 1920s. To begin with, Jesenská argued that women had a much greater obligation to attend to their physical appearance than men did. She stated that it was easy for a woman to win a man, but to keep a man's love a woman had to work on being attractive and pleasant. She wrote:

> Why do you not understand – all you married women who are dependent on husbands – that you are spoiling half your lives if you do not devote exorbitant care to yourselves? Why do you not understand that it is not enough to strive to hold on to your husbands' love, but that it is necessary to win your husbands back every day? Daily, every evening anew, you must be more beautiful than the rest. You must be victorious over the woman who drove past in the carriage, over the woman with whom he exchanged a glance on the street, over the woman he sat next to in the theatre, over the woman whose hand he touched when he entered the store at the same moment as she did! You must overcome a thousand opportunities, a thousand coincidences, offers, desires! Truly, it is high time that you banished from your heads the beautiful phrases of romances about how a woman should be the eternal lover and friend, the eternal escort, the eternal companion and altogether something terribly

political, noble and eternal for her husband! I advise you to forget that
and to take care instead that you are always pleasant to your husbands!
That he finds it pleasant to enter the theatre at your side, to sit with you
in a restaurant, to walk with you down the street. That he finds it pleasant to return home. That he never once sees you be unpleasant![65]

The desperate tone of this advice probably reflected the difficulties that Jesenská was experiencing in her marriage to Pollak. For
several years, she continued to argue that women had an obligation to please their husbands. In an article about marriage, she
stated: 'it is the duty of a woman to remain pretty, clean and tidy,
despite all her cares, exertions and obligations. To prepare a dear,
cosy, comfortable, orderly home for her husband. The friendship
between husband and wife consists in this: that she gives him the
opportunity to love her forever.'[66] She believed that a woman was
under a particular obligation to attend to her appearance when she
was pregnant, so that her husband could endure the nine months
of her pregnancy with good humour.[67]

This view followed from her conviction that a woman's role was
defined by her sex. In 'A Few Old-Fashioned Comments about
Women's Emancipation', she stated that a woman could have all
sorts of jobs but only one true calling: motherhood.[68] In this article
she defended the work of a mother and housewife as being just as
important as the jobs that men held. In 'A Theme that has Nothing
to do with Fashion', she argued that the infidelity of a man and
the infidelity of a woman were of a different order. Because a
woman's mission was to bear children, she was under an obligation
to uphold the highest principles in her sexual life.[69] In other words,
Jesenská defended the double standard of sexual behaviour, which
had long been attacked by supporters of equal rights for women.

One notes a different emphasis in her article 'A Good Housewife'.
There, she criticised women who acted like martyrs and tyrannised
their families by complaining about the difficulties of maintaining
a household. The duty of a good housewife was to spare others from
worrying. Women should not exaggerate the importance of household chores. They should make sure that they had time for other
things, including good books.[70] It was not enough to ensure that
the household was clean and tidy. Women needed to be more self-
critical and to re-examine the popular ideal of a happy marriage. In
articles such as these, Jesenská began to challenge a traditional
conception of woman as obliged to sacrifice herself for the comfort
of others.

Although she continued to uphold the ideal of self-sacrifice,
Jesenská became increasingly outspoken in rejecting the view that

the most appropriate sphere for a woman was that of the household and family. In the article 'A Lady and a "Modern" Woman', she argued that the old style of femininity was dying out. The modern world had no place for the traditional gracious, modest housewife, who always knew how to be pleasant, but was ignorant of the great issues of the times. She was being replaced by modern women, who were:

> independent, hard-working, tough and brave; who could be companions for men, friends and helpmates; who could take responsibility for themselves and support themselves by their own efforts; who were not afraid of work. They could stand behind a counter, at a desk or a machine all day long, as patient, skilful and energetic as a man; they could look life calmly in the eye for what it was and they did not need the 'bloom of femininity' (that is, that artificial, greenhouse-cultivated ignorance) in order to be profoundly emotional women.[71]

Jesenská wrote about the double burden of women who were responsible for running the household as well as earning a living.[72] She noted that although women had political equality with men, they did not have social equality; for example, it was still impossible for women to walk in the streets at night without a companion.[73] She criticised the conservatism of women who wanted the advantages of independence, but still sought a man to protect and care for them. The other side of male gallantry, she observed, was despotism.[74] In an article about the negative stereotype of the woman driver, she expressed pessimism regarding the possibility of change. She stated that women would never be emancipated because there was a deeply rooted negative conception of the liberated woman. A woman did not encounter any problems until she demanded to be taken as seriously as a man.[75]

By 1929, Jesenská had rejected completely the view that a woman should cater to the demands of her husband. Women had changed, she asserted, but men had not. There could be no love in relationships between men and women when there was no equality. 'The independence of woman is a healthy, good, bright thing', she commented. 'It has become an indispensable need that we can never relinquish because through it we gain so much that is worthwhile, so much that is needed for a healthy mental life.'[76] In an article about motherhood, she also implicitly rejected the view that a woman's mission was to bear children. The sentimental conclusion does not dispel the impression developed in the first part of the article that a woman has no instinctive affection for her offspring.[77]

Jesenská argued that there was a parallel between the emancipation of women and changes in fashion: progress or regression in one area was reflected in the other. Increased opportunities in the lives of women meant that they needed simple, practical clothes. These clothes, in turn, symbolised the freedoms that women had won. The return to popularity of decorative, complex styles of dress that restricted freedom of movement was therefore to be regretted.[78]

## Jesenská and Kafka

Jesenská and Kafka were probably first introduced in Prague by common acquaintances. Their friendship, however, began as an exchange of letters, which quickly turned into a daily correspondence. At that time Kafka, who had been diagnosed as having tuberculosis in 1917, was staying in the spa of Merano, in the South Tyrol. By the time Kafka returned to Prague from Merano several months later, stopping in Vienna to visit Jesenská (29 June to 4 July 1920), their love affair was well underway. It is not clear, however, whether or not their relationship was ever consummated physically. Apart from the few days they spent together in Vienna and a one-day tryst in Gmünd, they only saw each other on a few other occasions when Jesenská visited Kafka in Prague. Their passion found primarily a literary expression and was preserved as a text, with recurrent motifs, topics and characters. In his letters to Jesenská, Kafka dwelt repeatedly on certain subjects that were for him interrelated: fear; illness and the body; Judaism; and marriage.[79] Even in the early letters, his references to these subjects manifest his fear that she would reject him because he was ill and because he was Jewish. For example, in the letter of 30 May 1920 he wrote: 'And on top of that Milena is still going on about anxiety, striking my chest or asking: *jste žid?* [are you a Jew?] which in Czech has the same movement and sound. Don't you see how the fist is pulled back in the word "*jste*," so as to gain muscle power? And then in the word "*žid*" [Jew] the happy blow, flying unerringly forward?'[80] In the letter from 12 June 1920, he wrote: 'as far as I'm concerned you are not a woman, you're a girl, I've never seen anyone who was more of a girl than you, and girl that you are, I don't dare offer you my hand, my dirty, twitching, clawlike, fidgety, unsteady, hot-cold hand.'[81] Kafka was attracted by Jesenská's health and energy. In April 1920, for example, he wrote of her 'farm girl's vigor'. On 2 June, he commented that she was 'like the sea, as strong as the sea with its masses of water, crashing down with all their might'. On 12 July, he wrote of her 'life-giving force'.[82]

Jesenská's responses in this exchange with Kafka were lost with her letters. Her newspaper articles, however, offer further insight into their relationship. They suggest that two tendencies competed within Jesenská: on the one hand, the celebration of life and vitality; and on the other hand, empathy for the outcasts from the world of health and happiness. After her experience of illness at the end of the 1920s, this empathy became more pronounced. In her writings from the 1930s, she celebrated rather the virtues of compassion and solidarity, praising in particular the solidarity of the Jews.

Throughout their correspondence, Kafka showed an interest in Jesenská's writing. He described himself as her 'best reader' and responded to her newspaper articles in his letters as if they had been addressed to him personally. His reactions to these texts give further confirmation of the dynamic of their relationship; that is, his dread, but also his certainty, of rejection.

In his first reference to a specific article, Kafka responded to Jesenská's piece about bathing costumes.[83] In it, Jesenská described two types of swimmers: those who loved exercise and the outdoors; and those who only dipped into the water without intending to get their hair wet. Jesenská made this distinction in order to point out that the elaborate bathing costumes designed for the indifferent swimmers hardly suited those who relished the water. Kafka identified with the second type, those whose 'bodies stand in the water like poles weighted at the bottom'.[84] He commented: 'Naturally I belong to the second group; this weight on the feet is really my own property and I do not at all consent to the publication of matters of mine which are strictly private'.[85] In interpreting her article, he classified himself in the group that was criticised by her as unable to appreciate the delights of the body and of nature.

Shortly thereafter he responded to her article 'The New Big-City Type. II', which he described as 'excellent, sharp and angry, anti-Semitic and magnificent'.[86] Nowhere in the article or in 'The New Big-City Type' did Jesenská mention Jews. Both articles treated the subject of people who had profited from the war and the misery of the general population. In the first article, Jesenská described a second-hand dealer, a latter-day version of the rag-and-bone man. Jesenská presented this 'man who buys anything' as cunning, lusting for money because of his poor origins and craving for security. She described him as a 'leech', 'an ugly, repulsive, sprawling spider' hoarding the goods that others had had to surrender.[87] In the second article, Jesenská provided a psychological portrait of wartime profiteers. The idea that the Jews had avoided military service and profited from the war was a commonplace of anti-Semitic discourse after the First World War.[88] Jesenská wrote of these profiteers: 'they are even sly, clever, talented people, with a hard, iron, bloodthirsty cunning, a cunning like that of the beast of prey; it leaps at its victim at just the right moment with a superb leap and does not give in, does not let go until the victim drops. They do not, of course, have a spirit.'[89] The idea that the Jews were fundamentally materialist rather than spiritual was another anti-Semitic *topos*, notoriously elaborated in Otto Weininger's (1880–1903) *Sex and Character* (*Geschlecht und Charakter*, 1903). According to Jesenská, the profiteer's desire to earn money stemmed from fear of poverty and insignificance. She contrasted the profiteer with the spiritual person who had no interest in money.

It seems clear that Jesenská never intended these types to be interpreted as Jews. Although she had absorbed certain conventional perceptions of the Jews, such as the notion of the eternal sadness and exile of the Jews, she was not anti-Semitic. Most of the serious erotic relationships in her life were with Jewish men: Ernst Pollak, Franz Kafka, Evžen Klinger. Kafka described Jesenská as an 'angel of Jews', casting her in the role of his saviour.[90] This role did not sit well with Jesenská. On several occasions in her articles she insisted that people first had to save themselves and only then could they find help. In addition, her articles suggest that she identified with the Jews; that is, she identified with what she regarded as one of their defining characteristics, their 'forlornness' or isolation in the world.

In 'Perfection, a Support in Uncertainty', she discussed a performance of John Galsworthy's (1867–1933) play *Loyalties* (1922); in her comments, she concentrated on the presentation of the Jewish character Ferdinand De Levis and his isolation in English aristocratic society.[91] Jesenská criticised Galsworthy's psychological and social analysis as naïve. She argued that De Levis, having once achieved a position in aristocratic society, would never do anything to threaten that position. Jesenská mistakenly assumed that Galsworthy attributed greedy motives to the Jewish character. She condemned the myth that Jews were preoccupied with money. Jews were only interested in money, she argued, in so far as it could provide them with a support in their 'forlornness' (*opuštěnost*) in the world.[92] She provided a German term for this fear of forlornness: *Heimatlosigkeit*. She argued that because of the difficult circumstances in which Jews had lived over the centuries, they had been forced to excel and make an enormous contribution to the world. These views were echoed in the articles she later wrote for *Přítomnost* on the eve of the Second World War.

In the article 'Words', published six months after her discussion of Galsworthy's *Loyalties*, she wrote about words that appealed to her for obscure reasons. One such word was *heimatlos* (homeless, stateless), which suggested a person who was, 'internally unstable, troubled, a wanderer; one pictures a big-city park with a bench and on it an adult, a stranger to the city, with a great grief in his heart and a hopeless emptiness in his eyes'.[93] The description strongly recalls Jesenská's portrait, in 'Mysterious Redemption', of her state of mind following the break-up of her relationship with Kafka.

While Jesenská identified with this feeling of alienation, Kafka assumed that it was a weakness she despised. In another response to a fashion article by Jesenská, he classified himself as the object of her contempt. In the article she treated the importance of shop-window displays, describing a picture of a hare that she had seen among the other displays: 'A delightful hare, running away over a field through the snow to the woods, with its white tail raised. It appealed to me. It seemed so forlorn [*opuštěný*] in the white world and its tail gave it an air of melancholy powerlessness.'[94] She explained that she grew weary of the picture after seeing it day after day, for weeks on end, just as one would grow tired of seeing the same person continually. Kafka interpreted the passage as a warning directed at him. He wrote: 'Even earlier, before you said you sometimes think of me when writing, I felt it was connected with me, that is, I held it pressed against me; now, because you have expressly said so, it almost makes me even more anxious and when for instance I read about a hare in the snow I can almost see myself there, running.'[95]

With the possible exception of 'The Café', however, one does not find references to Kafka in Jesenská's articles from 1920. In 'The Café', about artists and intellectuals who frequent cafés, Jesenská used the expression 'capitalists of the spirit' to describe the renowned artists who were the pride of these establishments.[96] The expression recalls Kafka's phrase 'capitalists of airspace'; it appeared in the letter of 30 May 1920 in which Kafka defended Franz Werfel (1890–1945) and 'fat people' in general against Jesenská's criticism: 'Don't you know that fat people alone are to be trusted? Only in strong-walled vessels like these does everything get thoroughly cooked, only these capitalists of airspace are immune from worry and insanity, to the extent it is humanly possible'.[97] Kafka commented on 'The Café' in his letter of 11 August 1920. Instead of identifying with one of the loners described in the article, he pictured himself as removed from Jesenská and her society. He wrote: 'While I was reading it I felt I was walking up and down in front of the café, day and night, year after year; every time a guest came or went I would peer in through the open door to check that you were still inside. Then I would resume the pacing and waiting.'[98]

Direct and indirect references to Kafka appeared in Jesenská's articles after Kafka had ended their relationship. When, in January 1921, he asked her not to write to him any more, she used her articles as a vehicle to express her feelings for him. 'My Friend', published on 27 January 1921, is about her concierge, Mrs Kohler, who sometimes conveyed messages from Kafka to Jesenská.[99] She described how the concierge revived her after she had attempted suicide.[100] In 'Retreat to the Helpless', published two weeks later, Jesenská wrote about people's attachment to their pets, the helpless creatures dependent on them. A paragraph in the middle of the article stands out from the rest:

> I know of no greater despair than the despair of the helpless faced with the grief of someone dear. You stand in front of a person with your heart full [...] you stand and you see that he needs help, like someone who is drowning. And yet it is as if you were standing behind a door and, with your face pressed to the keyhole, you waited to see what would happen inside. There is no greater unhappiness in the world than the inability of one person to help another. Sometimes you pace the room from corner to corner and you are closer to death than to life. And a person trembles in the corner, watching your steps, pale, tense, unable to do anything but wait and wait. How deadly this waiting is. Not only are the sick abandoned by the healthy, but the healthy are also abandoned by the sick. The command of the expulsion from paradise lies between people when someone is dying. All the horror of unconditional human solitude. A person has to save himself and only then can he be helped.[101]

The passage includes Kafka's comment from the letter of 6 August 1920: 'The healthy forsake the sick, but the sick also forsake the healthy.'[102] It also echoes Kafka's description of his relationship with Jesenská: 'Sometimes I feel we have a room with two doors on opposite sides and each of us is holding his doorknob and, at the bat of one person's eyelash, the other jumps behind his door, and now if the first person utters a single word, the second is sure to close the door behind him, so that he can no longer be seen.'[103]

Jesenská's article 'Mysterious Redemption', published on 25 February 1921, also constituted a description of frustration and grief. The reference in the first paragraph to lungs that struggle to break through walls of pain in order to breathe suggests that the piece was addressed to Kafka. This is confirmed by the reference to

Kafka in the concluding paragraph. There Jesenská paraphrased a passage from one of Kafka's letters about his disease: 'When the heart and the brain could not stand the suffering any longer, they looked around for something to save them and that's when the lungs spoke up. I know that my disease saved me. But that bargaining between the heart and the lungs, which went on without my awareness, was probably terrible.'[104] The two middle sections of the article can be read as portraits of Jesenská's predicament. She described a person's desire to escape from her life and her eventual resignation. She also described the anxiety and dread of waiting for a person to return home; this may have been a reference to her marriage with Pollak. In the impressionistic 'Melancholy in the Rain', from 29 April 1921, Jesenská portrayed a state of mind through descriptions of gloomy landscapes and accounts of bizarre and pitiable deaths.[105] The concluding paragraph again indicates the personal subtext; there she cited Kafka, translating in full his short prose piece, 'The Next Village' (*Das nächste Dorf*, 1920).

Kafka did not respond, although he continued to read her newspaper pieces. Of all her articles, 'Devil at the Hearth', published on 18 January 1923, was the only one to elicit a detailed written reaction from him. One can assume that she mentioned it to him in a letter. He replied: 'I'll get hold of the "Devil" once I can go out; for the time being I still feel some pain.'[106] In his next letter, he responded in detail to the article, which treated the subject of marriage. It was not the first time that Jesenská had written on the subject. Six months earlier, she had published 'Superficial Small Talk about a Serious Subject' in *Tribuna*. There she rejected the sentimental conception of love. It was not important that one love one's husband, she had written, but rather that one find him to be a pleasant companion. Marriage required commitment, responsibility and a relinquishment of certain freedoms.[107] The same views were expressed in 'Devil at the Hearth'. The article indirectly explained why Jesenská had not left her husband for Kafka. She argued that people should not marry to find happiness. There was no reason for people to be happy simply because they were together. Indeed, it was more difficult to live with someone else than to live alone. She went so far as to claim that it was a 'literary fantasy' to expect happiness from such a union. Two people lived together, not for the sake of happiness or romantic love, but for the sake of friendship. The home was intended to protect the individual from the world and from himself or herself, or, as she put it, from the individual's 'internal mirror'. Marriage required one to be faithful, loyal and tolerant of the other. Attention to the trifles of everyday life was more important than a grand promise. She concluded the article with the reflection that one could either choose to accept one's fate with grace, or one could seek out one's fate. The latter option, according to her, was futile: 'in seeking you will lose not only strength, time, illusions, proper and good blindness, instinct; in seeking you will also lose your own worth.'[108]

In his funny, sarcastic response to the article, Kafka reinterpreted it as a conversation between two partners in marriage: Jewry and an angel, 'who loves these Jews so much he marries the whole nation so it will not perish'.[109] Some lines from the article are ascribed to Jewry and some to the angel. The outcome of the conversation is that, 'at last, good heavens, the angel pushes the Jews back down and frees himself'.[110] Kafka commented that there was no reason to blame either side for the failure of the marriage: 'both are the way they are, one Jewish, one angelic'.[111] With this response Kafka insisted upon his interpretation of their relationship; that is, he was the Jew who could not fail to repel her, the angel, eventually.[112] There was a note of defiance in his insistence: 'There are no unhappy marriages, there are only incomplete ones and they are incomplete because they were made by incomplete human beings, human beings who have not fully evolved, who should be torn out of the field before the harvest.'[113]

Although Kafka had dwelt several times on the subject of marriage and his own failed attempts at marriage in his letters to Jesenská, he only wrote about sex on one occasion. He described how he had lost his virginity to a shop-girl who lived across the street from his parents' apartment. Twice he spent the night with her in a hotel, after which he never spoke to her again, disgusted by the memory of a trifling gesture she had made and an obscene word she had uttered. Yet, he wrote, it was this very obscenity that had attracted him: 'And it's stayed that way ever since. My body, often quiet for years, would then again be shaken by this longing for some very particular, trivial, disgusting thing, something slightly repulsive, embarrassing, obscene, which I always found even in the best cases – some insignificant odor, a little bit of sulphur, a little bit of hell. This urge had something of the eternal Jew – senselessly being drawn along, senselessly wandering through a senselessly obscene world.'[114] In the next letter, he explained: 'between this daytime world and that "half-hour in bed" you once wrote of with disdain, as if it were men's business, there is an abyss I cannot span, probably because I don't want to. Over there lies an affair of the night, absolutely and in every respect; here, on the other hand, is the world which I possess, and now I'm supposed to leap across into the night in order to repossess it.'[115]

In her articles about marriage, Jesenská did not write about sexuality, except in connection with the requirement of fidelity. She returned to the subject of fidelity a number of times, arguing that women were obliged to be faithful for physiological reasons. She did, however, treat the subject of sexuality in a different context; thus one can imagine how she would have responded to Kafka. In 'Modern Dances', Jesenská wrote:

> Dance is something erotic. Of course, it is an erotic courtship. There are people who criticise it for that and claim that it is therefore improper. Well, the erotic life of a person is something like the sun, like water, like air. Something joyful, vibrant, an elixir, something essential to life. There are, however, unfortunate people who associate the erotic life with notions of the underworld. Not a gift of life for which one must give thanks, but rather a punishment, a curse of the darkness. Such people are not beautiful in any respect. Not even in dance.[116]

Jesenská described sexuality as a natural aspect of the life of the body, an animal life that she celebrated repeatedly in her articles. In 'To Market', for example, she wrote: 'Here one encounters the life about which no one speaks because it is so obvious and necessary and common to all. Life in its prosaic nakedness, in its cruel health and insatiability. Things would turn out badly for the household if I went shopping every day. I would not return home for hours on end. There is nothing more beautiful than to roam through the market early in the morning in the bright sunlight.'[117]

This celebration of 'cruel health' and the body was manifest in the article 'Bathing Costumes' from 1920. In responding to it, Kafka had identified with those who were outside the healthy, natural current of life. It seems that Jesenská came to regard him in the same light. In a letter to Max Brod, she wrote: 'this whole world is and remains mysterious to him. A mystical enigma. [...] Frank cannot live. Frank does not have the capacity for living. Frank will never get well. Frank will die soon. For, obviously, we are capable of living because at some time or other we took refuge in lies, in blindness, in enthusiasm, in optimism, in some conviction or others, in pessimism or something of that sort. But he has never escaped to any such sheltering refuge, none at all. He is absolutely incapable of living, just as he is incapable of getting drunk.'[118]

In an article published shortly before Kafka's death, 'Unknown Acquaintances', Jesenská again wrote about a person who was incapable of living, a comedian from Munich named Valentin. The physical description of Valentin reminds one of Kafka: 'he is endlessly tall and endlessly lean and endlessly weak. He has thin, senselessly long legs, sunken cheeks that are pale one moment and hectic red the next [...] and a small voice that is quiet, gentle, broken, like someone whom the world has injured.'[119] Valentin's humour, Jesenská wrote, was like that of Charlie Chaplin:

> the comicality of a person defenceless against the sobriety of objects, against the practicality of the world, a person at the mercy of the cunning of lifeless things (a ladder that falls on his nose, a rock that will not move, hot water that scalds). It is the forlornness [opuštěnost] of sad people, weak to the point of sickness, consistent to the point of diseased stubbornness, incurable in their anxiety, fear and timidity, people who will never get anywhere and who will never win, but only because they are as sensitive as plants and feel the cold of the world even more intensely, lying on the underside of the Slav soul. Perhaps one has to laugh at them because they do not know how to live. But their 'unable to live' comes from such precious sources of the heart that one chokes with shame on one's laughter.[120]

Considering that Jesenská had addressed Kafka in her articles after their relationship had come to an end, confident that he would read them, one cannot help but wonder if she tried to communicate with him in her writings towards the end of his life. Although it remains a matter of speculation, her articles published in the spring of 1924, like 'Unknown Acquaintances', suggest that she did address him. In 'Life in Spas', published on 4 May 1924, Jesenská wrote about people who frequented spas because they were ill or convalescent. At that time, Kafka was at a sanatorium at Kierling, near Klosterneuburg. The last two paragraphs suggest her empathy for the patient at the spa, to whom she offered encouragement:

> All of our spas lie in beautiful regions; a few steps away from the establishment, you will not meet a living soul. Here you can lie in the grass and look at the clouds. And when you feel sad, not far away provisions have been made for recreation and enjoyment.
>
> Incidentally, I think that city-dwellers find it very difficult to endure the solitude of the woods and meadows, solitude in general. A person must have a certain love of nature to endure it. For some, it is oppressive and reminds them of their cares, instead of removing them. They can bear it only in moderate doses, swallowed from a soupspoon after lunch. They are usually intellectual and nervous people and would do well to seek out a spa even if they are completely healthy. In the middle of a crowd, it is pleasant to be alone. This kind of solitude does not oppress; it only revives.[121]

In an article published a few days later, Jesenská again offered words of comfort:

> The most valuable thing about sport is that it can help a person find an inner path out of life's difficulties. This usually happens mechanically, without any special effort. The soul is exhausted by something and does not know which way to turn – and the soul is almost constantly exhausted and burdened by cares. The body that measures the road, or peddles the bicycle, or swims in the river carries the soul out into the light of the real, decided world, smoothly, like a diver retrieving a treasure from watery depths. Because nothing in the world is as healing as happiness. Whoever said that suffering purifies was wrong. Suffering very often defiles a person, leaving him angry, mistrustful, stunted; happiness, however, cleans, strengthens and saves. Suffering only helps in so far as a person who is open to pain is also more open to happiness; where there is a greater intensity of grief there is also a greater delight in laughter. Perhaps hardship is good for this very reason: that it teaches the blessing, the depth and the miracle of happiness.[122]

In the article 'Into the Countryside', published on 25 May, she wrote again of the healing effects of leaving the city for the country:

> It always seemed to me as if a person perceived the world with redoubled intensity; as if the baulk full of thyme also signified something else; as if the windswept linden and row of poplars in front of the mill and the field of clover in flower were not only what they were, but something infinitely, miraculously healing, joyful, radiant, blessed. And all the while it was one's own heart, freed from the cage and one's own accumulated heat and the vehemence of one's love for the world, which all of a sudden spilled out in great joy, enthusiasm and happiness.[123]

Her reflections in an article published in September 1924, entitled 'Indian Summer', suggest how she wishfully imagined the end of Kafka's life:

> But in these Indian summer days, I wish the same thing every year: I always wish that I were recovering from a serious illness, lying in a sanatorium wrapped up in an easy-chair somewhere on a sunny terrace with a view of a chain of mountains. I wish that someone would take away my strength and carry me over into that blissful state of passivity that only convalescents know, a state in which one has to reflect on every movement and every word is a strain. You lie and you breathe and you are infinitely happy that you are lying and breathing and you want nothing more than for it to last like that forever. All decisions and cares and exertions lie somewhere behind you; not only are you unable, but also you are not supposed to worry about anything because the doctor has forbidden it. It seems to you that you should not move, or else the magic will vanish. And your heart weakly beats with love for the mountains opposite, with love for the sky and for life. You have a tender and good heart and you care for all people; you love yourself as well and

you are good and kind to all. Life seems to you far more beautiful than it is. [...] And the strangest thing of all: in such states it is beautiful to live, but it would not be hard to die. You are so good and reconciled and composed that you are somehow blissfully happy. Clear-headed, with an unearthly calm.[124]

In the obituary that Jesenská wrote for Kafka, she paid tribute to him as a writer and also described his 'inability to live' as connected with his talent. She wrote of his works: 'They are full of dry scorn and the sensitive contemplation of a person who saw the world so clearly that he could not bear it and had to die, not wanting to save himself, as other do, by falling back on intellectual, unconscious fallacies, even the noblest.'[125] She paid tribute to Kafka as a person, without mentioning him by name, in the article 'The Curse of Outstanding Qualities', published in her collection *Cesta k jednoduchosti* (The Path to Simplicity, 1926). There she related the incident of his gift of ten kreutzers to a beggar, which Kafka had described in his letter of 18 July 1920.[126] Jesenská had written about the same incident in the article 'Children', published in January 1921. In both articles, she also treated the subject of the impact of tyrannical parental authority on children.[127] This was fundamental to Jesenská's perception of Kafka: the belief that his personality had been defined at a young age by the conflict with his father. In this respect, she was also postulating on the basis of her own experience. Although she did not say so explicitly in 'The Curse of Outstanding Qualities', she implied that because of this conflict, the child had become aware of his own deceitfulness. This awareness gave rise to a split in the child's personality, a split that was manifest in the incident of the ten kreutzers, which for Jesenská was emblematic of Kafka's character. In her interpretation, the young Kafka had been unable to act spontaneously on his generous impulse to give the ten-kreutzer piece to the beggar. He felt compelled to conceal this generosity, which was at odds with his perceived character flaws and to split himself into ten different alms-givers, each one of whom gave the beggar a kreutzer. Her interpretation was congruent with Kafka's perception of himself as divided. For Kafka, this self-perception was connected with his understanding of being Jewish. In June 1921 Kafka wrote to Max Brod: 'Mostly young Jews who began to write German wanted to leave Jewishness behind them, and their fathers approved of this, but vaguely (this vagueness was what was outrageous to them). But with their posterior legs they were glued to their fathers' Jewishness and with their waving anterior legs they found no new ground. The ensuing despair became their inspiration.'[128]

In writing about Kafka, Jesenská was also writing about herself. She too felt defined by her relationship to her father. She believed that the conflict with her father had created a split in her consciousness and that in this respect she was typical of her generation, just as Kafka had felt he was typical of his generation of Jews.[129] In an article from December 1925 she wrote:

> I think that few have experienced such a sharp antagonism between the generations as has ours. A struggle, a turning point, in the real world was added to the usual and rather ordinary struggle between fathers and children. Between our fathers and grandfathers there was perhaps only a thousandth part of the abyss that lay between us and our parents. We were caught up by the war and all its psychoses. We fought secret battles on painful fronts, without understanding what we were fighting for. We wanted to go forward, yet we did not know what was forward or what was backward. Concepts lost their value and in the meantime we could not give them new value. We were not supposed to build on the spiritual heritage of the immediate past. Acting according to the laws of youth and impetuousness, we swore to rebel. We knew what we were running from but we did not know what we wanted: that is the most painful and hopeless struggle that a person can fight. Revolutions are not won or lost, they simply pass away. And that is what happened to us: the era passed and the 'unreasonable age' came to an end. We are not revolutionaries, but we are new. A new generation younger than us is growing up; they have firm muscles, concentrated knowledge and willpower. We belonged to a generation of emotionally divided people and we resolved our own fates accordingly. Our fathers were absolutely whole and our children will probably also be whole.[130]

## To Take One's Place Among the Rest

In a 1925 article Jesenská wrote: 'I hate the phrase: it is not his fault. [...] Even if nothing is our fault, the world still demands and we ourselves demand that we take responsibility for everything. [...] [W]e are asked to live not according to the way we are, but according to the way we should be. But as all people share this fate, like birth and death and the danger of illness, it is no longer really fate but reality and all that remains for us is a single great duty: to take our place among the rest.'[131] Among the articles that Jesenská wrote for *Přítomnost* from 1937 to 1939 there were no more pieces about clothes, but the themes of the fashion articles recur, above all the imperative to improve one's character and to show solidarity with others. In 1938, for example, she wrote: 'the greatest illness of the European individual is the easy willingness to retreat, to offer no resistance, to surrender and to conform "because one has to live, after all!" It is more urgent that we know *how* we want to live and that we consider this *how* to be as important as life itself. A difficult task faces each of us today – to find the precise boundary between prudence and cowardice, between daring and an outburst of passion. Today, not only the leading people of this state must find this boundary, but also every ordinary person, even the most ordinary.'[132]

Jesenská also returned to the theme of social ills, which had preoccupied her in the early 1920s. When writing as a correspondent from Vienna at the beginning of her career, Jesenská had encouraged her readers to show generosity to beggars and had criticised the inequity of a society in which a few lived in luxury while the majority starved. She wrote: 'there is only one thing I know for sure: as long as there is a single hungry person among us, the world is a bad place'.[133] In 1923, in an article about Christmas-tree decorations, she urged readers to give gifts to people who were alone over the holidays: 'The knowledge that there are forlorn people in the world should drive you out of your own homes on a day that is supposed to be one of joy for all! The knowledge that there are children without Christmas presents (and there are such children) and that there are old people who are forlorn and left with nothing on Christmas but a memory of a life gone by (and there are such people), must spoil the cosy atmosphere of your own celebration.'[134] In 1939, she argued in a similar vein that entrepreneurs should provide jobs for as many Czechs as possible, even if it meant a decline in their own standard of living.[135] It was better for all Czechs to share a poor fare than for some to suffer.[136]

Not only themes but also phrases from the earlier articles recur, allowing one to measure the extent to which her outlook remained consistent. In an article in 1927 Jesenská wrote: 'If we compared the ethics of all the ages, we would discover that they all have the same goal: to stand on the side of the weak, as long as there are some who are strong ("*so lange es Stärkere gibt, immer an der Seite der Schwächeren*").'[137] In 1938 she used the same German phrase when writing about the 'weakest of the weak, the persecuted Viennese Jews'.[138] The articles published prior to the Munich Agreement were outspoken in their treatment of anti-Semitism, the plight of the Jews and of refugees in general. In 'People on a Promontory', she wrote about refugees fleeing from the Nazis: 'This handful of refugees can teach us what the swastika is: they are the living witnesses of the great violence and the powerful lie. On their own skin they bear the testimony here among us and anyone of us who is like Thomas, who did not believe until he had checked for

himself, can go and lay a hand on them.'[139] The reference to Doubt-
ing Thomas recalls the earlier article 'The Letters of Eminent
People', in which she wrote about people's need to verify, in biographies and letter collections, that the wounds of famous artists
were deep.[140]

In the early 1920s, Jesenská had written about Viennese children,
deformed by the hardships of the First World War. In the late 1930s,
she wrote about children deformed by Nazi ideology, taught to spy
on and betray their parents.[141] In her earlier articles Jesenská had
treated the psychological and social consequences of poverty, in
particular how deprivation could drive the underprivileged to
exploit others and pursue luxury. In the 1930s, she turned her
attention to the suffering of the refugees, asserting: 'The sated will
never understand that hunger hurts the soul more than it does the
stomach.'[142] In her later articles, Jesenská argued that suffering had
political, as well as personal, consequences. This was one of the
reasons she showed so much understanding for the Sudeten
Germans. She insisted that not all of them supported Nazism. Many
had been vulnerable to Nazi propaganda because of the years of
financial hardship they had endured. Severe unemployment in the
Sudetenland had contributed to the radicalisation of the population.[143] In her opinion, the Czechoslovak state had not done
enough to support the Germans in the border regions. She wrote:
'today we will pay a high price because there were many things we
did not pay for in good time'.[144] She expressed the fear that the
Czechs, following the disappointment of Munich, would take
revenge on the refugees swelling the population of the rump state:
'Revenge has always been an expression of tormented injustice and
it has never been vented in the right direction, but rather in the
direction open to it. Revenge is an act of the weak against the
weaker.'[145] It has been estimated that in the autumn of 1938,
150,000 Czechoslovak citizens left the territories ceded to Germany
to seek refuge in the rump state.[146] Writing of those who, out of
despair, had given up hope of fleeing from the Second Republic, she
commented: 'Even to seek [emigration], one needs hope.'[147] The
statement recalls the last line of her 1923 article about marriage,
'Devil at the Hearth'. There she had asserted: 'to seek [one's fate],
one needs faith and for faith, perhaps more strength than for
life'.[148] In the late 1930s, Jesenská's personal philosophy, taken to
its logical consequences, acquired a political dimension. In her early
articles about infidelity, for example, Jesenská had urged women to
look critically at their own behaviour before they reproached their
husbands. In 1939, she gave the same advice to readers coping with

the changed political and social circumstances: 'Every time you receive a blow in life, focus your criticism first and foremost on yourself: how could that person dare to strike me? Only then complain of people's barbarity.'[149] Consistently, she advocated a message of personal responsibility in the face of difficulties.

## What Does One Czech Expect from Another?

While there was consistency with the early work, the choice of subject in Jesenská's articles from the *Přítomnost* period was influenced by the political developments and the changing censorship regulations. Some of the articles written prior to the Munich Agreement were censored; blank spots appear in the published texts. In the article 'What was the Cost of Henlein's Speech in Karlovy Vary?', Jesenská addressed the censor, complaining that sentences in her articles that could be interpreted as criticism of the Czechoslovak Ministry of the Interior had been deleted. This practice of censorship, she explained, led to the grotesque situation in which the fascist propaganda of Henlein's party was published, while warnings concerning conditions in the Sudetenland were censored. She asserted: 'In reality the result is that a person who ardently desires an effective weapon against the rising German fascism in Czechoslovakia is permitted to say less than the Czechoslovak German fascist. I point out this circumstance to the censor because I am a little ashamed of all the things one is forbidden to say today.'[150]

Censorship was considerably more restrictive following the Munich Agreement and the creation of the Second Republic. In 'The Daily News on the Back Pages', published on 19 October 1938, Jesenská asserted that journalists would have to learn to read and write anew, not only to master the strange new intellectual juggling, but also to say anything at all. Between the journalist and the reader there was not only paper, but also censorship. The contact between them would be less direct, but nonetheless, it would still be possible to speak the truth. She argued that newspapers, even when they were more or less silent, still gave testimony to their times.[151]

According to a resolution of the Council of Ministers of the Beran government on 6 December 1938, a preliminary review of the press was carried out by officials of the press supervisory service. These officials were appointed to all the Czech daily papers and conducted their duties directly in the editorial offices of the newspapers.[152] Guidelines were issued to eliminate from the press all news that might provoke criminal actions or disturb the peace.

The censorship was to be carried out so that blank spots would not be visible in the published texts. The press was forbidden to criticise government officials or the foreign or economic policies of the state. All news that might lead to hatred of national or racial groups was to be suppressed. Journalists were forbidden to criticise, directly or indirectly, foreign states or their representatives, state officials in active service, public figures or functionaries of national organisations. They could not criticise proposed reforms to the management of the economy, or the new labour organisations. Likewise they could not report on troop formations.

The occupation in March resulted in further restrictions on the press, which became the 'main mouthpiece of the official political line'.[153] The regulations concerning the activity of the press remained in force. In addition, it was forbidden to discuss the deployment of the German army, suicides that occurred in connection with the political changes, arrests or the activity of the Gestapo. Reflections on the future organisation of Czech national life or the new constitutional arrangements were also forbidden. The press was encouraged to point out the practical benefits that residents would derive from the establishment of the Protectorate. All newspapers formally became organs of the one permitted political party. The Czech press was subordinate to the press section, headed by Zdeněk Schmoranz (1896–1942), of the presidium of the Council of Ministers. Schmoranz, who had connections with the underground organisation *Obrana národa* (Defence of the Nation), was arrested on 25 August 1939. Wolfgang Wolfram von Wolmar, authorised representative of the Reich protector, then took over the management of the press section. Following the German invasion of Poland, the Czech press became completely subordinate to the Germans.

In their study of the Protectorate, Gebhart and Kuklík comment: 'In the spring and summer of 1939, most Czechs shared the basic feeling that there was a pressing need for national solidarity.'[154] In accordance with the aims of the occupation powers, which at first strove to maintain an atmosphere of relative calm, the Protectorate government encouraged the development of 'Czech cultural distinctness' in its propaganda.[155] Some journalists also advocated a return to the 'roots' of the Czech national tradition as a means of resisting the Germans.[156] The articles by Jesenská that extol Czech traditions and refer to the national myths should be interpreted in light of the censorship restrictions and the defence of Czech cultural distinctiveness. In these articles, Jesenská walked a thin line between concession and resistance to the authorities.

Given the effective ban on writing about topical events following the occupation, she concentrated instead on the 'national character' and the moral obligations that Czechs faced in the changed circumstances.

Jesenská's articles from the 1920s indicate that she rejected Czech nationalism. She frequently took the opportunity to criticise her fellow Czechs. In 1921, in 'New Year's Greetings', she accused Czechs of being spiteful: 'We have grown too accustomed to our bad manners. [...] Everywhere everything is achieved through fights, rudeness and cursing. These are the daily scenes of our street corners, shops, theatres, tram stops and offices. We snarl at one another like dogs over a bone. We fight for an advantage, for the first place, for a bit of comfort, like street urchins brawling over marbles. We deform our lives together through a kind of obsession, for which I can hardly find a name, a kind of new pathological self-ishness.'[157] In 1924, she light-heartedly outlined her understanding of different nationalities in an article entitled 'Courtesy'. According to her the Italians, who knew how to appreciate life, were at one end of the scale. The Germans were at the other end. She wrote of Berlin: 'Everything has that terrible German note of conceited taci-turnity, of pedantic order.'[158] While she praised the Viennese, she criticised the residents of Prague: 'That something, which was and is good in our people, that something, which is slightly robust, rustic, invigorating and close to the earth, sometimes degenerates into the loudmouthed character of the Berliners.'[159] Elsewhere she accused Czech women of being tasteless and bourgeois, lacking the charm of the Parisians and the discretion of the Americans.[160] She attacked Czech eating habits and criticised Czechs for being over-weight and dull-witted.[161] Czechs, she wrote, had a penchant for kitsch, unlike the British and the Americans, who appreciated simplicity and quality.[162] Jesenská's criticism did not mean that she was anti-Czech. Her confidence in her national identity was like that of the Czech Decadents at the turn of the century, who could 'love their nation, but feel frustrated by their nation's behaviour or characteristics'.[163]

Neither the Munich Agreement nor the occupation made a nationalist out of Jesenská. In the articles published prior to 1939, Jesenská repeatedly asserted that the Germans could not be lumped together in one group. That is, she rejected the fundamental basis of nationalism. Her criticism was focused on Nazis, not Germans. In later articles, she did not express open criticism of Nazism; such criticism could not have been published. Nonetheless, in articles such as '*Soldaten wohnen auf den Kanonen*', her criticism of German militancy is thinly concealed; the title of that article, published on 21 June 1939, is taken from an anti-war song in the *Threepenny Opera* (*Die Dreigroschenoper*, 1928) by Bertolt Brecht (1898-1956), who had fled from Germany in 1933. Allegedly, when Jesenská was called before the German censor to explain herself, she pretended ignorance.[164]

In the article 'How Should One Treat the Czechs?', Jesenská reiterated a longstanding tenet of the national mythology, according to which Czechs were inherently democratic.[165] By making this claim, she was implicitly asserting the right of the Czechs to reject the authoritarian government of the Germans. She wrote: 'In issue no. 6 of *Přítomnost*, a German National Socialist wrote that "a German is unconditionally a National Socialist and it is his natural right to be able to declare this conviction wherever he likes." One can only reply that we are not asking for anything more for ourselves than the natural right to declare our conviction and support for a form of thought that has not sprung up overnight, but over centuries.'[166] This was one of her standard techniques of argumentation: to insist on the rights of the Czechs on the basis of the rights of the Germans. Her underlying premise, sometimes explicitly stated, was that the two national groups were equal.[167] For example, she defended the right of the Czechs to protect their national identity through promotion of the national culture. In 'Excuse Me for Not Whispering', published in May 1939, she wrote: 'Didn't the leader of the German nation fight with his bare hands, with no more than an idea and words, when he led the German nation out of a state of fragmentation into a state of unity? Isn't an idea a weapon superior to the sharpness and menace of all other weapons? And isn't the Czech national idea just as valid as the national idea of any other nation?'[168]

Jesenská's expressions of patriotism communicated a message of resistance to the German occupation. For example, in 'The Czech Mother', she related an anecdote about her grandmother, who, during the First World War, had refused to adjust her clock to summer time because she considered this a Habsburg invention. Jesenská commented that her grandmother had been correct to insist that the real time was eleven o'clock, although everyone else had asserted that it was twelve o'clock.[169] The anecdote implied a parallel between the Habsburg and the Nazi oppression of the Czechs. It suggested that the latter, like the former, would be temporary. The Nazi ideology, like the Habsburg 'invention' of summer time, would eventually be superseded, no matter how many people supported it.

In her last article for *Přítomnost*, 'With "the needy and the naked"', published on 5 July 1939, Jesenská expressed the fear that the Czech nation would be diminished through emigration. Czechs who left the Protectorate to work in the Reich would gradually lose their Czech character (*odrodit se*). The idea that emigration was tantamount to betrayal of the nation was another longstanding theme of the national discourse. In reiterating this idea, however, Jesenská was not simply expressing a nationalist fear but also promoting one of the goals of the underground resistance: to discourage Czechs from working in Germany, where they would be supporting Hitler's war efforts. Even before the occupation, wide-spread campaigns had been launched to lure Czechs to work in Germany, where there was a shortage of labour. By 15 April 1939, the occupation powers noted that 30,000 citizens of the Protec-torate had committed themselves to work in the Reich.[170] In this and other instances, Jesenská's evocation of a national myth dove-tailed with the aims of the resistance.

While she promoted Czech solidarity and forthrightness in dealing with the German authorities, Jesenská did not refrain from criticising Czechs. In her article about the occupation, 'Prague, the Morning of 15 March 1939', she condemned Czech fascists and collaborators through statements that she attributed to unnamed Germans. She also challenged her readers to look critically at their nationalist sentiments. In the spring of 1939, the two permitted political parties in the rump state were dissolved and replaced by a single political party, which was also a political movement, *Národní souručenství* (National Union). The executive of the National Union was appointed on 21 March 1939. One of the aims of the Union was to promote Czech patriotism and solidarity. Czechs did indeed appear to be consolidated in the movement: almost 100 percent of the eligible adult male population of Bohemia and Moravia became members of the Union.[171] To begin with, a number of officials within the National Union cooperated with the organisations of the resistance movement. Gradually, however, the limited autonomy of the Union was compromised by arrests carried out by the Gestapo; the Union began to collaborate openly with the German authorities. Even in its inception, however, the Union made compromises to the authorities; one of the conditions for membership, for example, was 'Aryan origin'.[172] Jesenská responded to the establishment of the Union in her article 'Am I, First and Foremost, Czech?', published in May 1939. There she asserted that Czech nationalism had no inherent value. One's nationality was no more than a fact registered in one's birth certificate. One's moral obligation was not to be

Czech, but to be a good person. Not surprisingly, the article evoked a response from a reader who believed that under the circumstances, the most pressing duty of all Czechs was to declare their national allegiance. The letter was printed in *Přítomnost* along with Jesenská's reply that to be Czech was no accomplishment; she called upon Czechs to give their nationalism a positive content.[173] The statement indicates that Jesenská remained something of an outsider, for whom the moral duty to be a good person was more important than allegiance to a national group. In this sense, in resisting the occupation, she did not seek her fate, but rather adhered to the principles she had expressed in her writing from the beginning of the 1920s.

## Notes

1  This is the title of a recent biography. Marta Marková-Kotyková, *Mýtus Milena. Milena Jesenská jinak* (The Myth of Milena. Another Perspective on Milena Jesenská), Prague, 1993.
2  Sayer also looks at Jesenská from this perspective in Derek Sayer, *The Coasts of Bohemia. A Czech History*, Princeton, 1998, p. 212.
3  The following account is based on biographies of Jesenská: Margarete Buber-Neumann, *Milena. The Tragic Story of Kafka's Great Love* (*Kafkas Freundin Milena*, 1977), trans. Ralph Manheim, New York, 1997; Jana Černá, *Kafka's Milena* (*Adresát Milena Jesenská*, 1969), trans. A. G. Brain, Evanston, Illinois, 1993; Mary Hockaday, *Kafka, Love and Courage. The Life of Milena Jesenská* (1995), Woodstock, New York, 1997; Marie Jirásková, *Stručná zpráva o trojí volbě. Milena Jesenská, Joachim von Zedtwitz a Jaroslav Nachtmann v roce 1939 a v čase následujícím* (A Brief Account of Three Kinds of Choices. Milena Jesenská, Joachim von Zedtwitz and Jaroslav Nachtmann in 1939 and later), Prague, 1996; Marta Marková-Kotyková, *Mýtus Milena. Milena Jesenská jinak*; Alena Wagnerová, *Milena Jesenská* (1994), trans. from the German by Alena Bláhová, Prague, 1996.
4  On Jesenská's experimentation with drugs and the alleged abortion, see Hockaday, *Kafka, Love and Courage. The Life of Milena Jesenská*, pp. 17, 28.
5  Milena Jesenská, *Mileniny recepty* (Milena's Recipes), Prague, 1925; *Cesta k jednoduchosti* (The Path to Simplicity), Prague, 1926; *Člověk dělá šaty* (The Individual Makes the Clothes), Prague, 1927.
6  Rostislav Švácha, *The Architecture of New Prague 1895–1945* (*Od moderny k funkcionalismu*, 1985), trans. Alexandra Büchler, Cambridge MA and London, 1995, p. 463.
7  Hockaday, *Kafka, Love and Courage. The Life of Milena Jesenská*, p. 136.
8  Jirásková, *Stručná zpráva o trojí volbě*, p. 31.
9  Buber-Neumann, *Milena. The Tragic Story of Kafka's Great Love*, p. 2.
10  Jesenská appeared in a Vienna court charged with theft on 11 August 1919. She admitted her guilt and explained that she had wanted to buy nice clothes because she was experiencing a 'love crisis'. Marková-Kotyková, *Mýtus Milena. Milena Jesenská jinak*, p. 30.

11 See, for example, M. P., 'Kino' (Cinema), *Tribuna*, 15 January 1920, pp. 1–2; A. X. Nessey, 'Jak se dělá reklama' (How to Make an Advertisement), *Tribuna*, 14 October 1921, p. 3. Jesenská used various pseudonyms and ciphers: js-, j. s., Milena, Milena J., M., Mi, -Mj-, M. J., M. P., A. X. N., A. X. Nessey, Marie Kubešová, M. K., m. k., M. Kr.

12 A. X. Nessey, 'Sen. "Any where – out of the world"' [sic], *Tribuna*, 14 June 1921, p. 3. A translation of this article is included in Franz Kafka, *Letters to Milena* (*Briefe an Milena*, 1952), trans. Philip Boehm, New York, 1990, pp. 262–264. Boehm notes that in the title Jesenská quotes the English epigraph to book xlviii of Baudelaire's *Le Spleen de Paris*. Ibid., p. 297.

13 A. X. Nessey, 'Sen. "Any where – out of the world"', p. 3.

14 Milena, 'Dopisy' (Letters), *Národní listy*, 8 March 1923, p. 4.

15 Milena, 'Hodiny' (Clocks), *Národní listy*, 13 January 1924, p. 10.

16 A. X. Nesey, 'Tanec nad propastí' (Dance over the Abyss), *Tribuna*, 5 November 1920, pp. 1–2.

17 M. J., 'Děti ve Vídni' (Children in Vienna), *Tribuna*, 25 March 1920, pp. 1–2.

18 Ibid., p. 1.

19 Milena Jesenská, 'Statisíce hledají zemi nikoho' (Hundreds of Thousands Looking for No-Man's-Land), *Přítomnost*, 27 July 1938, pp. 477–479, see p. 479.

20 See her article: A. X. Nessey, 'Moje přítelkyně' (My Friend), *Tribuna*, 27 January 1921, pp. 1–3.

21 A. X. Nessey, 'Bývalá idyla – dnešní drama' (Former Idyll – Present-day Drama), *Tribuna*, 30 November 1920, pp. 1–2.

22 M. P., 'Život ve Vídni' (Life in Vienna), *Tribuna*, 11 March 1920, p. 1.

23 Ibid.

24 A. X. Nessey, 'Cibulička almužnou' (A Charity Onion), *Tribuna*, 9 December 1920, pp. 1–3.

25 M. P., 'Jak se ve Vídni lidé živí' (What People Eat in Vienna), *Tribuna*, 27 January 1920, pp. 1–2, see p. 2.

26 M. Jesenská, 'Nový velkoměstský typus. II.' (The New Big-City Type. II), *Tribuna*, 7 August 1920, pp. 1–2; Milena Jesenská, 'K psychologii nové společnosti' (On the Psychology of the New Society'), *Národní listy*, 30 July 1922, p. 2.

27 Milena, 'Skleník pro živé rostlinky' (Greenhouses for Live Plants), *Národní listy*, 6 December 1925, p. 11.

28 Milena, 'Omnia mea mecum porto', *Národní listy*, 13 March 1924, p. 5.

29 Milena, 'Sláva jednoduchost!' (Glory to Simplicity), *Národní listy*, 3 September 1925, p. 5.

30 Milena, 'Pro odpoledne' (For the Afternoon), *Národní listy*, 27 September 1925, p. 10.

31 Milena, 'Klobouky' (Hats), *Lidové noviny*, 25 August 1929, p. 22.

32 Milena, 'Trench-coat čili Ten in one' (The Trench-coat, or Ten-in-One), *Národní listy*, 15 February 1925, p. 12. Republished in *Šť'astnou cestu* (Have a Good Trip!), Prague, 1927, pp. 92–95.

33 M. J., 'Malované šaty' (Painted Clothes), *Tribuna*, 29 August 1920, p. 6.

34 Milena, 'Moda a standardní ideal' (Fashion and the Standard Ideal), *Národní listy*, 13 December 1925, p. 17.

35 Milena, 'Modní a moderní' (The Fashionable and the Modern), *Národní listy*, 20 June 1926, p. 15.

36 She also idealised the British. By contrast, she criticised the Germans for their excessive love of order and the Czechs for their provincialism. On her attitude to nationalities, see, for example: Milena, 'Anglické kostymy' (English Suits), _Národní listy_, 16 March 1924, p. 13; M. J. 'Americká žena' (The American Woman), _Národní listy_, 7 December 1924, p. 11.

37 Milena, 'Dorůstající dívky' (Adolescent Girls), _Národní listy_, 14 December 1924, p. 14.

38 Milena, 'Pro tennis' (For Tennis), _Lidové noviny_, 27 April 1930, supplement, p. 2.

39 Milena, 'Pro sport na trávníku' (For Lawn Sports), _Národní listy_, 20 May 1923, p. 9.

40 Milena, 'Všeho s měrou' (Everything in Moderation), _Národní listy_, 1 May 1924, p. 9.

41 Milena, 'Župany' (Dressing-gowns), _Lidové noviny_, 13 October 1929, p. 20. She also wrote about her experience of illness in 'Radio', _Národní listy_, 14 October 1928, p. 13.

42 Milena, 'Boty a střevíce' (Boots and Shoes), _Národní listy_, 6 April 1924, p. 10.

43 Milena, 'Francouzské kostymy' (French Suits), _Národní listy_, 30 March 1924, p. 10. The general trend of the time in Czechoslovakia, however, was adulation of French fashion. See Eva Uchalová, _Česká móda 1918–1939. Elegance první republiky_ (Czech Fashion 1918–1939. The Elegance of the First Republic), Prague, 1996, p. 17.

44 Milena, 'Ex libris' (Book-plates), _Národní listy_, 24 July 1924, p. 3.

45 Milena, 'Romantika psacích stolečků' (The Romanticism of Desks), _Národní listy_, 31 July 1927, p. 11.

46 Adolf Loos, 'Ornament a zločin', trans. V. N., _Tribuna_, 15 June 1922, pp. 3–4. Loos' essay is usually dated to 1908.

47 See Rostislav Švácha, 'Architektura dvacátých let v Čechách' (The Architecture of the 1920s in Bohemia), in _Dějiny českého výtvarného umění_ (The History of Czech Art), 1890/1938, vol. IV/2, eds Vojtěch Lahoda, Mahulena Nešlehová, Marie Platovská, Rostislav Švácha and Lenka Bydžovská, Prague, 1998, pp. 11–35, see p. 15.

48 Milena, 'Mezinárodní výstava Werkbundu "Die Wohnung" ve Stuttgartu' (The International _Werkbund 'Die Wohnung'_ Exhibition in Stuttgart), I–IV, _Národní listy_, 23 October 1927, p. 13; 30 October 1927, p. 10; 6 November 1927, p. 10; 20 November 1927, p. 10.

49 M. J., 'Prádlo' (Underwear), _Tribuna_, 30 May 1920, p. 10.

50 Milena, 'Krásná žena' (A Beautiful Woman), _Národní listy_, 29 November 1923, p. 5.

51 Milena Jesenská, 'Zvenčí a uvnitř' (Inside and Out), _Národní listy_, 1 October 1925, p. 6.

52 Milena, 'Masopust' (Carnival), _Národní listy_, 17 January 1924, p. 5.

53 Jesenská, 'Zvenčí a uvnitř', p. 6.

54 M. J., 'Moda a sport' (Fashion and Sport), _Tribuna_, 22 August 1920, p. 6. Uchalová notes that the fashion of trousers for women was promoted in the catalogue _Civilisovaná žena, Zivilisierte Frau_ (Brno, 1929) to which Jesenská contributed. This had been a theme in Jesenská's articles from 1920 on. Uchalová, _Česká móda 1918–1939. Elegance první republiky_, pp. 33–35.

55 Milena, 'Pláště' (Overcoats), _Národní listy_, 13 December 1923, p. 4.

56 Milena, '"Uličnické" šaty' ("Urchin" Clothes), _Národní listy_, 27 March 1924, p. 5.

57 Milena, 'Účes 1924' (1924 Hairstyle), *Národní listy*, 13 April 1924, p. 10.
58 Milena, 'Klobouk a účes' (Hat and Hairstyle), *Národní listy*, 19 September 1926, p. 16.
59 Milena, 'Masopust', p. 5.
60 Milena, 'Trench-coat čili Ten in one', p. 12.
61 Milena, 'Nedáme se' (We Won't Give In), *Národní listy*, 5 September 1926, p. 10.
62 Milena, 'Všední šaty' (Everyday Clothes), *Lidové noviny*, 1 September 1929, p. 22.
63 Milena, 'Dekorativní předmět?' (Decorative Object?), *Národní listy*, 18 October 1925, p. 10.
64 Ibid.
65 M. J., 'Žena doma' (Woman at Home), *Tribuna*, 30 March 1920, pp. 1–2, see p. 1.
66 A. X. Nessey, 'Povrchní povídání o vážném předmětě' (Superficial Small Talk about a Serious Subject), *Tribuna*, 17 June 1922, p. 3.
67 Milena, 'Budouci maminky' (Future Mothers), *Národní listy*, 23 March 1924, p. 5.
68 Milena Jesenská, 'O té ženské emancipaci několik poznámek velice zaostalých' (A Few Old-Fashioned Comments About Women's Emancipation), *Národní listy*, 17 February 1923, p. 1.
69 Milena, 'Thema, které k modě nepatří' (A Theme that has Nothing to do with Fashion), *Národní listy*, 22 November 1923, p. 4.
70 Milena, 'Dobrá hospodyně' (A Good Housewife), *Národní listy*, 25 December 1923, p. 13.
71 Milena, "Dáma a 'moderní' žena" (A Lady and a 'Modern' Woman), *Národní listy*, 14 January 1926, p. 5.
72 Milena, 'Obyčejný den' (An Ordinary Day), *Národní listy*, 19 June 1926, supplement, p. 1.
73 Milena, 'Moderní dívčí výchova' (Modern Upbringing for Girls), *Národní listy*, 17 October 1926, p. 13.
74 Milena, 'Ještě ta samostatnost' (That Independence Once More), *Národní listy*, 31 October 1926, p. 13.
75 Milena, 'Děvče u volantu' (A Girl at the Wheel), *Národní listy*, 29 May 1927, p. 13.
76 Milena, 'Křik po samostatnosti' (A Cry for Independence), *Lidové noviny*, 27 October 1929, p. 30.
77 Milena, 'Miminko' (Baby), *Lidové noviny*, 21 April 1929, p. 18.
78 Milena, 'Civilisovaná žena?' (Civilised Woman?), *Lidové noviny*, 1 December 1929, p. 20.
79 Sander Gilman treats the subject of Kafka's illness and his self-conception as a Jew in *Franz Kafka, the Jewish Patient*, London and New York, 1995.
80 Kafka, *Letters to Milena*, p. 21.
81 Ibid., p. 44.
82 Ibid., pp. 6, 28, 79.
83 M. J., 'Plavky' (Bathing Costumes), *Tribuna*, 1 August 1920, p. 6.
84 Ibid.
85 Kafka, *Letters to Milena*, p. 129. Date of letter: 1 August 1920.
86 Ibid., p. 153. Date of letter: 10 August 1920.
87 Milena Jesenská, 'Nový velkoměstský typus' (The New Big-City Type), *Tribuna*, 2 July 1920, pp. 1–2.

88  Sander Gilman, *The Jew's Body*, London and New York, 1991, p. 47. See also O. G. Blanický, *O antisemitismu v českém národě* (The Anti-Semitism of the Czech Nation), Prague, 1919, pp. 22–24.

89  M. Jesenská, 'Nový velkoměstský typus. II', p. 1.

90  See, for example, his description of the trip from Vienna to Prague in the letter of 5 July 1920. Kafka, *Letters to Milena*, pp. 64–7.

91  Milena, 'Bezvadnost, opora nejistoty' (Perfection, a Support in Uncertainty), *Národní listy*, 17 January 1926, p. 13.

92  It is difficult to say to what extent she was influenced by Kafka's views. He wrote about the insecure position of the Jews in the letter of 30 May 1920. Kafka, *Letters to Milena*, p. 20.

93  Milena, 'Slovíčka' (Words), *Národní listy*, 1 July 1926, p. 5.

94  M. J., 'Výkladní skříně' (Shop-Windows), *Tribuna*, 21 August 1920, pp. 1–2, see p. 2.

95  Kafka, *Letters to Milena*, p. 168. Date of letter: 26 August 1920.

96  js-, 'Kavárna' (The Café), *Tribuna*, 10 August 1920, pp. 1–2, see p. 1.

97  Kafka, *Letters to Milena*, p. 18. Their exchange finds an echo in articles in which Jesenská distinguished between the hungry and the sated, for example in 'The Art of Consolation'. There she wrote: 'Have you ever noticed in yourselves how difficult it is to see a person in a favourable and how easy in an unfavourable light? To acknowledge the good traits of others, one has to have some of one's own. People who do not have any, envy them in others. People who do have them do not need to envy; they are like the sated, who do not covet the morsel of another person. They are sated and therefore they have a good heart and a kind smile for everyone.' (Milena, 'O umění potěšit', *Národní listy*, 14 September 1924, p. 10.)

98  Kafka, *Letters to Milena*, p. 157.

99  Kafka mentioned Mrs Kohler a number of times in his letters. See, for example, Kafka, *Letters to Milena*, pp. 78–9, 84.

100  A. X. Nessey, 'Moje přítelkyně' (My Friend), pp.1–3.

101  A. X. Nessey, 'Útěk k bezmocným' (Retreat to the Helpless), *Tribuna*, 15 February 1921, pp. 1–2, see p. 1.

102  Kafka, *Letters to Milena*, p. 140.

103  Ibid., p. 30. Date of letter: 3 June 1920.

104  A. X. Nessey, 'Tajemná vykoupení' (Mysterious Redemption), *Tribuna*, 25 February 1921, pp. 1–2, see p. 2. See Kafka, *Letters to Milena*, p. 6. Date of letter: April 1920.

105  A. X. Nessey, 'Melancholie v dešti' (Melancholy in the Rain), *Tribuna*, 29 April 1921, pp. 1–2.

106  Kafka, *Letters to Milena*, p. 228. Date of letter: January–February 1923.

107  A. X. Nessey, 'Povrchní povídání o vážném předmětě', p. 3.

108  Milena Jesenská, 'Ďábel u krbu' (Devil at the Hearth), *Národní listy*, 18 January 1923, pp. 1–2, see p. 2.

109  Kafka, *Letters to Milena*, p. 229. Date of letter: January–February 1923.

110  Ibid., p. 231.

111  Ibid., p. 229.

112  See, for example, his interpretation of the relationship in the letter of 14 September 1920. Ibid., pp. 193–194.

113  Ibid., p. 231.

114  Ibid., pp. 147–48.

115  Ibid., p. 150.

116 Milena, 'Moderní tance' (Modern Dances), *Národní listy*, 14 February 1924, p. 4.
117 Milena, 'Do trhu', *Národní listy*, 28 February 1924, p. 5.
118 Quoted in Max Brod, *Franz Kafka. A Biography* (1960), trans. G. Humphreys Roberts and Richard Winston, 2nd enlarged edition, New York, 1995, pp. 229–230.
119 Milena Jesenská, 'Neznámí známí' (Unknown Acquaintances), *Národní listy*, 20 May 1924, pp. 1–2, see p. 1. She refers to the comedian Karl Valentin (Ludwig Fey Valentin, 1892–1948).
120 Ibid.
121 Milena, 'Život v lázních' (Life in Spas), *Národní listy*, 4 May 1924, p. 10. Her reference to solitude in the midst of a crowd recalls her description of those who frequent coffee-houses in 'The Café'.
122 Milena, 'Do vody' (Into the Water), *Národní listy*, 8 May 1924, p. 5.
123 Milena, 'Na venek' (Into the Countryside), *Národní listy*, 25 May 1924, p. 10.
124 Milena, 'Babí léto' (Indian Summer), *Národní listy*, 18 September 1924, p. 5.
125 Milena Jesenská, 'Franz Kafka', *Národní listy*, 6 June 1924, p. 5. The obituary has been reprinted in Czech in: Milena Jesenská, *Zvenčí a zevnitř. Antologie textů Mileny Jesenské* (Inside and Out. An Anthology of Texts by Milena Jesenská), ed. Ludmila Hegnerová, Prague, 1996, pp. 21–22. English translations appears in: Jana Černá, *Kafka's Milena*, pp.179–180; and Kafka, *Letters to Milena*, pp. 271–272. An excerpt appears in Wilma Abeles Iggers, *Women of Prague. Ethnic Diversity and Social Change from the Eighteenth Century to the Present*, Oxford and Providence, 1995, pp. 263–264.
126 Kafka, *Letters to Milena*, p. 95.
127 In her fashion columns, Jesenská repeatedly treated the subject of childhood. She wrote about Otto Gross's theories (M. J., 'Šaty a výchova' [Clothes and Upbringing], *Tribuna*, 31 October 1920, p. 5.) She argued that infants and young children were easily damaged by exposure to the sexuality of their parents. (Milena, 'Kolébky' [Cradles], *Národní listy*, 11 October 1923, p. 5; Milena, 'Veselá výzdoba dětského pokoje' [Cheerful Decoration of Children's Rooms], *Národní listy*, 17 July 1924, p. 4.) She believed that a person's character was formed by the age of five. (Milena Jesenská, 'Hračky' [Toys], *Národní listy*, 8 April 1922, pp. 1–2.) Children were influenced by the atmosphere in the home and the relationship between their parents. (Milena, 'Maminko, bud' hezká' [Mother, be pretty!], *Národní listy*, 19 April 1925, p. 14.) Children should be toughened up through physical exercise, fresh air and daily baths; they should be brought up not to fear. Automatic obedience, which resulted from fear, was an obstacle to the development of a healthy person. (Milena, 'Prádýlko pro děti' [Baby Clothes], *Národní listy*, 3 April 1924, p. 5) Corporal punishment of children was wrong. (Milena, 'Trestání dětí' [The Punishment of Children], *Národní listy*, 24 April 1924, p. 5.) Children became rebellious when their parents did not treat them with respect. (Milena, 'Rythmus vnitřních dění' [The Rhythm of Internal Developments], *Lidové noviny*, 16 March 1930, p. 18.)
128 Quoted in Gilman, *Franz Kafka, the Jewish Patient*, p. 32.
129 See, for example, his comment in a letter from November 1920: 'After all, we both know numerous typical examples of the Western Jew; as far as I know I'm the most Western-Jewish of them all.' Kafka, *Letters to Milena*, p. 217.
130 Milena, 'Konvence na ruby' (Convention Turned Inside-out), *Národní listy*, 31 December 1925, p. 5. Jesenská referred obliquely to Kafka in an article that she wrote in July 1927. There she described a dream of being transformed into an

enormous gopher that lived in a burrow with intricate corridors. The description reminds one of the rodent in Kafka's 'The Burrow' (_Der Bau_, written in the winter of 1923–24, published in 1931). Jesenská probably had not read the story. In his letters to her, however, Kafka had described himself as a burrowing animal. See Milena, 'Stěhovati se' (Moving House), _Národní listy_, 17 July 1927, p. 12.

131 Milena Jesenská, 'Zvenčí a uvnitř', p. 6.

132 Milena Jesenská, 'Soudce Lynch v Evropě' (Judge Lynch in Europe), _Přítomnost_, 30 March 1938, pp. 206–208, see p. 208.

133 A. X. Nessey, 'Cibulička almužnou', p. 2.

134 Milena, 'Vánoční stromeček' (The Christmas Tree), _Národní listy_, 16 December 1923, p. 13.

135 Milena Jesenská, '_Soldaten wohnen auf den Kanonen_', _Přítomnost_, 21 June 1939, pp. 390–391, see p. 391.

136 Milena Jesenská, 'S "ubohým a holým"' (With "the needy and naked"), _Přítomnost_, 5 July 1939, pp. 418–419, see p. 419.

137 Milena, 'O primadonství' (On being a Prima Donna), _Národní listy_, 18 September 1927, p. 10.

138 Milena Jesenská, 'Statisíce hledají zemi nikoho' (Hundreds of Thousands Looking for No-Man's-Land), _Přítomnost_, 27 July 1938, pp. 477–479, see p. 477.

139 Milena Jesenská, 'Lidé na výspě (Z osudů německých emigrantů)' (People on a Promontory [From the Fates of the German Emigrés]), _Nad naše síly. Češi, Židé a Němci 1937–1939_ (Beyond Our Strength: Czechs, Jews and Germans 1937–1939), selected by Václav Burian, Olomouc, 1997, pp. 5–13, see p. 13. Originally published in _Přítomnost_ on 27 October 1937.

140 M. J., 'Dopisy vynikajících lidí' (The Letters of Eminent People), _Tribuna_, 15 August 1920, p. 6.

141 Milena Jesenská, 'Anšlus nebude. II. Napříč rodinami' (There Will Be No Anschluss. Part II. Dividing Families), _Nad naše síly_, pp. 31–41, see p. 35. Originally published in _Přítomnost_ on 1 June 1938.

142 Milena Jesenská, 'Pověz, kam utíkáš – povím ti, kdo jsi' (Tell Me Where You Are Fleeing to – and I'll Tell You Who You Are), _Nad naše síly_, pp. 92–98, see p. 95. Originally published in _Přítomnost_, 21 September 1938.

143 Milena Jesenská, 'V pohraničí: kolik bodů pro nás?' (In the Border Regions: How Many Points for Us?), _Nad naše síly_, pp. 80–91, see p. 84. Originally published in _Přítomnost_ on 7 September 1938.

144 Milena Jesenská, 'Kolik stála Henleinova řeč v Karlových Varech?' (What was the Cost of Henlein's Speech in Karlovy Vary?), _Nad naše síly_, pp. 42–50, see p. 50. Originally published in _Přítomnost_ on 22 June 1938.

145 Milena Jesenská, 'Nad naše síly' (Beyond Our Strength), _Přítomnost_, 12 October 1938, pp. 650–651, see p. 651.

146 Jan Gebhart and Jan Kuklík, _Dramatické i všední dny protektorátu_ (Dramatic and Ordinary Days in the Protectorate), Prague, 1996, p. 48.

147 Milena Jesenská, 'Denní zprávy na posledních stránkách' (The Daily News on the Back Pages), _Nad naše síly_, pp. 121–127, see p. 127. Originally published in _Přítomnost_, 19 October 1938.

148 Jesenská, 'Ďábel u krbu', p. 2.

149 Milena Jesenská, 'Změněné nakupování' (Shopping Changed), _Nad naše síly_, pp. 204–207, see p. 207. Originally published in _Přítomnost_, 26 April 1939.

150 Jesenská, 'Kolik stála Henleinova řeč v Karlových Varech?', p. 49.

151 Jesenská, 'Denní zprávy na posledních stránkách', pp. 121–122.

152 Tomáš Pasák, 'Problematika protektorátního tisku a formování tzv. skupiny aktivistických novinářů na počátku okupace' (The Problems of the Protectorate Press and the Formation of the Group of So-called Activist Journalists at the Beginning of the Occupation), *Příspěvky k dějinám KSČ* (Contributions to the History of the CPC), vol. 7, 1967, pp. 52–80, see p. 54. The following summary of the censorship restrictions is based on this article.

153 Ibid., p. 58.

154 Gebhart and Kuklík, *Dramatické i všední dny protektorátu*, p. 10.

155 Ibid., p. 12.

156 Pasák, 'Problematika protektorátního tisku a formování tzv. skupiny aktivistických novinářů na počátku okupace', p. 62, note 49.

157 A. X. Nessey, 'Novoroční přání' (New Year's Greetings), *Tribuna*, 1 January 1921, p. 18.

158 Milena, 'O zdvořilosti' (Courtesy), *Národní listy*, 25 September 1924, p. 5.

159 Ibid.

160 Milena, 'To nešťastné mikado' (That Unfortunate Bobbed Hair), *Národní listy*, 11 September 1924, p. 5.

161 Milena, 'Čaj' (Tea), *Národní listy*, 11 January 1925, p. 10.

162 Milena, 'Cetky a tretky' (Trinkets and Knick-knacks), *Národní listy*, 26 April 1925, p. 12.

163 Robert B. Pynsent, 'The Decadent Nation: The Politics of Arnošt Procházka and Jiří Karásek ze Lvovic', in *Intellectuals and the Future in the Habsburg Monarchy 1890–1914*, eds Lászlo Péter and Robert B. Pynsent, Basingstoke and London, 1988, pp. 63–91, see p. 82. See also: Sayer, *The Coasts of Bohemia. A Czech History*, pp. 154–155.

164 Buber-Neumann, *Milena: The Tragic Story of Kafka's Great Love*, pp. 141–143.

165 Milena Jesenská, 'Jak se stýkat s Čechy?' (How Should One Treat the Czechs?), *Nad naše síly*, pp. 166–171, see p. 169. Originally published in *Přítomnost*, 15 February 1939.

166 Jesenská, 'Jak se stýkat s Čechy?', p. 170.

167 She wrote: 'We stand next to the Germans as equals in terms of level of civilisation, skill in craftsmanship, industry and personal honour.' Milena Jesenská, 'Týká se nás všech' (It Concerns All of Us), *Nad naše síly*, pp. 236–239, see p. 238. Originally published in *Přítomnost* on 14 June 1939.

168 Milena Jesenská, 'Promiňte, že nešeptám' (Excuse Me for Not Whispering), *Nad naše síly*, pp. 219–223, see p. 221. Originally published in *Přítomnost* on 24 May 1939.

169 Milena Jesenská, 'Česká maminka' (The Czech Mother), *Nad naše síly*, pp. 200–203, see p. 203. Originally published in *Přítomnost*, 19 April 1939.

170 Gebhart and Kuklík, *Dramatické i všední dny protektorátu*, pp. 49–50.

171 Membership was restricted to the male population. Ibid., p. 33.

172 Ibid., p. 32.

173 Milena Jesenská, 'Stačí být Čechem?' (Is it Enough to be Czech?), *Nad naše síly*, pp. 224–228. Originally published in *Přítomnost*, 24 May 1939.

1. Milena Jesenská, photo probably taken to mark her graduation from Minerva, from the archive of Marie Jirásková.

2. Milena Jesenská, 1917, from the archive of Marie Jirásková.

3. Milena Jesenská, ca. 1920, from the archive of Marie Jirásková.

4. Milena Jesenská and Jaromír Krejcar, summer of 1926, from the archive of the Jílovská family.

**5.** Milena Jesenská, 1926, from the archive of the Jílovská family.

**6.** Milena Jesenská with her daughter Honza, ca. 1929–1930, from the archive of Marie Jirásková.

7. *Civilisovaná žena, Zivilisierte Frau* (The Civilised Woman), 1929, cover by Zdeněk Rossmann, a publication to which Jesenská contributed, photograph from the Institute for Art History, Academy of Sciences of the Czech Republic.

8. Milena Jesenská, photo taken by the Gestapo at the beginning of 1940, from the archive of Marie Jirásková.

9. Milena Jesenská with her tennis coaches, May 1911. Photo from the archive of Jaroslava Vondráčková, Museum of Czech Literature, Prague.

**10.** Franz Kafka, ca. 1920, at about the age of thirty-seven. Museum of Czech Literature, Prague.

**11.** Milena Jesenská, ca. 1930–1933. Photo from the archive of Jaroslava Vondráčková, Museum of Czech Literature, Prague.

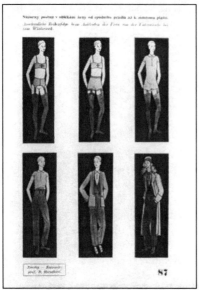

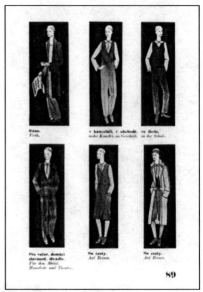

**12.** Illustration from *Civilisovaná žena,*
*Zivilisierte Frau* (The Civilised
Woman), 1929. The caption reads:
'An illustrated approach to dress
for women, from the undergar-
ments to the winter coat.' Photo
from the archive of Jaroslava
Vondráčková, Museum of Czech
Literature, Prague.

**13.** Illustration from *Civilisovaná žena,*
*Zivilisierte Frau* (The Civilised
Woman), 1929. The caption reads:
'Morning, at the office, in the
shop, at school. For the evening,
a party at home, the theatre. For
travel.' Photo from the archive of
Jaroslava Vondráčková, Museum
of Czech Literature, Prague.

**14.** Illustration from *Civilisovaná žena,*
*Zivilisierte Frau* (The Civilised
Woman), 1929. The caption reads:
'For work in the kitchen and in
the household. The mother of the
future. The mother of today.'
Photo from the archive of
Jaroslava Vondráčková, Museum of
Czech Literature, Prague.

# I. Articles from *Tribuna*, 1920–1922

# What People Eat in Vienna

## 27 January 1920, *Tribuna*

Most ordinary mortals eat in the so-called communal kitchens.[1]
There are various kinds – for journalists, artists, academics, clerks
and ordinary people – in various districts, one or two in almost
every district, as like one another as peas in a pod. They are all
equally cheap – 6.00–6.50 Austrian crowns for a lunch; they all
stink unbearably of sauerkraut and cheap grease. In all of them one
eats with bent tin cutlery at bare tables. There is the same thing
every day in all of them: the soup: dirty water with boiled barley,
beans or sauerkraut or sauerkraut or beans. On meat days, a bit of
stinking salami or mince is added, a strange gruel of salami and
breadcrumbs. Then a little piece of damson-cheese tart, made from
dough in which there is black flour, water and a lot of yeast so that
it rises quickly. For six crowns it is impossible to do more than that
and still make money. But it is also impossible to get full on this
fare and after a fortnight you cannot enter such a room without
feeling nauseous at the very smell. Yet: what else can one do? For
six crowns no one can cook even a carrot at home, perhaps not
even sauerkraut, that terrible damned sauerkraut, which all of
Vienna stinks of, every house from top to bottom. I am quite certain
that I will not touch sauerkraut as long as I live unless I have to –
one's nose, mouth, stomach, everything is always full of sauerkraut.

Students eat in these kitchens, as well as the wives of clerks
(clerks have their own canteens at the banks, where one pays a little
less and eats a little better, but still very badly), professors, all
theatre employees with great hopes but small salaries, teachers,
journalists and the widows of all sorts of executives and dignitaries.
Sometimes even entire families with their children and maid. All

---

1 The subject of the article was relevant to contemporaries because of the food
  shortage in Vienna following the First World War. Under the old Habsburg
  system, Vienna's main source of food had been Hungary. During the war,
  Hungary had cut off the usual food supplies to Vienna and Lower Austria,
  which then made greater demands on the farmers in the hereditary lands.
  These, however, preferred to keep food for themselves. When the war ended,
  this practice did not change. Because of the disruption caused by the war, food
  was often in short supply there too. See Elisabeth Barker, *Austria 1918–1972*,
  Basingstoke and London, 1973, p. 11.

those scores of souls in a big city who either do not have enough
money to eat decently or enough courage not to eat at all – that is,
to live ungoverned by convention and to make do with what the
Lord provides. This is the hardest hit population of Vienna – people
who do not have the opportunity to complain, protest, strike or
make demands, who silently divide up the kreutzers on the first of
the month and who, if they are going to wear shoes, cannot eat
that month; or if they are going to eat, must walk on tiptoe through
the mud because there is not enough money left over to sole their
shoes.

   In Vienna, however, one can also eat and drink one's fill, if the
pocket permits. There are hotels and restaurants that offer simply
everything. In every large restaurant in the centre of the city (the
Opernrestaurant, Imperial, Schöner Mozartrestaurant, Hopfner and
dozens of others) one can get poultry and roasts, cooked in various
ways, excellent soups, splendid cakes and pastries. The menu inno-
cently offers only what is permitted. When you are making your
choice, however, the waiter bends down over you and whispers
mysteriously: 'Will that be Hungarian sauerkraut?' Sauerkraut! You
are startled and ask: 'What's that?' 'Oh, something delicious,' he
answers condescendingly and compassionately. If you have to ask
what it is, you are not very 'posh', my dear; if you were, you would
have known. 'Well then, bring me sauerkraut,' you decide. A
moment later, with an undulating motion he carries over a plate
that looks like a heap of sauerkraut. Under that heap, however,
there really is always 'something delicious', for example, roast pork!
Or: roast veal! Wiener Schnitzel! A braised chop! A piece of chicken!
A leg of goose! A haunch of venison! Miracles!

   The same goes for pudding. On the menu is written: noodles.
Damson strudel. Semolina *Fleckerl*. If you know how to speak intelligently with the waiter, however, a sideboard appears in the corner
and on that sideboard, cakes with custard cream, fancy cakes made
with butter, wonderfully light jam-tarts, one could eat twenty at a
sitting, slices of sugared sponge-cake. In a restaurant like Sacher's,
where practically only foreigners eat nowadays, one can order the
most sophisticated dishes with mayonnaise and caviar, or chocolate
blancmange with cream, or peach Melba – ice cream with fruit and
cream. To be sure, at Sacher's one cannot eat dinner for less than
five hundred crowns. I think that in the whole of Prague one could
not find food as well-prepared, as tasty as in Vienna. And not only
Prague, but in many other cities. Oh, Vienna knows what a culi-
nary delight is and Vienna will not let that be snatched away, even
when hundreds, no thousands of its children eat sauerkraut in their

despair. From time to time, one of the famous restaurants is closed for a few days by the police. That does no harm, however. On the contrary – it is a kind of advertisement. Really, they probably knew why they closed it – the food was probably too good there!

One can eat just as well in the large hotels. In the Bristol, in the Grand Hotel, in the Hotel Kranz, where mostly Hungarians live and English, French and other people with plenty of money. Every day these foreigners receive milk, butter, white rolls, ham, eggs from the various shopkeepers who deliver it all right to their rooms and – for foreign currency, at a relatively low price. What are a few francs to a Frenchman for such an excellent breakfast? To be sure, for the shopkeeper, a franc is worth more than even the most shameless sum in Austrian crowns.

Recently, it has been possible to eat in the cafés as well. It would probably be hard to imagine a city that has more cafés than Vienna. There is no street that does not have at least one café; most likely there are three or four, always completely full. The cafés have their styles: each one different. There are bohemian cafés where the journalists, the writers, actors and artists sit – but also the strangest people, the most peculiar types, no one knows where they surfaced from, people with grotesque attire, grotesque faces and grotesque lives. People have been coming here for years and they know one another.

As far as the women are concerned, everyone knows when and who first brought them here. It is known with whom they were unfaithful to their first lovers and if they are getting divorced, why and because of whom. They move from table to table and see their former lovers and husbands every day at different tables and with other women. There are enmities here, friendships, factions, groups, opinions; all these people drag their lives around the little café tables for years and the café gets used to scenes, tragedies, comedies, to celebrations of newly published books, to curses over bad reviews. The café acquires its own style. Well then, one can dine even here and what's more – one can dine here on credit. The waiter, either Anton or Franz, is always here – and he knows his poets and critics and how much can be expected from them on the first of the month. And according to that, one can dine on credit – on cheese, or today corned beef, even boiled eggs and sardines. Of course, everything is terribly expensive. Yet it is sometimes cheaper to have an expensive dinner on credit than to have a cheap meal and pay – a mystery not everyone will understand.

There are other cafés with other styles. A band plays in the middle of the room. Sitting at the tables is a mixture of the most diverse people: young ladies who are chatting, lovers who are silent, elegant waifs who are seeking. There's an unbelievable noise here; tongues move to the rhythm of the Viennese waltz; people drink hot chocolate and eat wonderful pastries!

There are 'black-market' cafés. Here, almost all the people stand, fully dressed with their hats still on their heads. They get drinks from the bar and eat little sandwiches with cold meat, or rolls with butter and jam, while they stand. They make dizzying business deals. The mediator of all these deals is – the headwaiter. All you have to do is go up to him, stick a hundred-crown note in his hand – a waiter like that makes thousands every day – and say: 'Sir, I have so-and-so many trucks of coal, flour, candles, condensed milk and oranges' – whatever you happen to have – 'to whom should I sell?' – He answers: 'That gentleman at the third table on the left might buy perhaps, but not a whole truck.' Or: 'Oh, Sir, the one man you need just left. But tomorrow at half past three he will certainly be here!' Or: 'No, you won't sell coal today, but if you have medicine – you do? Well then, Sir, there in the corner at the table on the right you will sell it.'

Medicine that one cannot buy anywhere in Vienna passes through these hands and continues on immediately to countries with a stronger currency, medicine for lack of which people in hospitals and sanatoriums are suffering and perhaps even dying.

The headwaiters of the Vienna cafés, bars and pubs live like this: near Vienna, a villa with modern furnishings and comforts and a servant, where they go every third day and where a man is his own master. The other two days, he puts on a coat and accepts tips with a bow.

How many absurdities there are in the mechanism we call the big city!

# The New Big-City Type
## 2 July 1920, *Tribuna*

Five years of war shook the world like it was a sack of pears. Today, when the sack is standing relatively still once again in a corner of the universe, when we have time to examine our limbs and our heads, to look around ourselves and recover, we slowly count up all those changes, revolutions, consequences and results. Truly, they are great, for us they are great, for us they are practically incomprehensible. But if I think about it more: what is so incomprehensible? How has that old tune of the world changed? People who have money have full stomachs and are doing well. People who do not have money are hungry and are doing badly. Hasn't it always been like that in the world? It is just that different people are hungry today than before the war, than a hundred years ago, than before the revolution that was before the last revolution and before the one that was before that. It seems to me that in the eyes of God, it does not matter which one of us is wretched, whether it is this or that stratum of people and that it is almost irrelevant who is sated and clothed and who is hungry and in rags. When those who have money today achieve too much success in the world, the sack will be shaken and those who were on the bottom will be on the top again. Unless, of course, a miracle occurs and people on earth finally come to an agreement so that everyone has enough to eat.

Of course, if it is all the same to history what happens to people, it is not, cannot and should not, be all the same to us. Therefore it is correct, after all, when I say that the whole world has changed.

Not only the basic conditions of the world have changed, however; all the little parts of the world have changed as well, all the details, all the faces of the cities and streets. Something gained here, something lost there. Creatures have emerged about whom we all know and about whom the world does not yet know because they have not been officially identified. They are here. They edge in among us and when we are surprised for a moment and ask ourselves, 'how did they get here?', we have to answer, 'the war, of course'. Now that is clear, they remain amongst us, part of the landscape; now they are settling down, they are living, growing fat, taking over the present, they have a future.

One of them is the man who will buy anything. Do you know the man who will buy anything? Perhaps he is a descendant of that rag-and-bone man who used to call out in the courtyards: 'rags and bones, old glass!' The one they used to scare us with when we were naughty. I do not know. Perhaps he has no past. But he is here. He is here to stay; shamelessly he is striking root, he grows, gets stronger, prospers ...

Well then, one day the man who will buy anything knocks at the door – and, as the devil would have it, just at a time when you do not have any money. A man of his sort can smell that while still on the stairs, the way one smells the aroma of onion sauce – that is his job. You open the door and ask him what he wants. The man at the door oozes politeness. Do you have anything to sell? Clothes? Shoes? Linen? Hats? Duvets? Books? Furniture? Glass? Pictures? China? A tidal wave of questions. If you don't have shoes, you must have books. But at least old carpets! No? Then old bottles? Of course, you have old bottles: they are in the way, why shouldn't he take them away? But alas! Once you let the man who will buy anything into your flat, he certainly will not leave until he has bought something. He proceeds cautiously so as not to frighten you. He discovers a wardrobe in the corner. What a nice wardrobe! Sell it! He will pay well! You laugh. How could you manage without the wardrobe? The man who will buy anything, however, is unyielding. Slowly (please do not forget that this is a time when you have no money!) you begin to listen to him. One could, after all, put the linen in the other wardrobe, it's half-empty as it is; one could put a little table where the wardrobe stands. You give in. And what do you know? At that moment, all of a sudden, the nice – the very nice – wardrobe becomes an old useless cupboard for the man who will buy anything. It's got a battered corner here. It's old, old-fashioned and too small (or too big, as the case may be). It has five shelves, if only it had four instead! (If it has four, he says, 'if only it had five!') It's brown, if only it were black! (If it is black, he says, 'if only it were brown!') But the devil has already got into your head. All of a sudden an opportunity has presented itself to get rid of all the worries that have been tormenting you. (You forget that at the end of the next month you will have the same troubles, only worse because the wardrobe will no longer be there.) Now you want to sell the wardrobe at any price. The man who will buy anything stands there and thinks about it, hands in his pockets. He turns up his nose, shrugs his shoulders, babbles on endlessly until finally he agrees. Two hundred crowns! But because it's you, only because it's you! Otherwise? Oh, a whole two hundred crowns! You don't even know how much he will be losing on this deal! How could he ever get two hundred crowns for this rubbish? You stand meekly, eyes downcast. What a good man! What a beautiful soul! Only 'for you' he will waste time and money and carry away your wardrobe! What altruism!

Yes, that is the man who will buy anything. Take a look around: somewhere in the slum streets he has a little shop. There used to be only one junk shop in the city, in some proletarian nook. Today the streets have one junk shop after another, each more mysterious than the next. In a shop-window, not cleaned for years, a jumble of the most pathetic objects is lying about – shirts, blouses, shoes, china, mirrors, little tables, vases, a hat, a parrot cage.

When you stand in front of the shop-window, it almost hurts you. It must have been some terrible poverty or anxiety that brought that mirror, that statue of St George in a glass dome, that nightshirt with torn lace on the left sleeve, that pair of nice white shoes – here, amongst this rubbish, into the dark hole of this man. He sits on his goods, bought by haggling, like an ugly, repulsive, sprawling spider. In his dirty, torn jacket full of holes he looks poor and wretched – but in the drawer under the counter he has a slice of bread and butter, which he cuts with a dirty pocket-knife when no one is looking. And he has an old, many-pocketed leather wallet, filled with hundred- and thousand-crown notes, under his coat-tails.

Someone probably looked about at home in the flat for a long time for something he could do without, for something he could give up with the least regret. Some agonising necessity, some hideous, humiliating hunger, drove that person from corner to corner until he found this very clock with its little marble columns, until he wrapped it up and carried it here, in order to use the few kreutzers he snatched up to buy a few vegetables? A bit of bread? Some medicine? Soles for his shoes?

How many people throughout the war brought things 'that were not needed' to these holes. Poverty demonstrated that there was no need for the six linen chemises that were lying in the wardrobe for her daughter when she grew up. Hunger whispered that there was no need for three pillows under the head, that two, or even one, was enough. When sickness settled in somewhere, no one hesitated any longer – even the table and chairs moved out! There, even the winter coat departed! And last of all – oh, wretched, ragged poverty! – last of all that mirror with the little heart in the corner, that cheap, tasteless mirror! Look at it and tell me. Can you imagine that the person who sold that ridiculous mirror had anything left at all?

In these shop-windows there lies an entire dusty heap of those who are starving. Do you object, saying that it is not a tragedy? That there are other things in the world that are more important, more urgent and even more painful? Perhaps. But the desolation of that person walking down the street, not knowing what else to do but sell a worthless mirror, that, it seems to me, reveals more than the fact that someone was once hungry. For example: how merciless, how savage, we are to one another and how destitute the individual is, and how alone with his misfortune, what wretched, pitiable things we all are, all of us – if that unknown person has to sell his mirror.

The man who will buy anything, however, is making an excellent profit. He gets a hundred crowns for a shirt, which he paid twenty for; and for the wardrobe for which he paid you two hundred, he manages to get eight hundred. In one street there are ten, twenty of his shop-windows. But the man who will buy anything is not a wartime profiteer; that sort is, if you please, a different species. He is not the sort of person who throws his money around in handfuls, who pays for carriages and women, who sits in bars and boxes at the theatre. No, he is someone who does not indulge in anything except food. Who sits on his money like a tenacious leech, who, unlike the profiteer, does not want pleasure from life. Who wants security, shameless, cheap security, even faced with all these people who are drowning!

Wretched, insignificant, with his torn coat and bent back, with his face that says, 'poor friend, we two know what hunger and poverty are,' the man who will buy anything walks past a beggar.

# Bathing Costumes
## 1 August 1920, *Tribuna*

There are two kinds of people: those who go swimming for the exercise, for the pleasure of cool water, those for whom the river is a great joy, for whom clouds in the sky, waves in the water and warm air are worlds unto themselves.[2] They swim with long strokes; they swim on their backs; they swim under the water; they jump into the water; they caress and fawn on the waves and they are happy there. They would like best to swim naked; for them water is their element; the body is their element; the sun is their element; nakedness is good, joyous. Well, since it's not allowed and it's not possible, one has to have something on. So for those people: a close-fitting maillot, as short as possible and all black, which will not restrict movement and will cover the body only where it needs to be covered. The rubber cap to protect the hair is still not perfect: it's hot under the rubber; in the heat, the hair steams and sweats, is easily damaged and falls out. But never mind, in the sun it will dry in half an hour and it's healthy to have a good swim. So we shall soon be ready: a small black maillot and our toilet is complete.

The second kind of people are those who swim in the water and don't even pant, don't even splutter, don't even keep their chins under the water the whole time. No, they swim in a well-bred manner; their bodies stand in the water like poles weighted at the bottom; even their shoulders are out of the water; not a hair gets wet. This swimming business has nothing to do with exercise or sport; indeed it is only by chance that these people manage to keep themselves above water and not sink.

For sport one must always dress practically and if some people can combine practicality with good taste it's to their credit; but I still prefer old, torn, practical rags to elegant, expensive clothes in which one cannot move freely.

This kind of swimming, however, is not sport. It is a strange sort of entertainment, diversion. Fashion designers seized on this short-coming and fashion barged in somewhere it had no place to be, where it was a nuisance, unpleasant, superfluous, nasty. Only in

---

2 Kafka commented on the article in the letter of 1 August 1920. See Franz Kafka, *Letters to Milena*, p. 129.

recent years has fashion really begun to take over. Previously, swimming-costumes were used by fat ladies and people who wanted to swim but were not attractive enough to wear a maillot and that was all right because the human body can be a beautiful thing and likewise it can be painful and embarrassing. To go in the water today, however, does not mean undressing, running, jumping and swimming – it means doing one's toilet, dressing, decking oneself out – and then it's almost a waste of all that effort to go into the water.

There is the greatest variety of modern swimming-costumes. Very often made of expensive fabrics, they are, on their own, really beautiful items to look at – in the shop-window. All that lacing and embroidery in the front and in the back and on the sides looks very pretty, in particular if it is white on a black background. The little sleeves tied with ribbons are adorable and the balloon-shaped knickerbockers with flounces and embroidery are charming. How one swims in them is another matter. Usually the knickerbockers are separate, covered by a one-piece garment put on over one's head, a short skirt like a tunic, with all kinds of decorations, buttons, trimming and so on sewn onto it.

Well, even that would be all right.

The outfit, however, also demands a hat, shoes, stockings – horror of horrors! – even gloves! Any kind of hat, suitably heavy and hot; under it, one's hair must be curled and one must take care that the curls don't droop into the water. Black silk shoes – you even see silk high boots in the big-city bathing places, a girl looks almost like Esmeralda from *The Bartered Bride* – ribbons criss-crossing all the way up the calves, and black silk, coloured, or fish-net stockings – always, of course, very fine, transparent.[3] The illustrations in foreign magazines even carry photographs of women with long sleeves down past their elbows. How one can swim in such garb, I really don't know; I can't even imagine it. Although the body is practically covered, however, it seems to me it would be more appropriate to speak of impropriety here, because semi-nudity is

---

3 Jesenská refers to a character from the popular opera *The Bartered Bride* (*Prodaná nevěsta*, 1866), a comedy of Bohemian peasant life composed by Bedřich (Friedrich) Smetana (1824–1884). Her description of elaborate bathing costumes is similar to the description of turn-of-the-century English costumes provided by Doreen Yarwood: 'Bathing costumes were still highly unsuitable: they included stockings and a knee-length dress with short sleeves, worn over knee-length full knickerbockers. Various colours and materials had been introduced by now, either plain or in checks, stripes and floral designs. Shoes, laced up the leg, and a cap completed the outfit.' Doreen Yarwood, *English Costume from the Second Century B. C. to 1967*, London, 1967, 3rd edition, p. 256.

always more provocative, more sophisticated, than simple nakedness and if this semi-nudity is intentional, it is also repulsive. I
think that the world and fashion have invented it for German
comic films, where things are usually 'funny' that in reality are
either sad, embarrassing or ugly: a drunkard, a hunch-back, a spin-
ster, infidelity in marriage, obscenity.

The luxury of a beach robe is another matter. A soft, shaggy robe
is such a delight when you run out of the water, tired and chilled
to the bone. Not a lot can be said about them – you know them –
those brightly coloured, shaggy, hooded things. But it's no tragedy
if you don't have one. Five minutes in the sun on the boards by
the swimming area and it's so hot that you're back in the water.

# The New Big-City Type II
## 7 August 1920, *Tribuna*

There is no need to spend time drawing your attention to the type I would like to write about.[4] This one is not 'the man who will buy anything', that inconspicuous, shabby little man with a wallet stuffed with banknotes, engrossed in his money and sated by the mere thought that there is money, that it is here, in his greasy coat in a secure pocket fastened with a button. The type I am writing about is not stuck away in a dark hole in the slums and does not have a little shop with pathetic articles for sale. The type I am writing about sticks out like a sore thumb; he is a social and cultural eyesore. You will find him wherever things are expensive and you will find him in all countries, in all cities, in all resorts, in all hotels; you will even find him on the front pages of satirical magazines and in the leading articles of newspapers. The wartime profiteer! Of course! Who else?! The wartime profiteer. The mushrooms that spring up after a catastrophe. Thus far, after every catastrophe, people have cropped up who 'know their way about'; people who suck out what there is to be sucked out from an atmosphere imbued with fighting and charged with mental electricity, at a time when others feel the ground giving way under them, when others are losing their minds and sacrificing their lives. What a surprise, over and over again it turns out that there is plenty to be sucked out.

A psychological portrait of a certain class of people is never invariably accurate, but it can apply at least approximately to the majority. If it can shed light on only one part of the whole, it has accomplished something.

The general conventional psychological portrait of the wartime profiteer runs thus: a stupid, shallow, money-minded person. The 'why?' He is someone who takes his luxury to impossible extremes of ostentation – and so on.

First and foremost, it is not true that wartime profiteers are always stupid – no, not at all. Just because in bars they have the most terrible musical pap played for them, in theatres they yawn during the good and guffaw during the bad plays, in their libraries

<hr>

4 Kafka commented on this article in the letter of 10 August 1920. Kafka, *Letters to Milena*, p. 153.

they have the collected works of the great authors, which they have ordered from the bookseller, never read and have left their pages uncut, because they have the stupidest possible opinions concerning all political, cultural, moral and aesthetic matters, that still does not mean they are stupid. Sometimes they are even sly, clever, talented people, with a hard, iron, bloodthirsty cunning, a cunning like that of the beast of prey; it leaps at its victim at just the right moment with a superb leap and does not give in, does not let go until the victim drops. They do not, of course, have a spirit. A spiritual person, however, can never be a profiteer because he is not able to concentrate that much energy or interest on *a matter of money*. Not that he is incapable of energy or interest in general, but a spiritual person is not grounded *in the world*. Even if he has difficulties, even if he is hungry, even if he has the certainty of economic *un*certainty, even when he places great hope in money, he is in the end indifferent to it, at the very bottom of his soul and even only in one corner of his soul – *and for this reason he has already lost it.*

There are people who decided, out of despair at their own poverty, to do business. If Mr X., who is a dolt compared with me, can be successful, why can't I be successful too? Look, Mr A. is successful, but our man is not. Why? Perhaps the shares fell at the last minute. The Z. company did not agree to the price of iron he had negotiated. He didn't catch the soul of the enterprise, Mr J., at home in time. Or it was necessary to make a telephone call and he could not get a connection. Those are, of course, only the external causes; the 'bad luck' is not the cause itself but only the external sign of the cause. Our man was not successful because actually he did not care about it, actually he did it with disgust, distaste, contempt. He simply did not have the businessman's passion: that feverish, frantic passion and unswerving, singular will to get *money*.

Secondly: the traits that are laid at the door of the wartime profiteer are usually only secondary traits. The frenzy for luxury, the sloth, pride, conceit and so on – that is all refuse that the turbid water brings to the surface. The strongest impulse, however, the impulse behind the horsepower that drives such a person, is ambition. Every ambition, even that of great statesmen, of great financiers, even that of great industrialists, every ambition, perhaps even that of Napoléon Bonaparte, has a bizarre, unsuspected, surprising source: not a longing to go forward, but a fear of what lies behind. The fact that a person wants money is not the main thing. The main thing is fear of poverty. If all he wanted were money, a small amount would suffice for a peaceful and contented life. This person, however, has an unhealthy fear of poverty, of being inconspicuous, insignificant; for that reason he rushes forward with terrible force, as far as possible from poverty, inconspicuousness, insignificance. Only a poor person can be afraid of poverty, only an inconspicuous person of being inconspicuous, an insignificant person of being insignificant. A person is never afraid of something he does not know, if he does not at least know how much it hurts. Since poor and insignificant people do not have and can never have enough conclusive proofs of their wealth and importance, they produce excessive proofs for themselves and for the world, proofs after proofs. *Only an insufficiency exaggerates. Sufficiency is firm and balanced.*

Yes, proofs. It is a matter of showing myself and the world that I am confident, that I am secure. How will I show it? First and foremost, through pleasure and luxury. Pleasure for myself, luxury for the world. It is said of profiteers that they throw money away in handfuls. Throw it away? They do not throw even a heller away. The profiteer does not save, nor does he throw money away – assuming that to throw money away means to spend it on something unimportant and unnecessary. The profiteer will pay thousands for a bottle of champagne, for a car, for a stay at a French resort, for a woman, for clothes, for dinner. For something tangible that provides pleasure and confirmation. For what is most important to him. The profiteer, however, will not give a single crown to a beggar-woman if no one is looking. The profiteer makes the most terrible fuss if a servant orders a limousine *unnecessarily* and pays forty crowns for something *he does not use*. The profiteer will donate several thousand to a charitable organisation if it will be in the newspapers, but his relations and illegitimate children are hungry and poor. Woe betide the parasite who manages to 'squeeze' a few crowns out of the profiteer who then finds out that they were not used for vital things. That perhaps they were used, say, for a cheap ticket to the theatre, in addition to food. The profiteer will be outraged: what does that person think? That the profiteer makes money so that *other people can amuse themselves*? As long as other people are not dying of hunger, the profiteer will not acknowledge that they are hungry. As long as they are not walking about naked, he will not acknowledge that they need clothes. He will never acknowledge that anyone in the world has a need for luxury. How could he? After all, luxury is *his* proof, for the profiteer alone.

The man 'who will buy anything' will be secure (not rich, but secure) for his entire life. His children will inherit the capital. His children will certainly be raised in such a way that they will be able to maintain and expand this capital and from time to time 'treat themselves' to something. The wartime profiteer does not have this certainty at all. He does not know how to save, nor is he concerned with security. He is like a person who, out of fear, escapes, runs, falls and drives himself frantically forward, upwards, as long as his strength holds out. Finally, he trips and then he falls, overnight, just as he had risen overnight. He went too far because he had no sense of proportion. Up until now, at least, all those mushrooms that sprang up after the rains of catastrophe have imperceptibly rotted, without leaving a trace, except for their own frenzy. So perhaps there is hope for us too?

# The Café
## 10 August 1920, *Tribuna*

The human need for congregation, for a neutral place for conversation, is as old as the world. Loners always have and always will be eccentric and in any case, the need for solitude and the need for company are not so mutually exclusive as it would seem. There are people who are only able to think and work in the midst of the movement of their surroundings, in a din, against the changing backdrop of a busy street. They walk alone with their brooding through the largest crowd of people. There are people who sit every day in the company of others who are conversing and they do not say a word about themselves or their private lives and thus they pursue solitude in a crowd. There are people who can stand pensively for hours on end on a street corner and observe the currents of humanity. There are people who spend hours sitting in a night café, without meeting anyone, without uttering a coherent sentence. There are different kinds of loners – but I do not want to talk about them today. All I want to say is that even for a loner, some company is necessary, if not the centre of it, then the periphery, or at least a view of it.

People used to meet in the forums, in the monasteries and in the salons. Today, there are no forums or monasteries for this purpose, or salons with this atmosphere. Today, there are cafés. I do not mean those elegant cafés where mothers take their daughters on Sunday afternoons and where one goes to drink hot chocolate or eat a few pieces of cake. Nor do I mean those that during the day are tired, dim and sleepy, that hang a red lamp on the gable and come to life in the evening with a band, a few girls wearing makeup and a few 'soldiers of fortune'.

I mean those distinctly 'literary' cafés, known far and wide, known to the entire city, the meeting places of the intellectual and bohemian world, such as the Prague 'Union', the Vienna 'Central', the Berlin 'des Westens', the Parisian 'Montmartre'. Cafés with a rather strange existence that no one can understand until he penetrates it to the core, until he fills his lungs with its air.

The first guests are the great ones. Those who already have a name in the official world, those who are the pride of the café and whose pictures and caricatures hang on the walls of the bar; those who, when they arrive, sit like capitalists of the spirit behind a table and only a few are permitted to sit beside them. In any case, these are rare guests. It is strange that as soon as a person establishes himself somewhere, whether financially, socially or intellectually, as soon as he settles somewhere to such an extent that one can presume he will remain there until death, from that moment on the dissolute life of the bohemian is almost despicable to him. Although he certainly emerged from such a dissolute life himself, or at least lingered in it for a while, still, all of sudden he considers it undignified – simply, in a word: he becomes bourgeois. The popular division – on the one side the bourgeois, on the other the revolutionary – is not entirely accurate. From a certain point on, even the revolutionary becomes bourgeois (indeed, the bourgeoisie and the revolutionary spirit are purely intellectual and spiritual concepts). Even if he remains a member of a radical party and even if he continues to write for a radical paper, in his life and in his soul he has become bourgeois. Instead of dividing people into revolutionaries and the bourgeoisie, one could divide an individual human life into a revolutionary and a bourgeois period, totally unrelated, of course, to age. In so far as a person is a pioneer of a new idea, in so far as he has a new thought or inspiration, every person is a revolutionary. From the moment that he creates only from the idea that he once had (and every truly great person has only *one idea*; those who have more, don't have any, or at least, any of their own); that is, when he has already spent himself, when his only movement is at most a perfecting of form – from that moment on he is bourgeois. From that moment on, he is not a pioneer but a proprietor who saves and gets fat. That is, one can also get fat in an intellectual sense.

Well, those are rare guests, the honorary guests at the café tables, honorary guests and ungrateful alumni. Today, all of them either have a villa outside the city, or an eager publisher, or a full lecture hall, or an editorial in the most important daily. They all have a place to turn to and do not need the shelter of the café.

Those who create the real foundation, the real atmosphere of the café, are the journalists from every sort of newspaper, the famous, the less famous and those who are not famous at all. The crowd of writers, those who carry their first poems in their breast pockets and read them aloud now and then when the opportunity presents itself. And those who have already had something published here and there, who are prospering, who are well on their way to capitalism of the spirit. And mainly: the crowd of castaways, the crowd of the strangest characters with the most mysterious lives, people who will never get anywhere and will never manage to achieve anything, the bravely resigned and quiet melancholics about whom the world does not know and never will know anything. Sometimes the real geniuses of the world are buried in these strata, the bearers and creators of ideas, those who simply did not have the strength to give their ideas form. For the most part, however, they are ghostly creatures, like Dostoevskii's General Ivolgin and Korolenko's ex-clerk Voikov, like all those whom Russian literature treats with such kindly delight and warm humour and whom Czech literature prefers to ignore, although they are all around us.[5]

The individual types in this environment would take up twenty articles and could even take up twenty novels. But they are not the matter at hand. The strangest thing of all is the common life of the café, including the owner, the scorer, the waiters, the busboys, the old lady in the cloakroom, the old lady taking money at the toilets, all of them together, the entire community, its laws, its jargon, all that is so completely cut off from the rest of the world.

People have known each other for years; they know each other's lives, advances, successes, defeats. For years they have kept an eye on each other, like neighbours living off a single gallery. The women who are brought along move gradually from table to table, either 'for no reason', or because of marriage, infidelity, divorce. In the end they belong to the café; they lose their surnames and are called simply by their nicknames; they turn into friends. With the growing number of cigarettes smoked and the growing number of lovers, they lose their true femininity and become stale, boring, ugly. In the last few years, when there was nothing to eat, no heating at home and nothing to wear, the café was transformed into a communal home for the bohemians, who were very badly off during the war. Some have gone, killed by hunger, madness, disease. Some continue to warm themselves with cups of Turkish coffee. In the café, one writes, makes corrections, converses. In the café, all family scenes are played out; in the café, one cries and rails against life. In the café, one eats on credit; in the café, the most reckless financial transactions take place. In the café, one lives, one idles and the hours pass.

The creative person is alone. The uncreative person seeks distraction. He seeks entertainment appropriate to his intellectual level: conversation, literature, at least a taste of creativity. And just as disease is contagious, every intellectual atmosphere is also contagious and whoever once succumbs to the lazy, sluggish pace of life in these cafés will hardly ever get ahead. Of course, of course, it is not exactly like that because he who is capable of getting ahead simply will not succumb.

---

5 Fedor Mikhailovich Dostoevskii (1821–1881); Vladimir Galaktionovich
   Korolenko (1853–1921). General Ivolgin is a character in Dostoevskii's *The Idiot*
   (1868).

# The Letters of Eminent People
## 15 August 1920, *Tribuna*

For the moment, I will leave aside the question of the right to publish the letters of eminent people because it is not the main issue. It is not so much a question of whether or not we have the right to look into the privacy of eminent lives. Rather, it is, first of all, a matter of establishing the meaning that these intimate accounts and displays have. Only then can one resolve the other, secondary, question.

You very often hear it said: a personal acquaintance with an artist is dangerous and often disappointing. You hear that a person whose music, poems or paintings are inspiring is a very odd man with mystifying traits. For example, he hoards like a hamster; he is as timid as a hare or as coarse as a guttersnipe; he is dirty, unshaven and greasy; or he wears a nightcap; or he passionately loves his parrot.

The same person who has such a passionate relationship to eternity, truth and deeds wears a nightcap? Yes, my dear Miss. Artists, fortunately or unfortunately, do not always look like Waldemar Psilander.[6] If you are disappointed by an artist as a person, however, an artist whose talent has been conclusively demonstrated by his work, then it is simply your fault. It is the fault of your outlook on life, the fault of your conventionality that compares the artist to a bank clerk and does not understand that the difference between an artist and someone who is not an artist does not lie in human qualities, but in property. The person who is not an artist has no more than he possesses at a given moment: ten thousand, stocks, a nice nose, two strong hands. The artist, however, also has that which he does not possess as intensively. The material of the artist also includes his works and longings, his desires, his imagination and even the entire world. If you are disappointed, my dear Miss, it is only because you do not know how to find him and you do not know how grotesquely astonishing the human soul is.

Or is it not, for example, grotesque that the profound moralist of *La Comédie humaine*, someone who understood the splendour of

---

6 Waldemar Psilander was a Norwegian actor in silent films. See the note in: Kafka, *Letters to Milena*, p. 297.

pomp and elegance as well as Balzac did, was a thick-set, ugly heffalump, always carelessly and even shabbily dressed, whom his friends had to watch constantly to prevent him from committing some silly, senseless, embarrassing impropriety? Or that the sweet melancholy Czech Dvořák was a country youth of robust nature and questionable morals? Or that Maupassant was an irritable loner, despairing and suspicious, who for thirty years tormented himself over his inadequacies and for thirty years burned all his novellas, out of despair that they might not be perfect? Or that Napoléon, formidable, daring Napoléon, master of the world Napoléon, was a tiny, weak, hideous man who was afraid to be alone in the dark?[7]

And so on, a long line of eminent people of all pitches and keys. Hence the interest in their private lives and intimacies: one is not satisfied by the work alone, the creation alone. One wants to know where it came from; one wants to throw light upon the inner act that preceded it. All the more so as every great artistic act is in itself incomprehensible and new because the artist does not say *what is, but rather what is not – and because he says it, it happens.*

Since the time that Shakespeare wrote *Hamlet*, the world has known the indecisive individual who cannot decide if it is better to be or not to be. Since the time that Dostoevskii wrote *Myshkin*, the world has known a good, not a nice, but a genuinely good person, a miraculous person, a man-idiot, a man-saviour. Since the time that Němcová wrote *The Grandmother*, we have known the wise, shining, country soul of an old woman. Since the time that Zola wrote *Nana*, we have known the harlot of the Parisian demi-monde. Not that there wasn't a Hamlet in the world before Shakespeare, or a Myshkin before Dostoevskii; the world turned even before Galileo and there was electric current before Galvani. But the world did not know about it; the world did not recognise it; the world was without it. The world did not assume it was there or even have an inkling of it. Likewise, the world had no inkling of Hamlet before Shakespeare, or of Onegin before Pushkin.[8] *That* is the property of the artist: his exclusive perception of the world. His ability to see *for the first time*, his ability to see the world anew.

---

7 Honoré de Balzac (1799–1850); Antonín Dvořák (1841–1904); Guy de Maupassant (1850–1893); Napoléon Bonaparte (1769–1821).

8 She refers to Fedor Mikhailovich Dostoevskii and the main character of *The Idiot*, Prince Lev Nikolaevich Myshkin. The Czech writer Božena Němcová (1820 – 1862) and her novel *Babička* (1855); Emile Zola (1840–1902) and his novel *Nana* (1880); Galileo Galilei (1564–1642); the Italian physicist and physician Luigi Galvani (1737–1798); and Aleksandr Sergeevich Pushkin (1799–1837) and the novel in verse *Yevgeny Onegin* (1833).

Of course, we ask ourselves: my God, how simple, how is it possible that I didn't see it before? How did he discover it? We reach eagerly for the letters; we uncover the humanity; we devour the pages: how did he discover it? Through what kind of pain? What kind of desire? What kind of illness? What kind of tension? The letters flesh out the work for us, like a geographical map fleshes out the world. The letters justify, they provide logical support for us unbelievers, for whom a miracle is not enough and who need a tangible explanation.

Biographies are another thing altogether. Interesting in a totally different way. Stendhal's biography of Napoléon presents Stendhal's ideas about Napoléon rather than Napoléon himself.[9] It is a work of art. I do not expect art in a letter; from letters I expect *humanity*.

Of course, the ideas of eminent people about eminent people are of the utmost interest and value. Simple accounts 'without claim to artistic quality', however, written on the assumption that they will interest the world, show a complete lack of understanding of the meaning of intimate glances into the lives of the great. The world *should not* be interested in Miss Lola Šetelíková, who sees fit to write down what Milan Štefánik did, where he went, why he did not marry and what he said when he visited someone.[10] A mere, simple fact, if it does not provide a profound insight into the mind, some kind of justification or clarification, cannot be of interest. It is not a matter of *betraying* something to the world, but of enriching the individual through understanding. It is a matter of the logical connection between the world of the insignificant and the world of the elect.

We have a right *to this*, as long as we are so imperfect that the utterance itself is not enough for faith and understanding and as long as we need, like Thomas, to stick our fingers in the wounds to be convinced that they exist and that they are deep.

---

9 Stendhal, a pseudonym of Henri Beyle (1783–1842), and his *Life of Napoléon*.

10 She refers to Lola Šetelíková's biography *È morto … Paměti lásky Štefánikovy* (The Memoirs of Štefánik's Love), Královské Vinohrady, 1920. The Slovak Milan Rastislav Štefánik (1880–1919), a general of the French army, organised the Czechoslovak legions in Russia, Italy and the USA during the First World War, and with T. G. Masaryk and E. Beneš, promoted the idea of an independent Czechoslovak state during the war.

# Shop-Windows
## 21 August 1920, *Tribuna*

A street is not a dead thing. A street is alive, like a thing of flesh, it has eyes, an expression, colour, scent. It moves and shouts, looks and listens. It is always unique. In any city, in any noisy foreign street, you can remember the corner of Vodičková Street and Wenceslas Square, but you will never find any foreign streets that are similar. You will never find another corner of Vodičková Street, nor will you ever find another Můstek.[11] Not because our Můstek is anything unusual. But a street is singular, just as a person is singular. And another street is different just as another person is different. A street is alive and has a living relation to and impact on the individual. It is pleasing. There is a place in the city that you dearly love. When you walk there, you feel more at ease than elsewhere. When you think of your city while abroad, you recall that street first. Something ties you to it, something that is not an event or a definite memory of an event, but rather the essence of the street itself. In the same way, there are some streets that you do not like. Even if your way leads through one such street every day, you prefer to avoid it; you make a detour. You cannot stand it; you do not like each other, you and the street. You do not know why; it has never done you any harm. But it has an ugly face. It has a repulsive, blinking, suspicious face, or else it strikes you as insolent, cunning, or haughty. You will never be reconciled to it. You have a bad conscience in front of it, as you would face-to-face with a person whom you cannot abide, although he has never done you any harm. You try to be more pleasant towards the street, but it just won't work, damn it. All effort is futile. In the end, you would rather avoid it if you can.

The street also has attire: the shop-windows. Shop-windows are layout, sets and direction. Good or bad direction. The shop-windows are the eyes of the street, sleepy and dull, or keen and beautiful. Shop-windows are scenery: a fitting or poor choice. Shop-windows are the most important feature of the expression. They can save or destroy the street. They can turn a young beauty into a boring, ugly old woman. They can turn a loner into a society

---

11 She refers to streets in the centre of Prague.

woman. They can turn a progressive and modern spirit into a philis-
tine. They have power, they have terror in their hands and they
make full use of it.

The owners of shops on the main avenues should be officially
obliged to treat their shop-windows with elaborate care. I even dare
to claim that it would be a good job – to be a director of shop-
windows – and that such a job would require as much talent, skill,
training and expertise as arranging stage sets. The shop-windows on
a main street can add or detract from the beauty of the entire city.
There are objects that can easily be arranged in a tasteful and interesting way. Truly, a seller of flowers, a seller of books, ceramics or
fabrics has a relatively easy task. It is worse, for example, at the
jeweller's, where the small size of the object on display makes the
work more difficult; taken as a whole, a jeweller's shop-window is
always boring. A seller of Nestlé powder for children or gramo-
phones could also say: 'that's easier said than done.' That, however,
is the matter at hand: every shop-window, one next to the other,
should be designed in a truly architectural and artistic fashion. A
display case is a little stage. It is ridiculous to think it is a matter
of putting up everything you have. You will create a formless, bleary
impression. What matters is that you have an idea! That you
compel the pedestrian to stop; that the window attracts and flirts
with the passers-by. One tasteful vase with a few flowers and some
drapery is better than bowls of flowers crammed together. A little
mahogany table, with three different pairs of gloves on it and an
elegant parasol leaning against it, makes a perfect picture. If you
hang gloves in the display case like wet laundry out to dry, who
will be surprised? Two suits, an appropriate hat in a matching
colour, a discrete fabric draped in the display case, will stop the
pedestrian on the street. Our wax dummies with wooden chests, on
which suits droop as they would on a hanged man, tend to drive
everyone away. A shop-window is also the most important advertisement for a business. There are days when you wander and do
not know which way to turn. You say to yourself: I will go see what
is new in X's shop-window. You know for certain that the display
in X's shop is never disappointing. It is always interesting. It offers
advice. It starts you day-dreaming. When you decide to buy something, you prefer to go the long way round to X and say: 'You used
to have such-and-such here. Do you still have it?'

But unfortunately, how many shop-windows do we have like
that?

One of the conditions necessary for a good shop-window is that
it be changed often. In big cities many stores change their displays

daily. Understandably so. I remember that every day I used to walk past a shop-window where there was a young hare on display among the other pictures. A delightful hare, running away over a field through the snow to the woods, with its white tail raised.[12] It appealed to me. It seemed so forlorn in the white world and its tail gave it an air of melancholy powerlessness. Well – but after a few weeks the hare annoyed me terribly: rain fell, the sun shone and the hare kept on running away, with its tail raised, morning and afternoon. Then it even made me cross; every day even from a distance I had to check, willing or not, to see if it was still running away. In the end, the hare drove me out of that street; I preferred to walk down another. A display that is the same for several days is like a person with whom you are constantly together. Even if he appeals to you to no end, one day you will still need to run away from him. A blouse on display for six weeks will make you detest all the blouses in the world. Pickled herring, drying at the back of a display for the third week, will destroy your faith in herring altogether. Our shops are distinguished by this very stubbornness. What you found there a month ago, you will most certainly find today and perhaps even a month from now. Only dustier, dirtier, gloomier.

Yet at least this cross – from the Powder Tower to the National Theatre and from Můstek to Museum – should sparkle and shine with diversity and ideas, colours and tastefulness.[13] Or else – that I might also 'savour' for once that nice Czech phrase – 'What will the foreigners say, for God's sake?'

---

12 Kafka made reference to this image in the letter of 26 August 1920. Kafka, *Letters to Milena*, p. 168.

13 She refers to landmarks in the centre of Prague. From the National Theatre on the Vltava River, one follows National Avenue onto Na příkopě Street to reach the Powder Tower in the Old Town. This route is intersected by Wenceslas Square, which runs from Můstek Square to the National Museum.

# The Household and Overalls

## 24 October 1920, *Tribuna*

If in this column, headed 'Fashion', I were to report only on the most recent developments, from winter to summer and from summer to winter, I would soon bore myself and you as well. We are not, after all, so pathetic as to think constantly only about what new pleat, what new colour, what new skirt fashion has brought into the world. We are concerned not only with modern, but also with attractive clothing, which is not always the same thing. We are concerned with everything connected to clothes and with all relations between clothes and life. For this reason, I would like to write here about everything (in addition to news about all sorts of developments in clothing) that concerns fashion even only remotely and yet concerns us very closely. Today, for example, I want to tell you something about American housekeeping.

The American housewife has two worries in common with the Czech housewife: first of all, even in America it is incredibly expensive; and second, even in America there is a shortage of servants. The factories swallow up working women just like they do in Europe and the American housewife, just like ours, has all the housework on her hands.

American women, however, have settled the question of looking after the household in a different way than we have. Our housewives and mothers cannot be accused of being less skilful, less healthy or practical than Americans, but rather of being more *sentimental*. For the Czech housewife, the household is a kind of mission in life; every plate and every dinner is something deadly important. In Czechoslovakia, an entire day of religious reflection is devoted to domestic chores and usually the housewife tyrannises those around her with her precision, her scrupulousness and self-importance. In Czechoslovakia, curtains exist so that no one can smoke at home, the polished floor so that no one can walk over it and parlours so that they can be draped in linen dustsheets. A sentimental importance is attached to every jar of preserves and every parquet floor and a person might suppose that the purpose of life was to clean, do dishes and do the washing and then repeat it over again, continuously until death. The more importance is attributed to this work, the more slowly, of course, it is carried out. The Czech housewife drudges all day long and does not even have time to read a book, or run out to the cinema, or listen to music, or dress properly. Fifty percent of Czech women become homely, worn-out servants of the household, who have, of course, one satisfaction: all their lives, the stove gleams like a mirror.

America is different. For Americans, filth and disorder are just as intolerable as they are for us, but there attending to cleanliness is treated as a necessary evil, one of the vulgar human functions about which one does not talk much. One prefers to hide it from the world and from one's husband, to put it away somewhere quickly, so that no one will see it. For this 'quickly', of course, something is needed that we do not have: modern appliances for domestic chores. The Czech housewife is like a peasant from Mokrá ves: ploughing with a plough, reaping with a scythe, sticking money into a sock in case lightning should strike, by the will of God. A broom, dust rags, a washing-up basin, a scrubbing brush for the parquet floor – these are our tested weapons and tools; with these one can clean all day long, nice and slowly, but surely.

Perhaps the American woman paid a lot of money once for the new inventions. But now she has them and the advantages that go along with them. A vacuum cleaner instead of our dirty rags. A rug cleaner instead of our 'scrubbing brushes'. A delightful roller-brush on a pole, which she runs lightly over the parquet floor and in a few minutes it is shining. A utility stove is a matter of course. You can find a revolving machine for washing dishes in every household: a large basin with a handle in the middle and two movable bottoms; the dishes are placed inside, you turn the handle, water pours over the plates and cups in a strong current and a moment later they are perfectly clean. Slow-cooking pots, such as one also sees in Czechoslovakia, at least in the shop-windows, are not rare in American households but can be found by the dozens. The food is inserted in the morning and it cooks slowly by evening, so that all one has to do is put the meat in the pot, bring it to a boil, turn down the heat, then put the lid on the pot.[14]

In addition, the husband and the state help the housewife, which, of course, does not happen in Czechoslovakia. The American woman does not go out to shop, but orders what she needs for cooking from the shop by telephone and in half an hour a little

---

14 In a later article, Jesenská also wrote about a remarkable American oven that shut itself off when the cooking time was up so that the food would not burn. M. Jesenská, 'O moderní domácnosti' (The Modern Household), *Národní listy*, 25 December 1926, p. 13.

boy brings everything she wants in a basket. American cities have shops where one can get milk, as well as fruit, vegetables, meat and cocoa. These shops have hundreds of delivery-children who take care of the telephone orders. There is, of course, central heating everywhere. In every apartment there is an automatic refrigerator installed in the wall and likewise outlets for ashes and dust, hoists from the attic and cellar leading directly into the kitchen and, of course, the inevitable building, city and room telephones.

Well then, the American woman does not give much thought to her work. In a few hours she is finished with everything. But that is not all. The American woman never permits herself to be a burden on any of the people living with her. And she well knows that an untidy, unattractive woman, a woman's underskirts and 'mules' are more of a burden than anything else. In this respect too she has helped herself: while the American woman does not wear overalls on the street, she certainly wears them when she is working at home. Loose clothes, sewn in one piece, with wide trousers and a belt, a double row of pockets and a short fold-down top. Sandals on the feet and a cloth cap on the head. Today that is how not only cleaning ladies and laundresses look, but also the wives of officials, workers and small businessmen. Not only do they look tasteful and neat carrying out the most break-neck tasks, they gain practical advantages as well: they can move freely and their clothes do not hinder them in their work.

One thing is certain: we are constantly learning from America. America gave us the entire new technical world, with all its advantages of timesaving and all its disadvantages of factory crudity and capitalism. We accept one thing after another and we forget that when we accept the material and not the inner relationship to it, we do not make the most of it. All we get are the disadvantages, while the advantages vanish. While American matter-of-factness has much that is unhealthy, Czech sentimentality also has much that is unhealthy. It would be good to loosen the laces where the shoe pinches. To live with feeling, to perceive with feeling – fine. But to dust with feeling, to cook breakfast with feeling and to scrub the floors with feeling in soggy underskirts – who ever heard of such a thing?

# Dance over the Abyss

## 5 November 1920, *Tribuna*

Perhaps every city today is a Babylon; they say that in Berlin it is even worse than in Vienna and Paris, apparently, lags behind both of them. I do not know what it is like elsewhere. But here – God knows – there is pandemonium, one absurdity after another, degeneration, madness, luxury, poverty, hunger, champagne, everything all mixed up together like it is in a carnival. I do not know where to begin. There is no beginning; I do not know what should come first.

The frosts have suddenly struck. The wind whistles through the streets. In a single night, it tears all the leaves from the trees and tosses them in a frantic carousel from the pavement up to the roofs. The sky is a light blue and from five o'clock on, the frozen disc of the moon hangs there. The frost strikes in the day and strikes twice as hard in the clear, limpid nights and this unexpected frost has set all of Vienna in motion. The word 'quickly' can be heard everywhere. The frozen apples from the gardens are quickly cleared away; vegetables are quickly transported to the city; wood is quickly distributed; and butchers quickly sell frozen meat. It has started early this time and Vienna has only one consolation: it can hardly get worse.

The frost will not get much worse, but otherwise shopkeepers are predicting a horrible winter, such as Vienna has never experienced before. The exorbitant taxes that are, according to the new regulations, in effect as of 1 November this year and that raise the price of rent, food and fuel by 30 to 40 percent, lie over all of Vienna like a heavy cloud. An egg which today costs fourteen crowns, will, they say, cost thirty crowns by Christmas! One will not get a kilo of meat, not even the cheapest, for less than 250 crowns. But much has changed since last winter. In food stores, one can get everything one's heart desires, but at such prices that no one is able to buy anything. An abundance of butter, eggs, flour, cocoa, rice, condensed milk, all kinds of meat, peas, semolina, chocolate, fruit, sardines, simply everything, even smoked meat (ten decagrams of ham, fifty crowns, ten decagrams of salami, twenty crowns, two sausages, thirty-five crowns, one frankfurter, eighteen crowns), are on sale. The shop-windows show a magnificent abundance and for a person who has money, it is possible to live as one did in peacetime. But only a few hundred foreigners who reside downstairs in the expensive hotels and several hundred wartime profiteers living in the palaces and ten-room apartments of the ninth and fourth quarters or the villa districts outside the city, only they can eat and drink their fill. The hundreds of thousands of other residents, the thousands of clerks, doctors, manual and intellectual labourers, all the people who support themselves through work rather than stock-market deals, suffer from the most terrible hunger and poverty imaginable, a hunger more terrible than in past years because they are starving in front of fully stocked shops. Everyday the newspapers announce in small news items that the ambulance took this or that person to the general hospital because he had collapsed in the street from hunger. At court, there are trials every day for thefts and murders and hunger, poverty and need are the constant motives. People seem to have gone wild; hunger (fear of hunger) drives them to the most terrible extremes. One cannot rely on anyone; everyone steals and cheats and most of all the adolescents and children who grew up in the war years and the youths, returning from the battlefield.

For that matter, it is not only food that is so senselessly expensive. The prices of shoes and clothes have risen to such giddy heights that soon even overalls, a work outfit that has caught on in Vienna and costs three thousand crowns, will be a luxury! By what miracle scores of people in Vienna walk about in splendid clothes, by what miracle people wear fur coats, beautiful dresses and shoes and splendid hats is a mystery to me. (By the way, on the basis of the new tax, a Viennese seamstress charges nine thousand crowns to sew one suit and that does not even include the price of the material!) How a university professor or a postal clerk can support his wife and children is another mystery. These are things that only God understands. Anyone who thinks that Vienna looks gloomy, however, is mistaken: there are hundreds of cabarets and dancehalls here, luxurious cafés and sweetshops and tea-rooms crammed with people; automobiles and horse-drawn carriages throng through the streets in an impenetrable stream. People are having a good time. Vienna is laughing. The hundreds of thousands of starving are behind the scenes and, like a gloomy theatre, are presented, at most, to the reparations commission. But in the cabarets, people are dancing the latest dances, they drink champagne and are cheerful. I have heard that one of these modern hells, the 'Parisien', is particularly lively. Only men in tails and women in evening dress are admitted. A bouquet of violets costs three hundred crowns. The waiters – imagine! waiters wearing makeup – carry around slender glasses of sparkling wine. The headwaiter earns thousands every day. Every day hundreds of thousands are squandered here. But a shelter for sick girls, which housed several dozen, was shut down a few weeks ago – for lack of funds.

Pictures of the Vienna train stations at various times of day would make an interesting sight. The train to Amsterdam and the Hague leaves from the western station every morning. It has long narrow cars, only first and second class and the tickets are numbered, like tickets to the theatre. Beautiful ladies and gentlemen sit behind the large windows of the restaurant car and drink hot chocolate from silver cups. The platform is swarming with hotel servants and vendors of foreign newspapers and magazines; here and there, a beautiful greyhound threads its way, or a Great Dane, the noble escort of its master. Five minutes before the departure of the train, the platform turns into an exhibition of fashionable clothes of unusual splendour: nowhere else in the streets or in the bars is there such gleaming elegance as there is here, the moment before the train departs. But hardly has it been swallowed up by the opening of the sky beyond the station when a crowd of gaunt, frozen figures in rags rushes over the platform, women with terrible coughs, irritable, unshaven, embittered men, loaded down with rucksacks, satchels, bags, milk-cans. At five o'clock in the morning, hundreds of people depart from the surrounding villages in order to hunt up what there is to be had: a little milk, bread, an egg, potatoes, wood. The Austrian farmers are prospering; the mortgages on farms and land under crop were paid off long ago during the war. They have more food than they can consume and they exchange the surplus for things that the famished city dwellers bring them: linen, shoes, clothing, even furniture and bedding. One peasant woman, when they had brought her everything she wanted, asked for – opera glasses. And she got them, in exchange for several kilograms of potatoes. Hardly has the platform recovered from the noise, arguing, shoving, squabbling and curses when a trainload of children sets off for a foreign country. The platform is full of small, pale pilgrims with little bundles, full of mothers and goodbyes. The children, happy to be leaving behind their ill-fated native city, their care-worn parents and their daily menu – sauerkraut and sauerkraut – wave their handkerchiefs, gabble like geese and look forward merrily to their journey into the world.

If there is one thing I am afraid of in Vienna, it is the rancid odour of sauerkraut, of which every house and every street has reeked for three winters now, like the poisonous effluvium of human poverty. The very thought of those pieces of dirty cabbage that float in boiled water and are recycled for lunch, tea and dinner almost daily in all the public kitchens, hospitals and households, is enough to turn one's stomach. In the summer, we hoped that the sauerkraut was gone for good but there is twice as much of it this winter.

What do the streets of Vienna look like? On the walls and lamp-posts frayed colourful rags flutter, the remnants of the Viennese elections that turned out so dismally.[15] They fly with the dry leaves in a frenzied rage from sidewalk to sidewalk; there is more than enough dust and filth. Here and there, a house or a staircase is being painted. Otherwise everything is worn out from the war: the facades, the windows, the stores, the shop-signs, the shop-windows. Only downtown in the city is there a little island of elegance and splendour, but that contrasts with the desolate gloomy slums on all sides.

As for the rest, Vienna is Austrian, the same as before – in the republic things are managed as kindly, with as many smiles, from ten until five and as utterly senselessly as in the empire. The following incident will serve as proof of this.

A poor but famous painter who had stayed in Vienna for several days was departing for Munich. After much standing and running around, he received a ticket in a ticket office that was valid – as such tickets usually are – for several weeks. Dear G. had the ticket confirmed and got a stamp for Tuesday, wrapped his luggage (two dirty shirts and a handkerchief) into the evening paper with the intention of going. But in the café he started talking at great length – they were solving some earth-shattering problems. G. became agitated and – did not depart. The next day he went to the office and asked them to extend the validity of his ticket. The clerk considered the matter from the right side and from the left, from above and from below and finally announced that it was impossible. G. begged until he was practically crying with anger – he had spent the last money he had on the ticket. G. thundered, swore, begged again, turned everything there upside down, but in vain.

---

15 In the elections held on 17 October 1920, the Christian Social Party won seventy-nine seats in parliament, the Social Democratic Party sixty-two seats and the German National Party eighteen seats. The Christian Social Party was a Catholic conservative party with a mainly rural electorate, founded by Karl Lueger (1844–1910) in about 1889. See Elisabeth Barker, *Austria 1918–1972*, pp. 15, 20–21. On the demagogic politics of the opportunistic Lueger, see Carl E. Schorske, *Fin-de-siècle Vienna. Politics and Culture*, New York, 1981, pp. 133–46.

Regulation, duty. G. ran around to all the higher competent authorities, from the station master to the director and everywhere he was
told that it was impossible, everywhere he was thrown out. Finally,
he broke down, borrowed the money and returned abjectly to the
office. He stood for another two hours before he was admitted and
finally he guiltily asked for a new ticket. Over the rims of his glasses,
the clerk inspected him and asked triumphantly: 'Well then, was I
right or not?' G. timidly assented. 'It really is impossible.' 'Well
there you go, you should have listened to me in the first place. And
now I will extend that ticket for you.'

   We laughed so hard we cried. Tell me, should one laugh or should
one cry?

# Children
## 9 January 1921, *Tribuna*

There are no children in the spiritual sense of the word. A child is
a complete person; a child is a perfectly developed soul. There is
nothing that a child cannot understand or sense. It sees and understands and thinks not only with its heart and mind, but also with
all of its skin, with all of its being; and if its heart and mind come
to a halt before a mystery, its being does not. The child's soul
absorbs the atmosphere of mystery and converts it into horror and
fear, or a false explanation. Usually this fear remains inscrutable to
the person and those around him for his entire life, even when the
mystery has long ceased to be a mystery and even when the mind
has answered the questions with which his instinct wrestled in
childhood. A child is a person and I firmly believe that the decisive
features of human character are formed in early childhood, in the
seeds of sensibility, at a time when the child is still a small animal
and when it is usually treated as such, as a creature that does not
see, hear, or understand. If a person changes from childhood to
adulthood, it is at most a formal change, a change of expression,
self-control, a mature cleverness that conceals what has to be
concealed, or a deceit that pretends to be what it is not. In essence,
every person is the same as he was at the age of four or five and
when he reacts to something suddenly, unexpectedly, he reacts
essentially with the same internal gesture that he had as a child.

Usually we treat children – in life and in literature – as if they
were pretty dolls, half jokingly, using a half-lisping tone and yet no
one is more repulsive to a child than a person who is constantly
'hugging and kissing'. For a child, only a person who treats it seriously is a friend and it senses precisely when seriousness is affected
as a joke and when it is genuine, shy, candid. A child demands
inner freedom from everyone it meets, just as radically as an adult
does and it is never open or direct with a person who, in some way,
lets his superiority be known. Parents who force their child to obey
simply because it is a child and they are parents, teach it to be a
liar because a lie is the only defence a child has against an authority it does not understand. Parents who beat a child for its first lie
commit a crime; a child never lies if it is not driven to do so by
some necessity of defence or resistance against something that it

opposes with its entire being, although its brain is not able to oppose.

In all the world, only Russian literature approaches the world of the child with attentive, profound seriousness, with shy appreciation, yes, sometimes with a humble plea for forgiveness for the wrongs so often perpetrated against these little ones. Dostoevskii was right to say that when investigating a crime, a judge should look first at the earliest childhood of the accused person and that this would often explain the cause of the later aberrant development. It is not only Dostoevskii who describes children in such a moving way. All the others do the same, Tolstoi, Goncharov, Gogol', Turgenev, and likewise the younger generation of Chekhov and Korolenko.[16] Here and there a child's soul glimmers in their work and it is always presented with profound truthfulness and the most serious interest. It is never presented with false playfulness or indulgent condescension, as in Czech literature. The Russian writer stands before the soul of a child as humbly as he does before any human soul and he never dares to say that he understands it. He extends his hand to every child as a comrade and speaks to it as an equal. We Czechs have never been able to do this. Not our teachers, our women or our artists. Yet we need it as much as our daily bread.

A child is as distinctive and fantastically unusual as every person is and just as there are no so-called ordinary people, there are no ordinary children.

Surprisingly, however, they clearly have one trait in common: they are not good. Ninety-nine children out of a hundred are not good. Not that they are evil – not even we grown-ups are evil, a truly evil person is a rare exception – but they are not good. If a child lends a toy to another child at all, it does so hesitantly, uneasily and uncertainly; it is not satisfied until the toy is returned. A child never wonders about the poverty or misery of another child, unless it is urged to do so. Then it does a 'good deed' hesitantly, in a complicated fashion and is not satisfied until it receives some word of praise. Perhaps because it does not understand well what a *difference* is. Any kind of difference: social, intellectual, physical. Every difference seems comical to a child. Children who chase after a lame beggar or an idiot are not like evil Oldřich in the primers; they are not evil at all. But a child finds it funny that that person

---

16 Fedor Mikhailovich Dostoevskii; Lev Nikolaevich Tolstoi (1828-1910); Ivan
   Aleksandrovich Goncharov (1812–1891); Nikolai Vasil'evich Gogol'
   (1809–1852); Ivan Sergeevich Turgenev (1818-1883); Anton Pavlovich Chekhov
   (1860–1904); Vladimir Galaktionovich Korolenko (1853–1921).

is so different from other people. Compassion for suffering, deformity and pain is not an innate emotion, just as suffering, deformity and pain themselves are not innate. A child does not know them and cannot know them because they are not from God, but from people. A child comes to know about them only when it comes to know about people.

This year I saw a handful of city children who were blowing soap-bubbles into the air through a straw. It was on the edge of a meadow, the sun was shining and the bubbles were lustrous and colourful, so alluring that I too stopped to watch them. The group was cheerful, friendly, in high spirits and everything was going well – until an obstacle appeared. Attracted by the unfamiliar splendour, a little girl who tended geese came closer and closer until she was right by the group. She was quiet and did not interfere at all. The children, however, lashed out at her so angrily that I was amazed. The little one had to go away; but she could not hold out for long. The bubbles drew her back like a magnet and after a while she returned, standing close to the little boy who was blowing bubbles and she devoured the coloured spheres with her eyes. But this time it really was bad. Not a single child defended her; it did not occur to a single one to be good to the girl. Perhaps they would even have hurt her if I had not interfered. The strangest thing, however, happened next: when I asked why they did not leave her be, one boy answered, embarrassed, 'I don't know.' An older girl, who perhaps guessed that this explanation would not satisfy me, added, 'She's so strange.' Truly, the little girl was 'strange'. She did not have shoes or stockings, her straw-blonde hair was bleached by the sun and she had a comical little pigtail and ugly freckles. 'But it is a pity. She would like to watch and have fun,' I tried to explain. 'So let her look then,' the children decided. But we understood clearly, myself and the little gooseherd: it was not kindness but rather – they obeyed. I had completely spoiled their game. They did not laugh anymore and after a while they left.

When a child does a good deed, it always does so in a complicated fashion that is most characteristic of the child's mind. I know two interesting cases of boys (today they are grown men) who wanted to give a *Sechserl* to a beggar-woman.[17] The first one did not have any money, but he saw the beggar and made up his mind that it would be nice to give her a *Sechserl*. He ran home, burst into the kitchen, grabbed his mother by the apron and said: 'Mummy, please, for heaven's sake give me a *Sechserl* quickly.' His plea was so

---

17 A *Sechserl* was a ten-kreutzer coin.

desperately insistent that he got it and no one asked for an explanation, although at that time – about thirty years ago – it was a
great fortune. The boy flew back to the beggar and pressed the *Sechserl* into her hand. The beggar, of course, was extremely surprised
and pleased and the boy stood there, his chest heaving, his heart
pounding – on account of what? Not only the kindness, but also
the glory. He had acted like a nobleman, he had acted like a knight;
he had done something terribly glorious; a burning warmth coursed
through him and he started to cry. That was the first one.

The second one met a beggar-woman in the Old Town Square
and he had a *Sechserl* in his pocket and in his heart, a need to give
it to the beggar.[18] But to give a beggar a ten-kreutzer coin was a
great and noisy deed, most likely it would also have great and noisy
consequences and his beautiful soul was embarrassed by greatness,
noise and glory. The *Sechserl*, however, burned in his pocket and his
heart was on fire. So he changed the money into ten kreutzers, gave
one to the beggar, ran around the Old Town hall and approached
her from the other side, like a totally new donor. He gave her a
second kreutzer and flew away again – and did this ten times. Of
course, afterwards he was completely exhausted in mind and body,
but with the exhaustion came a mundane anxiety, uncertainty,
regret. In the end, he cried until he received another *Sechserl*.
Clearly, he could not bear it after all that he had not been rewarded
for his truly rare kindness.

In the large European cities, strange and remarkable buildings
have been erected: courts for children. They are large, spacious
buildings, a little like reformatories where children end up who
have committed a crime but are not yet old enough to be convicted.
The young delinquents are tried according to the same laws as
adults. Only the punishments are different: the children end up
under the supervision of the state for a time. They live in the above-
mentioned buildings; they study there and are supervised by people
who understand pedagogy and psychology. They are treated kindly
and gently and are not punished. On the contrary, they lack for
nothing and their guardians try to teach them rationally why virtue
is beautiful and evil is ugly. I will give more details about these
buildings on another occasion; here, I do not have space. I will only
say this much: if this undertaking has obvious shortcomings, just
as every collective confinement has shortcomings as far as morality and sexuality are concerned, it is, nonetheless, a worthy

---

18 Kafka gave an account of this incident in a letter to Jesenská on 18 July 1920.
Kafka, *Letters to Milena*, p. 95.

undertaking that Czechs have never attempted. If a normal child deserves the greatest care and attention, a child that has committed a crime deserves a hundred times more care, a hundred times more love, respect and attention. The modern era is finally beginning to understand that it is not enough to thrash a guilty child; that it is first necessary to discover what caused the illness to grow up in the child's soul and to strive to cure the illness. All modern cities have set this task for themselves and certainly no one would refuse support or help. Why should we Czechs lag behind?

# My Friend
## 27 January 1921, *Tribuna*

People have a capacity for friendship only when they are very young. Haven't you noticed this before? Later, as soon as they start to grow old, or, let's say, to mature, they make friends only with great difficulty, irritably, as if they did not want to and the friendships certainly do not last. But sometimes such a friendship is forced on one by life, a friendship that is sometimes very strange and, if you like, not a friendship at all. Beethoven's close friend was, they say, an old, broad, carved armoire that stood in the corner of the room. My friend is my concierge, Mrs Kohler, who stands by my bed every morning at seven o'clock with a tender expression on her face and a mop in her hand and waits compassionately, shuffling in her tattered slippers, for me to leave the room so that she can clean.[19]

Do you think I am planning to write a caricature? Not at all. I am moved as I write, with tears in my eyes. This woman of the people, a true, uneducated, proletarian bumpkin of the last generation, has the best heart in all the world and I love her tenderly and profoundly. I always grow sentimental when I think of her. Please forgive me if I express myself in an unusually maudlin manner. The image of her round moony face, in the precise geometrical centre of which is a little dot of a nose and a wide, scantily toothed mouth, a face that is eternally sweating in some kind of strange embarrassment before the world, always makes me feel tender-hearted. It was a long time before I could distinguish which of the distortions of her features indicated happiness, pain or anger, but in time I committed to memory the unerring signs of her moods. Thus, for

19 Kafka referred to her a number of times in his letters. Mrs Kohler (Jesenská writes 'paní Kohlerová') was the concierge and housekeeper at Lerchenfelderstrasse 113, where Jesenská and Ernst Pollak rented an apartment in May 1918. According to Marta Marková-Kotyková, Mrs Kohler was Adelheid Koller-Simmel (11.9.1884, Gyermely, Hungary – 7.11.1972, Vienna). When the young married couple moved to Lerchenfelderstrasse 113, she was a thirty-four-year-old widow, caring for two children. She was two years older than Ernst Pollak and twelve years older than Jesenská. She stayed in the same building after Jesenská left Vienna and continued to look after Pollak's household. She married again and remained in the same building until her death. See Marta Marková-Kotyková, *Mýtus Milena*, pp. 99–100.

instance: when she is happy, her lonesome upper lip juts out at the world, threatening and when she is sad, her little eyes turn purple, as if she is going to cry and her nose swells to unheard-of dimensions. When she wants something, she bustles around me in haste, wipes my inkpot three times in a row, remembers without prompting that she has to get flour and makes a fire without opening the windows, which hardly ever happens. But if something terrible has happened, her face becomes truly gruesome, pale, stiff, sort of lifeless and her figure seems to turn on an axis, as if a mallet had struck her unexpectedly on the head. When I see that expression on her face, I freeze in genuine horror to the core of my soul: it never errs.

The nicest thing about her is the regularity of her actions. I can be absolutely certain that she will do everything exactly an hour late. You must admit that if this is followed as a steadfast principle it is a good trait. If I want her to light a fire at six, I ask her to light it at five and by six-thirty, the room is warm. This regularity is manifest in all sorts of ways. I know for certain that she will not steal more than four pairs of stockings a year from me, one pair for every season, which entirely suffices for her. No more than five cubes of sugar have ever disappeared at once from my sugar bowl. No more than a small piece is ever sliced from the lump of butter in the refrigerator and at most two coffee-spoons a day disappear from the box of condensed milk. She never takes more than she needs from me and she needs very little. A year ago, inspired by noble thoughts of friendship and equality, I suggested to her that she not steal anymore, that I would prefer to give her what she regularly took. I frightened her to death, the poor soul. Because she could not detect any guile in my face, she did not dare to claim that she did not steal and she had no idea how to react. Her anxious eyes looked at me first in reproach and then in indignation. I acknowledged that she was completely in the right and since that time, everything has gone on as before.

We have been through quite a lot together. For the three years I have been living in this cursed city, she has been my consolation. I know that her love for me is as great as mine for her and that I can depend on her. But I did not always know that. I did not even suspect it when I had that silly idea – admit it, who in the world has not had such an idea? – to poison myself.[20] When I lay for a week in the empty flat, not recognising a living soul, half-unconscious, I was woken every day at noon by the powerful shaking with

---

20 Wagnerová links this suicide attempt to use of cocaine; according to her, Jesenská's circle of acquaintances in Vienna experimented with the drug.
Wagnerová, *Milena Jesenská*, pp. 83 and 91.

which Mrs Kohler called me back to life. In the haze of my confusion, a tearful round face, fluid as water, floated before me and hands stinking of kerosene stuffed a large, round, black dumpling into my mouth. She cooked these for me herself, having a kind of sentimental notion of what Czech dumplings were because I had always dreamed of them aloud. This continued until I had enough strength to vomit up the black ball. I think I will never poison myself again. Not because I am afraid of death, but because it is difficult to believe that we two will ever part from one another. That is, to be honest, because I am afraid of more of Mrs Kohler's dumplings.

That was not the worst, however, that we have lived through together. It happened that, cut off from our homelands by the political situation, I from Bohemia and she from Hungary, we sat for months, without a heller, our stomachs rumbling, on the box of ashes in her hole in the cellar by the flickering light of the kerosene lamp and racked our brains for a way to get money. Hunger is a terrible thing and a big foreign city can be cruel. The second-hand dealer in the building next door swallowed up our shirts and all our rings lay in the pawn shop; from these proceeds, we ate lunches, dinners, breakfasts and teas of red beets and dirty sauerkraut for as long as we could. But nothing can go on infinitely. In this finitude, I proved to be the weaker fighter. My stomach could not tolerate the sauerkraut and general weakness prevented me from showing any further interest in our common menu, which seemed to me terribly pointless, like life itself. But Mrs Kohler was victorious for both of us. The more apathetic I became, the more lively this little creature grew and her gout-swollen legs performed wonders and her brain thought up transactions worthy of the stock-exchange. With a blunt conviction that one must live, she performed miracles that remain a mystery to me to this day. There wasn't a crown that she didn't share with me; there wasn't a piece of bread that she didn't break to give me the larger half. Where would I be today without her? At that time I decided that when I became a millionaire, she would get half of my fortune and I will stand firmly by my promise. You will see.

Dear God! What three years can do to a person. At that time, we were what is known as a bohemian society. All of us together did not have enough to eat and because at our place it was a little less cold than on the bench at the train station, it often happened that one of the desperate members of this little society lived in the closet behind our kitchen, where today wood is piled to the ceiling, gloating in its bourgeois conceit and prosperity. With touching devotion,

Mrs Kohler befriended all these folks. Missing buttons, torn shoelaces, threadbare collars, muddy boots – under her motherly hand everything recovered a smooth, decent appearance. She called people by their first names and got angry if they left without swallowing a little of the black, mushy coffee and chicory she had made for them. She cut out clippings of their poems and carried them proudly to show the neighbours. She got the police on their backs because she thought that one of them was a communist but she 'wouldn't let them touch a hair on his head.' She followed our progress with genuine pleasure and today the former starving vagabonds are grateful. When W. returns from Italy, where he went to pick up the payment for his last novel, or when L. comes from Prague on an important assignment for a major journal, or when P., who today is a travelling wine salesman, or S., who is a bank official, visit our nest, they stop by her kitchen downstairs. She cheerfully admires the creases in their trousers and shakes the hands of 'the gentlemen', first wiping her own on her apron. But when we both feel lonely and sad, we remember together those three out of all our many friends who succumbed to the poverty of the times and died. They did not know how to 'become bourgeois'. Mrs Kohler's little eyes fill with tears and her compassionate, loud nose-blowing resounds through the twilight of the room.

Mrs Kohler is a widow. Her husband fell in the war and if you saw his photograph, you would be surprised. He was very dashing, with long moustaches. But Mrs Kohler has no shortage of suitors. She is courted by the old and the young and because of them Mrs Kohler has the reputation of a siren in this street, a reputation that she does not deserve, as all the blame can be laid on her good heart, which is unable to deny anyone anything. Her love, however, belongs only to one man, who has a terrible 'character flaw': every sixth Sunday, he gets stone drunk and staggers to Mrs Kohler's place at midnight. Kicking up a row, he bursts open the front door (if it happens, by chance, to be locked, which it usually is not – Mrs Kohler is not that petty) and beats her so hard with his drunken fists that the next day my floors are not swept or polished. For the next six weeks he is as gentle and peaceful as a lamb; he goes to fetch the coal and brings her little bouquets and pieces of chocolate. On the sixth Sunday, however, the same thing happens all over again. Then, in her grief, Mrs Kohler breaks plates while washing the dishes in my kitchen, shakes her head and complains: 'Not someone like that! A red-headed monster like that.' I feel for her deeply. There is just one thing I do not understand: why, in her anger, does she curse her one and only 'red-headed' sweetheart

when his beautiful hair is as black as night? But maybe I'm confus-
ing him with that other one.

That is my friend. You see, I cannot imagine life without her. If
I move to America, she will be my bulkiest piece of luggage. I
cannot wake up in the morning if she is not standing by my bed
in a stained apron, mop in hand. If something happened to me, I
could not confide in anyone if she was not nearby and I could not
enjoy my dinner if I knew that she had not stolen her share, which
sometimes happens, through an oversight. We have silently made
a pledge not to part. So when you meet me, you will also meet Mrs
Kohler and when you look up Mrs Kohler, I will not be far off.

# Mysterious Redemption
## 25 February 1921, *Tribuna*

The bond between people and things is closer and more mysterious than we imagine.[21] Surprisingly, the happier we are, the easier it is to approach people. The worse off we are and the more we suffer, the more connection and companionship do we have with things. There are moments when a person is surrounded by objects that have suddenly acquired a face; suddenly they move and suddenly they have an entirely different expression, significance and size than ever before. Pain shuts you up in a narrow cage, without doors or windows; there is no exit and no air. People walk by you, mute and blind; but all of a sudden some roof, cart or bit of sky seems to open wide the walls of pain, the invisible gates fly open and the lungs, liberated, exhale.

Sometimes the four walls of the dwelling you know too well spit you out onto the street you know too well, in front of the shopwindows and posters you know off by heart. A kind of anxiety sits at the back of your skull, a kind of strange, feverish suffering and at the sight of the familiar face of the wardrobe, a horror of futility overwhelms you. The long, dead street uncoils upwards towards

---

21 The order of the sentences as printed in the original article was jumbled and has been altered in translation. The article appears to be addressed to Kafka. It was published two months after Kafka had ended their relationship by asking Jesenská not to write to him. He made this request while he was at a sanatorium in the Tatra Mountains in the winter of 1920–21. Jesenská wrote to Max Brod at the beginning of January 1921, expressing her despair. *Dopisy Mileny Jesenské* (The Letters of M. J.), ed. Alena Wagnerová, Prague, 1998, pp. 54–55. For an English translation of the letter, see Max Brod, *Franz Kafka. A Biography*, pp. 231–232. She wrote: 'I do not dare to write a word, a question, to him; and I don't even know what I want to know. Jesus Christ, I would like to press my temples into my brain. Only tell me this one thing – you must know, you were with him lately: Am I at fault or am I not at fault? I beg you, for God's sake, don't write comforting things to me, don't write that nobody is at fault, don't write me any psychoanalysis. I know all that, believe me, I know all that sort of thing that you could write to me. I trust you, Max, in what is perhaps the most difficult hour of my life. Please understand what I want. I know who and what Frank is: I know what has happened, and I do not know what has happened; I am on the verge of madness; I've tried to act, live, think, feel rightly, guided by conscience; but somewhere there *is* a fault. That's what I want to hear about.' Ibid., p. 232.

the sky, like a dusty ribbon. You know: it will take hours before you get to a place you have never been before. The little boxes of human dwellings, crushed together between the spread crosses of cross-roads, kilometre after kilometre, four storeys high; people's kitchens, beds and garbage and the tiny flower-pots behind people's windows all of a sudden make you feel uneasy, dizzy, disgusted. You would not go back upstairs for all the world; from the street you look up at the little square window and you wonder anxiously how you could have lived weeks, months, years, there behind the glass case between the sky and the pavement; you live out your anxieties and wishes there; you go back there *every evening*. Five meters long and six meters wide sustained what you call life and through the little glass pane there lies what you call the world. All of a sudden you jump into the first tram that comes along, onto the platform, up to the front and it's like you are fleeing from something. My God, what an amazing thing a tram is! It whirrs and rumbles through the streets with a gong underneath and people in its stomach. It surges through the streets, busy and full of haste; it slides over the tracks, taking air into its motor lungs from both sides. It descends further and further into streets you don't know, past houses with unfamiliar faces. At some crossroads, you get out and change trams. Suburbs, gardens, a church, a grocer's, corners lit up, curving streets. In the middle of the noise and the city, you sit there, lonely and alone. You see hundreds and hundreds of windows like the one that terrifies you and your horror of absurd-ity changes into a quiet, lamenting surrender to the law. You look at the faces of people and the faces of animals and it seems to you that you know something they do not. In your heart you caress them and you wonder at how strangely they live and how hard they have to work to get by, to live in a home, to love, to feel. At the end station, a muddy road continues into the countryside; you don't know where it leads, but you caress it because it goes into the world. You stand for a while where the road begins and finally you renounce your desire to follow it and you go back into the bowels of the city, slowly, aged and wise. You look up at your window without dismay and if it happens to be lighted, you run upstairs, open the door and say: hello.

Someone once told me:

'By afternoon, I knew he wouldn't come home. It chased me out onto the street and grabbed me by the throat, dragged me from corner to corner, through the passages, the squares, the parks, the embankment: the suspicion that he wouldn't come home. I felt like stopping strangers, telling them everything and asking what they thought: would he come, or wouldn't he? The streets rose over steep hills towards the sky and collapsed under the vehicles into the depths; I staggered over the pavement, on level ground stumbling over the boulders that fear put in my path. The grocery store, the tobacconist's and the window of the pub opposite threatened even from a distance to confirm it. The windows were dark. The staircase dark. The apartment empty.

The infinite burden of the time I would have to wait settled on my chest. Hour after hour, the street in front of me trickled into the past. One corner of the room threw me into the other, like a wretched ball, back and forth, back and forth. A stain from the street lamp crawled onto the carpet, darkness settled on the furniture and the game came to an end. The window was the one point in the apartment that was not empty. At one end, me, in the other, expectation; we took up the whole room and we settled down quietly. Beyond the curve of the street, footsteps sometimes sounded. But it was a foreign gait that drifted at the turning and around the corner, darkness swallowed the stranger. All night long. Blows fell from the tower, a quarter past, half past, three quarters of the hour. Behind me, on the wall of the room, the pendulum clacked, smick, smack, back and forth. All night long. Morning slipped over the roofs, grey, clear, formless, colourless and carried away hope, carried away hope, carried my companion, expectation, out the window. With long poles over their shoulders, the lamplighters of the suburban street-lights marched one after another at regular quarter-hour intervals, as if issuing in the day *which no longer interested me*. The street stretched, yawned, turned on its side and fell back asleep, for one more hour.

The untouched bed in the room at that early hour acted as if someone was dying. The glass of water set out for the night, the plate with fruit and the scattered slippers stabbed with such a terrible anguish that I lost the courage to step down into the room and stayed by the window.

Transfixed by a single horror from head to toe: how to survive the coming day? All the hours ran through the mind in a deadly anxiety, limbs were paralysed, the head hurt, the heart stopped, the chest stopped breathing. The pavement far below seemed to rise to a height and death ceased to be terrible.

All of a sudden, a jerky clatter cut through the silence and the first suburban vehicle drove into the street as if on a whim; the little horse tossed its head, tossed its mane, it had a chafed hide and a cart behind its back – and a miracle happened. The world fluttered, breathed in the daily activity; the shops, the passages, the pubs, the tobacconist's, everything stirred, the bells stirred in the tower, the windows stirred in the houses with a broad movement all along the street, all over the city, all over the sky; the day spread far, far and a quiet blessing went through the air.

As in the half-second between the operation and the swoon, in the half-second that embraces the entire space, all the sunlight, all the sky, all the world, the realisation shook me until I broke into a tired weeping: how sweet, how sweet, how sweet it is to live!'

Hasn't it ever happened to you that you lay in the dark in your room, looking through the dark to the ceiling and could not move for dread and pain and somewhere up above a child was crying *for you*? Hasn't it ever struck you in the theatre that people die and fight and sing *for you*? Haven't you ever seen a bird flying with spread wings *for you* across the horizon, peacefully, happily, far away, never to return? Haven't you ever found a road on which there were as many steps to the crest as you needed to free yourself from grief?

I firmly believe that the world helps. Somehow, some way, all of a sudden, unexpectedly, simply, compassionately. But sometimes this salvation is almost as painful as the pain itself. I know a person with diseased lungs. He is tall and thin, his face angular, sharp, beautiful, evil and exceedingly good. He said this about his disease: 'When the heart and the brain could not stand the suffering any longer, they looked around for something to save them and that's when the lungs spoke up. I know that my disease saved me. But that bargaining between the heart and the lungs, which went on without my awareness, was probably terrible.'[22] It sounds like a fairytale. Like a strange fairytale from another world and yet it is the truth, existence and suffering. Here the sick lungs brought redemption. No, do not be surprised. One does not have to be surprised. One has to cry over it. One has to press one's head between one's hands and ardently, ardently love life, so that it will be appeased by such a great love and redeemed from damnation.

---

22 Jesenská here paraphrased Kafka's description of his illness in one of his first letters to her. Kafka, *Letters to Milena*, p. 6.

# Melancholy in the Rain

## 29 April 1921, *Tribuna*

Ah yes, there are towns that blossom under palm trees, white towns high above the blue sea. There are mountains, eternally covered in snow, with overhanging roads, with dazzling views; there are roads lined with thuja, sad roads, like paths to a cemetery and islands surrounded by waves and magnificent solitude, with rocks at their centre where birds nest. There are towns encircled by potato barrens and sealed off by factories. Desolate landscapes with ravines full of acacias and blackthorn bushes bordering stony farm tracks.

But the sun rises and sets over them all, the rain falls, the wind blows, the mist rises and night comes on.

In Dubrovnik, I saw an old woman who was dying; she stood at the window with a face of yellow wax.[23] In Vienna, I saw a woman who was dragged by a tram and died under the car and no one was able to help her. In Prague I saw a person who jumped from a bridge into the Vltava River and drowned and the next day he lay, a swelling, livid corpse, on the pavement of the towpath; and another person who fled without a hat or a coat from the policemen chasing him and when he saw that flight was futile, he shot himself in the mouth and collapsed on the pavement. I saw a hunch-back clown who hanged himself in a circus carriage on a brightly coloured rope and his pointed hat lay at his feet. I know a woman, a young, pretty girl who became a prostitute to support an obscene slob who beat her when he was drunk. I knew a person who died of hunger and another who lived with his wife for three months in a cave, along with the rats and when he recognised – he was a doctor – the signs of incurable madness in his wife, he poisoned her. Today he is dead; he died of starvation in Berlin; and their child, a red-headed, sickly little girl with rickets who lives in

---

23 Dubrovnik is a port city in Croatia, located on the southern Adriatic coast.

Vienna with a proletarian family, carries alone the unfinished tragedy of those two people into the world.[24]

But are these the experiences that shape our lives? Isn't a little girl crying in the street, or a young woman wearing a tight, shabby bodice just as strange and unforgettable?

And the young prisoner of war, with matted hair and a pale face, the soldier who flashed past at the window of the train when you were standing under the tracks on Sunday, what will happen to him? What had happened to him? And the worker you meet by chance and the old servant with the worn shoes? And each one of those who sit next to us in the tram and in the waiting-room at the train station, where do they come from and what will happen to them? And those, the strangest of all, whose lives are not novels and in whose lives nothing ever happens, day or night?

Have you ever seen a person sleeping? More terrible than a dead man! A person sleeping is full of guile, full of thoughts, wishes and desires. No one knows what is happening inside him. He breathes and does not know himself what is happening inside him, how he will wake, what will happen tomorrow.

And the paved little courtyard with blades of grass in the cracks of the stones and the flaking wall of broken brick and the rumbling telegraph poles by the ditch of the dusty road, the bean field with stakes poking from the earth and the baulk and the field of potatoes with purple July flowers and the ditch behind the barn with the rusty pot without a bottom and the boot without a sole, the back of the goat-shed and the foot-path to the neighbouring village, what unforgettable, bitter-sweet landscapes!

There is a shop-window and behind it, a little pub. There one can see an Indian and a woman with a snake. There is also a gramophone and one can listen to music, two crowns for a song. Mozart, Verdi and Spanish dances and *Aïda* and *Don Giovanni*; but in *Rigoletto* there's a place – *'Tempi buone, tempi buone'* – and Caruso sings

---

24 The story of the cave may not be far-fetched. Janik and Toulmin write: 'Vienna had always had a housing shortage, and the rapid growth of its population (from 476,220 in 1857 to 2,031,420 in 1910) merely aggravated a long-standing problem. By 1910, the average Viennese dwelling housed 4.4 persons, with an average of 1.24 per room (including kitchens, bathrooms and front halls); "a considerable number of persons" were even reduced to "living in caves dug in railway embankments, in boats, in hiding places under the bridges, and in other emergency refuges."' They quote Charles O. Hardy, *The Housing Program of the City of Vienna*, Washington D.C., Brookings Institution, 1934. See Allan Janik and Stephen Toulmin, *Wittgenstein's Vienna*, New York, 1973, p. 50.

it like the booming of a drum.[25] So much beauty and enthusiasm in the midst of so much filth and misery and poverty is unbearable. Tears fill my eyes.

In front of me there lies a little postcard, a little photograph of Charlie Chaplin in a stiff hat, shabby clothes and a tattered waistcoat without a collar. He sits on some steps with a little dog beside him. The film is very funny and is called *A Dog's Life*.[26] But Charlie sits there, so helpless and touching that you do not know if you should laugh or cry. The dog beside him looks just like him. He sits there leaning against his master. His paws, which are still big and soft, have slid down a little on one side. But the master is even gentler, more pitiable and his big eyes look even more unhappily at the world. May God help them both.

Do you know the little station between Prague and Paris? If you go by train, you will see in the window a woman who rises and children who grow up and become people. Daily the trains go by and the people sitting in them will see the Seine and Montmartre the following day; with a light and a bell, the little station gives the signal to proceed and every day with a series of chains it sends off the express train on the Prague-Paris line. If you see it, you will witness a scene of sweet Laforgue comedy and you will ask yourself in wonder why people sleep, eat, love and live there.[27]

'My grandfather used to say,' the writer Kafka wrote somewhere: 'life is amazingly short. Now, in recollection, everything is so compressed that, for example, I can hardly understand how a young person can decide to go to the nearest station without being afraid that – not to mention the possibility of an accident – the length of an ordinary life passed in happiness will not suffice by far for such a ride.'[28]

---

25 She refers to Wolfgang Amadeus Mozart (1756–1791) and his opera *Don Giovanni*; and Giuseppe Verdi (1813–1901) and his operas *Aïda* and *Rigoletto*. Enrico Caruso (1873–1921) was a famous operatic tenor.

26 The film *A Dog's Life* was released in 1918.

27 She refers to the French poet Jules Laforgue (1860–1887).

28 This quotation constitutes the text of a short prose piece written by Kafka. It was translated by Willa and Edwin Muir as 'The Next Village': 'My grandfather used to say: "Life is astoundingly short. To me, looking back over it, life seems so foreshortened that I scarcely understand, for instance, how a young man can decide to ride over to the next village without being afraid that – not to mention accidents – even the span of a normal happy life may fall far short of the time needed for such a journey." See Franz Kafka, *The Complete Stories* (1971), ed. Nahum N. Glatzer, New York, 1983, p. 404. The piece, *Das nächste Dorf*, was first published by Kurt Wolff in May 1920 in the collection *Ein Landarzt* (A Country Doctor). See Joachim Unseld, *Franz Kafka: A Writer's Life* (1982), trans. Paul F. Dvorak, Riverside CA, 1994, p. 378.

# Superficial Small Talk about a Serious Subject

17 June 1922, *Tribuna*

One of the errors of the present age is that it is too profound. Forgive me, but this is not at all a frivolous paradox. Certainly, profundity of thought, emotion and knowledge is one of the most beautiful things in the world. But this profundity appears to have been exploited in recent years. No one can enjoy even a single hour free of profundity. Have you noticed this too? You meet an acquaintance at the market at ten o'clock in the morning and you are thinking about butter and hogs' tails, but your acquaintance immediately strikes up an abstract conversation as if he could not do otherwise. You are forced to forget about hogs' tails and turn either to the eternity of the human soul or, at least – at best – the question of human happiness and the right to free love. Matters that are very unpleasant and inappropriate at ten o'clock in the morning, perhaps as inappropriate as eating radishes with marzipan.

Today, it is as if we have succumbed to the spell of complexity. There is hardly anything left in the world that is simple, clear and obvious and that one can sum up intelligibly in a few words. There is hardly anything in the world that is not the subject of long public debates, conjectures and conversations. For people with a certain degree of intelligence, it is easy to string together a few psychological phrases, cast up by the times in a colourful geometrical pattern and by using the word 'subconscious' – a golden word for intellectual loafers and idiots – you can prove what you want to any victim. If you tell someone, for example, that his subconscious homosexual inclinations place constraints and obstacles in the way of an honest life and compel him to steal silver spoons – it sounds wonderful. If the person under attack says, 'but Sir, I simply am not homosexual', you reply, 'but my friend, what do you know about your subconscious?' The result is that he somehow (another of those convenient words) cannot help stealing the silver spoons. A beautiful thing, the subconscious.

That is how it is with everything these days. People whose responsibilities have become onerous, people who want to wrench themselves free from anything whatsoever required by law, all of a sudden discover terribly funny things in their subconscious. They produce a torrent of psychoanalytical volleys and exclamations and in two minutes you are convinced that they are right. Always subject this conviction to a test: try to remember what the person has just said to you and how he convinced you. If you can remember a single coherent sentence, I will give you – but you won't remember.

A rather long, but necessary introduction for the matter at hand. I was thinking about why it is that modern marriages are so problematic, short and unhappy. Today, even if you search in broad daylight, you cannot find a couple whose life together is simple and uncomplicated. If a marriage does not end in divorce after two months, it drags on with a whole host of problems and terrible inner catastrophes. I do not believe that marriage is different today than it was before. But people have a different attitude towards it than they did before. Perhaps a more intelligent, but definitely a worse, attitude. I will deliberately drop the 'profound tone'. (I can wave it about as well as anyone else.) I will try to speak superficially. Perhaps it will be more profound.

Most people who marry today make several mistakes a priori: first of all, both somehow, for some completely incomprehensible reason, imagine that the moment they marry they will be happy for the rest of their lives. Why they believe this is a complete mystery. A person who is alone is condemned to life-long unhappiness – (something very common, but little known) – so why should two people be happy? Why? By what right, by what prerogative, by what oversight of Fate? For a couple, life is a difficult, accountable, painful thing, requiring exertion. Why we go through it is as much of a mystery as why we are born and die. What compels one person to live with another is the power of life, the necessity of sex, the necessity of the mission – it is all the same what name we give it – simply, necessity. If people regarded their wedding as a necessity of human mental and organic existence, they would make things much easier for themselves.

The second error is that the majority of people today get married as an experiment. Marriage does not mean more duties. People do not take responsibilities upon themselves. Something occurs to them and they get married. Every marriage in the world, even the happiest one, is troublesome. It means a loss of freedom, a certain loss of pleasure. But no one today wants to give up pleasure. Pleasure is a kind of terrible heritage of the war, a reaction, a kind of desperate mistake and people consider it the goal, the adornment of life. Thus everyone combines marriage and pleasures. If a husband or a wife feels inclined to be unfaithful, a lot of phrases about sexual needs are at hand to help. Marriage today is not what it was or the one thing that it should be if it is to have any meaning: a sexual secret between two people, a secret that is betrayed and annulled by infidelity. A secret with a profound moral aim: a child, ultimately the one aim in the world that is worth pursuing. Marriage should serve to provide a child with a firm, moral ground under its feet.

The third error is that often, too often, the words 'I love you' are confused with 'I care about you', words that are very, very different. The first phrase, forgive me for saying so, is not worth a cent. The second, all of life itself. A man says 'I love you' to a woman whom he meets in the evening, only to find her repulsive and incomprehensibly foreign when he wakes the next day. The words 'I love you' have many meanings, many possible interpretations. 'I care about you' is a simple, solid, good promise. It is gold money that does not lose its value. When you marry, it is not important that you love your husband. But it is important that you care about him; that is, that in all situations in life (and how many situations are there in life?) you find him to be a dear, pleasant, good friend; you are well off if, after eight years of marriage, you can say that every day you look forward to the hour when your husband returns home. In that case, you are happily married.

Other errors follow once the marriage is contracted. Novels for girls end in a wedding. In life, the wedding is the beginning. But it is as if people did not live according to life, but according to novels for girls. As if, after the wedding, one no longer had to bother. A lot of trivialities follow, which douse the great passion. Untidy hair, teeth that are not brushed, that familiar, confounded comfort that a person indulges in at home. Usually women surrender their bodies entirely to this comfort and later to pregnancy. A pretty girl turns into an unpleasant, unfamiliar, unattractive person worn down by cares. But it is the duty of a woman to remain pretty, clean and tidy, despite all her cares, exertions and obligations. To prepare a dear, cosy, comfortable, orderly home for her husband. The friendship between husband and wife consists in this: that she gives him the opportunity to love her forever.

What is necessary is a little good will and, mainly, a firm decision. Today, people live without making decisions. That is, they live life as it comes. Yet what is necessary is for each person, at a certain hour, to identify his path, his inner calling, to set out on it and take all the consequences upon himself without exception. It is in this respect – bearing the consequences of one's actions – that the present era fails.

# II. Articles from *Národní listy* and *Lidové noviny*, 1922–1929

# On the Psychology of the New Society

## 30 July 1922, *Národní listy*

Do you remember the barefoot boys who used to run through the streets during the war and beg for a *Sechserl*? At first, we were moved to pity and gave. The more boys there were, however, the more we grew tired of giving. On the one hand, a more distressing poverty reared its head; on the other hand – and this was perhaps the main thing – it appeared that the boys, as soon as they got a *Sechserl*, ran to the snack-bar on Wenceslas Square and ate canapés.[1] With sardines and mayonnaise. We asked ourselves: why do boys need canapés? And we stopped giving.

Certainly we were right in a moral sense. But were we also right in a psychological sense? You forget what is always being forgotten, over and over again. You forget that our bellies were full. That does not mean I want to talk about the obligations of the sated to the hungry. But our bellies were full and we knew that the next day they would also be full. The sated, however, cannot understand the hungry. They do not differ from them in that they eat three times a day and are not hungry. They differ from the hungry in terms of their mental, spiritual and emotional structure. Those with full bellies see the world from a different perspective. Their wishes, passions, ideas, longings and functions are different. A slice of bread is something different to someone who is sated than it is to someone who is hungry, not quantitatively, but qualitatively.

Those who have gone hungry for several days do not know anything about it. The hunger that ladies feel when they undergo a slimming cure is perhaps something very amusing. Hunger that can be satiated at any moment is not desperate. But a hunger that might never end is like a curse that changes a person into someone completely unlike full-bellied people. If, by chance, you found your-selves in a situation in which you were ceaselessly hungry for a long time, without any hope that your condition would change, you would discover a strange thing. You would discover that after a period of starvation, you could not tolerate meat or bread; your

---

1 Wenceslas Square is a main avenue in the centre of Prague.

stomachs would immediately vomit it up. On the street you would find yourselves standing in front of a delicatessen shop-window, in front of a hotel entrance, with a caustic, corrosive, frantic longing for – pheasant, for example, lobster and pineapple, the most wonderful, exotic and savoury things. You would dream of sophisticated foods; on your hungry tongues you would taste the sauces of the most tender roasts. (In a suburb of Vienna I once saw a scrawny little girl who was 'telephoning' God through the bars of a sewer, saying that she would like a plate of pineapple strawberries. In reply to my question, she answered shyly that she had never eaten them before and did not know how they tasted. That child had not had anything in her mouth for two days, but she did not telephone for a piece of bread, but for something that was, to her mind, the best thing in the world.) If someone put food in front of you, however, you would not be able to swallow it. A long period of treatment and careful diet, slowly getting accustomed to food, would be necessary before you regained your health. Because hunger is a sickness most terrible for the soul.

Destitution, when a person suffers from hunger, is almost always confused with poverty, when a person suffers from privation. This is because destitution and poverty are neighbours. They are undoubtedly neighbours. They lie, however, on opposite sides of the border; that is, the border that, from a psychological perspective, divides economic life into two parts. On the one side, there are financially secure existences; on the other, those that are not secure. This is the realm of destitution. Over the border begins the realm of poverty and it soon comes to an end; in this sense, destitution and poverty are neighbours. They are closer together quantitatively than a certain degree of affluence is to poverty. Measured in quantitative terms, of course, a rich person is further removed from a poor person than a poor person is from a hungry person. But there is a border between poverty and hunger; a poor person differs from a hungry person in qualitative terms. A poor person has a small, secure capital. A hungry person has nothing but uncertainty, or the certainty of hunger. A hungry person is like the damned in hell. The despair of infinity mingles with the ceaseless pain of the present.

Let us return to our boys. Our urchins have got hold of a *Sechserl* and gone to eat canapés. Even if you discount the fact that it is wasteful, it is also senseless, silly, unhealthy, useless and thoroughly disgraceful. But you do not take into account that life is illogical; that there would be no luxury at all if there was no destitution. Luxury and hunger are not connected to satiety. There is not the least barrier between them. Hunger is the most terrible thing in the world, not so much in itself as in the fact that it is irremovable. People who have suffered from hunger for a long time have a feverish fear of it, even when they eat their fill; a fear so great that it destroys their souls, hearts and minds. It is a terribly difficult, perhaps impossible task to satisfy a person who has at one time truly stood face to face with destitution. The most awful despair is rooted in destitution: the despair that lurks behind haughtiness, Mammon, surfeit, drunkenness. Hunger does not drive one to a full plate; hunger drives one to profligacy. I will never believe that people prostitute themselves out of hunger. But I do believe that they become millionaires out of hunger.

From a psychological perspective, the behaviour of our boys is entirely understandable; it is not only the behaviour of little urchins, but the logical progression of the whole world, of history and of this century. It is not only the hunger of the stomach, but also the hunger of ambition. Not only the suffering of empty bellies, but also the suffering of humiliation.

Here and everywhere, the world is indignant and amazed by the dissipation, insatiability, voracity and conceit of the new social strata. You forget, however, that when the sack of the world was turned upside down, tens of thousands of hungry people – symbolically speaking – were given an opportunity to satiate their hunger. But a hungry person is not able to satiate his hunger. First and foremost, he must escape from his hunger. A person like that has a destructive fear of insignificance, of the hunger of the soul and seizes the first opportunity to escape from it. Only an indigent person, however, is afraid of destitution, only an insignificant person of insignificance. A person never fears the unknown. Because the indigent and insignificant do not have and can never acquire enough proofs of their significance, they stage extravagant displays for the world and for themselves. Only an insufficiency exaggerates. Sufficiency is firm and balanced. One automobile is not enough, but rather four. One fur coat is not enough, but rather a full wardrobe. Lunch only at a luxurious restaurant. Opera only with a private box. They take no pleasure in things, but rather in the fact that they can pay for expensive things.

The world of waiters pays obeisance to them; the world of the envious ridicules them. But even the contempt they provoke is exaggerated. They are like a hunted herd: the thunder of world revolutions has driven them out from the shadow of insignificance. The children of their children will be moderate. Because only he who has not experienced want in his youth can be humble. Only he who has not been humiliated can command. Only he who has learned to appreciate music can listen to it from the galleries. And so on ad infinitum.

But the era has given us new classes and people. It is necessary to wait until they are satiated. Just as we were not in the right, however, in psychological terms, when we reproached the boys for their canapés, we are not in the right today, in psychological terms, when we reproach the *nouveaux riches* for their dissipation. It is the bane of the world. But because it is elemental, reproaches, anger and contempt will not suffice. Do not laugh at them. Teach them.

# Devil at the Hearth

## 18 January 1923, *Národní listy*

Why all, or almost all, modern marriages are unhappy (as if the old ones were happy), is one of the fashionable questions around which, in all seriousness, a vast literature turns as does, in all frivolousness, every five-o'clock conversation.[2] Every question in the world is a suitable subject for social tattle as well as for philosophical essays and even we journalists pick up topics that are practically lying around in the street. This question, however, always astounds me; not because I could not give an explanation as to why modern marriages are unhappy – what can't a journalist explain? But because I always have to ask again and again: why should they be happy?

This is how it begins. Two people – two small, isolated human lice, exposed to so much hopelessness, distress and a life without prospects, two little people on the enormous globe, so inconceivably, appallingly, disturbingly large, both of them, according to innate, natural and correct law, unhappy – are suddenly supposed to be, at one stroke, at half past nine in the morning, for example, having been shut up in the same apartment, in the same name, in the same property, in the same fate, all at once are supposed to be, immediately and only because they are two, happy?

It seems to me that when two people get married because they want to be happy together, at that moment they sign away and eliminate the possibility of happiness. To marry for happiness is just as mercenary as to marry for two million, for a car or a barony and happiness, like two million, a car or a barony, does not suffice for happiness. If there is one thing that backfires in this world, it is scores and figures in matters of the heart. Two people can have only one sensible reason to marry and that is that they cannot not marry. They simply cannot live without one another. Leaving aside all romanticism, sentimentality and tragedy, such a reason does exist. One comes across it every day and whether it is love or something else, it is decidedly the strongest and most justified feeling in the world. But then, how many people are there who neglect and suppress, minimise, avoid or destroy this very thing in their lives?

2 Kafka referred to this article in letters to Jesenská written in January-February 1923. Kafka, *Letters to Milena*, pp. 229–234.

Two people marry so that they can live together. Why, I ask, is happiness needed, in addition to the immense, boundless gift of this possibility? Why are people never satisfied with true, unembellished greatness and choose instead a beribboned lie? Why do they promise one another something that neither they nor the world, nature, the heavens, Fate or life, can procure and no one anywhere is ever able to achieve? Why do they affix conditions of literary fantasy, such as happiness, to the real, actual, holy, earthly contract? Why do they expect more of the other than they themselves are able to give? Why do they expect anything at all, face to face with an event so great, so serious, so profound, as a life together?

If we were to reflect on marriage with understanding before we entered into it, we would appreciate, as a matter of course, several things we had not thought of before. For example, that a life with someone else is not easier but rather more difficult than a solitary life.[3] The individual gets many benefits along with his solitude: for example, half the responsibility; freedom; self-sufficiency; or the possibility of simply departing for Australia. Marriage is, however, so difficult because the moment you make the bond, you have to relinquish everything – psychologically – that it does not include. That is the second issue over which modern marriages shatter: people get married without positively deciding in favour of one another. Or rather, without deciding to give up all the rest.

It is fantastically difficult to get to know another person. I think I do not exaggerate when I say that it is possible to get to know a person after the first half hour of conversation and a second time after ten years of living together. I also think that it is almost impossible for two people to even suspect before the wedding who they are and whom they are marrying. Even if they know each other's deeds, ideas, enthusiasms, convictions, faiths and confessions, they still do not know each other's stockings, sleepy eyes, way of gargling or brushing teeth in the morning or way of tipping a waiter – because in the depths a person deceives, but on the surface you will know him. Thus, every marriage hides within itself a thousand risks of disappointment and all the possibilities of inner foundering, against which there is only one weapon: to accept them all beforehand. Convention the world over requires that a person be forgiven in the name of love for all different sorts of inner disposition, such as nationality and political and religious affiliation and we forgive him. But let us go deeper: let us forgive his superficiality. Let us put aside the modern Karenina hysteria and forgive ears that stick out

---

3 Jesenská later changed her mind. See her article: 'O žárlivosti' (Jealousy), 18 December 1927, *Národní listy*, p. 11.

and cravats tied crookedly. Every individual is a self-contained world unto himself. The more distinctly formed a person is, the more complete he is. The fewer opportunities and talents he possesses, the more certainly and profoundly does he possess them. If he has only one, it is the most valuable of all. But just as one cannot demand of a fair-haired person that he have at the same time – for example, on Tuesdays and Fridays, for a change – dark hair, one cannot ask of a pedant that he enjoy dancing the shimmy, of a dunce that he understand Kierkegaard, of a painter that he be interested in mathematics, of a dismal person that he sing songs, of a loner that he hold soirées. This is very simple accounting and surprisingly few people understand it. Usually people reproach one another for the very essence of their inner lives and it does not occur to them that it is the task of marriage to tolerate the essence of the other and to tolerate it in such a way that the other person feels justified in being the way he is. In the end, it is always a confirmation of himself that a person seeks from another. Proof that he is loved 'despite the fact that'. Every one of us has such a 'despite the fact that' and for that very reason is unhappy. People do not live together – I will never believe it – only because of sexual, erotic, financial or social necessities; people live together so that they can have a friend. So that, in the solitude of the world, they can have someone who confirms that their existence is justified, with all its errors and shortcomings – because, what is friendship but support for a crippled self-confidence? So that they can have someone who spares them from punishment, revenge, criticism, justice, a bad conscience. Or do you really think that a home has any other function than to protect and protect and protect an individual from the world and mainly from his internal mirror? The greatest promise that a woman can give a man or a man a woman is that profound sentence, spoken to children with a smile: 'I won't let them get you.' Isn't this more than 'I will love you unto death', more than 'I will be eternally faithful to you'? I won't let them get you. It encompasses everything. One's consideration for the other, one's truthfulness to the other, home, fidelity, allegiance, commitment, friendship. How great are these promises in contrast to paltry, shabby happiness.

Well, in other words, it almost seems to me that our marriages are so unhappy because we make it too damned easy for ourselves. It is very easy to accept a promise from a person that he cannot keep and a year later, when he has broken it, to get offended and run away. I think it would be much more difficult to make a promise one can keep and actually keep it. All those fantastic profundities are excuses that shatter against the first truly difficult situation when it is necessary to act with consideration. But why don't people promise, for example, that they will not scream when the roast is burned, or when one of them comes home late for dinner? Why don't people promise that they will never be too lazy to bring home an orange in their pockets, a bouquet of violets, a brand-new *Koh-i-Noor* pencil, or a cornet of raisins? Why don't they promise to appear at breakfast in the morning washed, fragrant with water and soap, fresh and carefully dressed, even on the day after the golden wedding and every day in between? Why don't they promise that they will strike a blow in anger rather than make reproaches for some little ugliness, cowardice, annoyance or nastiness? Why don't they promise always to be interested in each other and each other's pursuits, whether of art history, football or butterfly collections? Why don't they promise to give one another the freedom of silence, the freedom of solitude, the freedom of space? Why don't they promise one another all these endlessly difficult 'trifles', promises that can be fulfilled and yet never are fulfilled, instead of something as incidental as happiness?

If marriage is to have any meaning, it must be established on a broader and more real basis than the longing for happiness. Good Lord, let us not fear a little suffering, a little pain and unhappiness. Try it sometime: on a starry night, stand face to face with the starry sky and look at it intently, directly, completely absorbed, for an entire five minutes. Or stand somewhere in the mountains where you can see a bit of the earth from a height, as if from the sky. You will see that after a moment you believe in the importance of life and the unimportance of happiness. Happiness! As if the possibility of happiness did not lie in ourselves alone! As if the talent for happiness were not a particular talent, like a talent for singing, for writing, for politics, for cobbling! Give one person everything he asks for, shower him with love, presents, advantages and everything he wants and he still will not be happy. Beat another person until he can hardly breathe and perhaps he will be going along the street, see a heap of carrots, sprinkled and fresh, red carrots with green tops and he will be happy.

There are two possibilities in life: either to accept one's fate, to decide and act accordingly, to know it and be bound by the advantages and disadvantages, the happiness and unhappiness, bravely, honourably, without haggling over a kreutzer, generously and humbly. Or to seek one's fate: but in seeking you will lose not only strength, time, illusions, proper and good blindness, instinct; in seeking you will also lose your own worth. You will be poorer and poorer all the time. What will come is always worse than what was before.

And then: to seek, one needs faith and for faith, perhaps more strength than for life.

# The Bath, the Body and Elegance
## 28 January 1923, *Národní listy*

Clothes don't make the individual: the individual makes the clothes. A woman with a lofty, graceful, trim and agile body can dress herself in anything and the elegance of her movements will permeate the clothes, which will settle on her in marvellous folds. Clothes are not as important as is thought. The individual is important. Her gait, the movement of the shoulders, which push the body forward, the line of the throat and the head as she turns towards the wind, the complexion and the scent of the hand, which we press. Every individual has her inexpressible, invisible, erotic charm, a kind of fluid radiance and I am convinced that this quality alone is decisive in human loves and hatreds. Why else is it that we all know people whom we would forgive everything and others to whom we are unjustly severe? This instinctive directive that governs human relations is never unjust. The scent of human skin and the expression of the human face, the gaze, the gait, the handshake and every movement of the physical individual express her spirit just as much as her qualities do, or even more so. Everything a person does, she does from the one source of her spiritual vitality. Even the way she bathes.

A person's relation to water is the most important condition of human physical existence. Perhaps it does not seem that way for the first thirty years. After fifty years, however, a person's appearance clearly reveals whether or not she loved water. People who look after themselves as if it were second nature still have pure, glowing, firm skin, pink nails and the elasticity of youth when they are fifty. Age is the greatest human test. Here life gives unerring marks for behaviour. A person who is fifty will not deceive those around her by any means. Her face, her gait, her appearance tell how she lived. She is no longer developing; that is over. And every deed leaves a trace on her face, just as the use of good soap does.

I do not have much faith in the care of beauty salons. They are too preoccupied with artificial methods and not enough with water. I do not deny that electric massage of the face and hands is an unusually pleasant, healthy and good thing. It seems to me, however, that it is only a substitute for those who do not know the massage of the wind and rain. Nothing helps the skin as much as hearty exposure to sun, wind and water.

Love of the body is one of the most justifiable of human delights. Isn't it the body that always carries us once again out of anxiety, suffering, depression, pain? Isn't the body the one friend we can rely on? Isn't it the leading factor in all our fates, victories and defeats? What right do we have to deprive it of the education it deserves, of the intelligence it demands? The body that is cared for every day is more independent, more intelligent, more proper and self-confident. Not only the bath, however, is needed but the entire broad apparatus of physical education, which includes sport, well-aired rooms, windows open in the bedrooms, clean linen and a cultivated need for water, a need so strong that it is elemental.

There should never not be enough time to wash. People who can dress in a quarter of an hour are people who do not know how to wash. At least half an hour is required for washing. Half an hour and good soap, good toilet water, a large sponge and a hard scrubbing-brush. The harder the brush you wash with, the softer your skin will be. If you want to have firm and healthy skin, you should use a brush with a large handle for at least five minutes every day and literally scrub your entire body, after washing in cold water. Treat your body at least as adroitly, carefully and intricately as you would the washing of delicate cloth. Skin needs soap, a lot of soap, massage, movement, hot and cold water, water and more water. There is never enough water. There is no such thing as a harmful excess of water.

Toiletries, of course, are also part of washing. I love the superb English toiletries, in simple tin boxes, in simple porcelain containers and I loathe the German trash in chic cut glass. The English are certainly the most physically cultivated people in Europe. Their soaps, wrapped in simple paper and toothpaste, kept in sober, practical tubes and boxes, demonstrate that for them washing is not a luxurious affair, but a matter of course, like shoelaces, over which no one makes a big fuss. Efforts are being made to ensure that their excellent A. F. Pears wash balls and first-class F. E. Atkinson's Lavender Water will be available to all classes.

Certainly no one can accuse us – as a certain French woman did not long ago – of not knowing what to do with baths. We have the 'Crown', which is certainly wonderful and we have baths in practically every new home.[4] The only thing we can be reproached for

---

4 The Koruna (Crown) Building, constructed in 1911 at the bottom of Wenceslas Square in the centre of Prague, included baths and a swimming pool in the basement.

is insufficient hardiness, insufficient love for those open windows, fear of coughs and colds. My advice is: starting in the summer, sleep with the windows open and bathe in cold water every day. If you do this regularly every day, you will get through autumn without even knowing how and will find yourselves in the middle of winter with the windows open and won't even feel the cold at all. This is nothing strange or difficult. All one has to do is begin – as with everything else in the world. After a few months it will become a need you cannot live without.

# A Few Old-Fashioned Comments About Women's Emancipation

## 17 February 1923, *Národní listy*

Usually, all the world's – more or less aesthetic – problems are subject to nature and are resolved by their very own weight and by the unstoppable advance of time, regardless of all newspapers, campaigns, battles, lectures and parliaments. All debates are therefore pointless, a priori pointless because behind every debate there stands a specific person with a specific face, upbringing and fateful constancy of character. It would be a serious question to consider whether people are dependent on an opinion, or an opinion on people; that is, whether it is people who cannot help themselves and must have this kind of opinion, or whether it is the opinion which cannot help itself and must have this kind of people. But in the end, the entire modern invention of psychoanalysis resembles a dog chasing its own tail and may this splendid introduction be dedicated to the hailstorm of disagreement I will provoke.

So, about the equal rights of men and women. It has always seemed to me very simple: one cannot have equal and identical rights without identical attainments. (I would add that this *feuilleton* is the most humble opinion of the poor journalist that I am and not a contribution to the social controversy.) One cannot have identical attainments without identical abilities. In defiance of all the battles that have been waged and proofs of abilities that have been submitted in this matter, stands the great, unchangeable and terrifyingly unproblematic natural law, according to which a woman needs nine months to give birth to a child and a man needs a few moments to beget a child. I do not believe that one can get around such basic and fundamental things through any kind of ordinance. Even if – I repeat: even if – this purely physical obstacle could be surmounted in everyday life; even if a woman at the office, in the factory, in the scientific laboratory, in the state bureaucracy, in the political forum or on the field of sport, knew how, was able and was permitted – in the interest of the child was permitted – to ignore her pregnancy and carry on with her work without interruption, as if she were not pregnant, she could not and would not know how to ignore it internally. This is simply because physical laws have been given to us for a reason; they are symbolised in our souls, in our brains, in our hearts; they are re-evaluated by the invisible, mysterious laws in our beings that evade all agendas. I am not sure if God knew what nonsense he was doing when he made a human being. But he did not, after all, create one person; he created two. If it had ever been possible to speak about likeness and equality, the body of a woman would not have to differ so much from the body of a man, or the bodily functions of a woman to resemble those of a man so little. Things would not be arranged in the world in such a way that clothes were necessary. It is possible and perhaps even advisable to argue with everything that humans have produced: parliament and the republic, prostitution and tram lines. But it is quite dismal to struggle against and debate with nature, which is unchangeable and hardly subject to human wishes – fortunately or unfortunately – and which has established the principle of the difference between the male and female sex for sparrows, dogs, elephants, earthworms, carp and chrysanthemums, just as it has for people. Whatever one can say about this principle, it is rather hard to believe that it is coincidental. Likewise it is hard to believe that it could be deceived or bribed, even with the best intentions in the world.

This declaration of identity and equality of rights always seemed to me to belittle woman. I do not know who in the world could decide who was more valuable, man or woman. What kind of nonsense is it anyway, to hold such competitions? It always seems to me belittling to deny people their place in the world and to assign them some other place, regardless of whether it is a smaller or a bigger place. It is always best, most dignified and decent when people stay where they belong. It is not true that the world does not have a place for all of its children where they can make themselves useful, as long as they are honourable and brave. I firmly believe that every person in the vast world is good at something, whatever that might be. I adamantly believe that all people in the world can get by if they work at what they do well. This is, so to speak, a natural law and the earth would have to be ashamed if it were otherwise. In the same way, however, one cannot belittle anything in the world that is done thoroughly. I do not understand – I really do not understand – why making a good pair of boots should be a lesser art than delivering a good speech in parliament, why cooking excellent dumplings, drawing a good poster, turning out a beautiful table, should be more contemptible than building a house or drafting a law. Aren't boots just as necessary as laws? Isn't every occupation in the world a little link in the work of great culture and isn't all work honourable, useful and beautiful if it is carried out honourably, usefully and beautifully? I think that one of the mysteries of human dissatisfaction is that many people do not understand that pleasure and the fulfilment of obligations overlap, or at least complement one another. For this reason I have never been able to understand why so-called woman's work is so underrated; a woman, it is said, isn't in this world just to look after the household. But aren't the household and home a little state, a little world and isn't woman its soul? It is superficial to claim that running a household consists of cooking, sewing, washing laundry and generally cleaning up. All of these jobs are really secondary. (But isn't it in itself an enormous task of patience and love and a kind of miraculous wise skill to submit to work that is really so futile, that vanishes every day without a trace, in order to reappear the next?) The soul of the woman is most important, the expression of her personality, her abilities, the soft, quiet, creative gift in this world of a few rooms. Life also consists of daily trifles! My God, let us finally understand that there are no great or small things. That there is only one life, one great current of life, beautiful and sad and just as powerful everywhere and in all things. Or is it perhaps a trifle to transform the three rooms of a private life, the three rooms with bare walls, filled with furniture, into a world to which a husband happily returns? A world where children grow up into healthy and capable people, not burdened by the conflicts of youth or upbringing? A world where friends do not feel oppressed by an unpleasant atmosphere of erotic struggle, erotic indifference or erotic perfidy? A world where one can simply breathe, live, work, believe in life? Only women who have done this know what tremendous sacrifices, self-denial, labour and strength are required for such an achievement. A far greater achievement for a woman than a speech in parliament is, don't you think?

To bear offspring is not difficult. Any cat can do it – and much more bravely and wisely, without any fuss. To raise children is an enormous task. If you think that every mother can do it as well as every cat, have a close look sometime at what a resolute, healthy, unsentimental and yet loving, vain and yet reliably conscientious and hygienic mother that four-legged animal is. For the period that a cat is giving birth to, feeding and raising her young, she does not entertain a single thought or feeling for her mate. For that period, the tomcat is for her a useless thing, which is always getting in the way, a big grown-up kitten with which she has to be patient; but her offspring are the essence, the mission, pride and meaning of her life. Do not try and tell me that animals have less worth than people. You do not know them if you can say such things. The very fact that every animal is beautiful and so few people are beautiful demonstrates that an animal is proper and people are flawed. Where will you find in people such bodily harmony as a tiger, a horse, a dog or a goshawk has?

Raising a child does not mean slapping it when it wets the apron. Raising a child means, first of all, being a resolute, courageous, mature, upright person. It means having a tremendous, infinitely great heart. Is that a trifle?

And the woman's role, the woman's place beside her husband, isn't that a tremendous thing? For all their great achievements of energy and intellect, men always remain children, seeking in their wives a mother, a friend, someone to bear up all the scaffolding of life. Weak people usually have the tremendous strength of endurance. If woman is weaker than man, then her ability to endure – certainly overdeveloped by the fact of nine-month-long pregnancy and painful labour – is something that far exceeds the strength of man. The heroism and bravery of weakness, the courage and perseverance of natural passivity – a passivity again dictated by a woman's physical and sexual structure – isn't that a mast that can withstand all, a strength that never disappoints, a proffered hand that always rescues?

I repeat and over and over again I find this confirmed: such problems usually resolve themselves on their own. One of the precious qualities of a woman is that she becomes the sort of person she has to be. If she has to earn money to provide for her children, even for her husband and for herself, she can certainly do so – and perhaps more conscientiously and persistently, if not efficiently. She can run factories, drive automobiles and trains, she can study, she can hold official posts, she can fight courageously for her life. During the war we demonstrated this countless times and we will demonstrate it over and over again, whenever necessary. But all of these jobs will never be more than jobs; none will become a calling – for a true woman. At the bottom of her heart a woman remains what God created her: a woman and a mother. Fortunately, she will not change despite all the banners of the woman question and that is her greatest worth.

I inform all those who are of the opinion that I deserve a beating for these paltry lines that I am usually at home on Saturdays from

2.00 until 5.00 p.m. What else did you expect? A person should be ready to sacrifice herself for her beliefs.[5]

5 The columnist 'ksg.' (Karel Scheinpflug, 1869–1948) published a response to the article in *Národní listy* on 25 March 1923, pp. 1–2. In this article, 'O emancipaci žen' (The Emancipation of Women) he commented that her views seemed very reasonable, but he disagreed with her statement that 'male' occupations would never be 'callings' for women. He also suggested that the woman question had already been resolved, that a woman could choose any profession she wanted, vote and sit on juries. He noted, however, that woman was a slave to fashion. Jesenská responded to his comments in the article 'Pro muže, aby neřekli' (For Men, So That They Won't Say). She asserted that men were just as much slaves to fashion as women (3 May 1923, *Národní listy*, p. 4).

# A Theme that has Nothing to do with Fashion

## 22 November 1923, *Národní listy*

Last week I found among the many letters that I receive a strange sheet of paper, the end of which, by some inexplicable chance, was missing. Thus I do not know the name or status of the writer. I did not even learn why the hurried, distraught lines of appealing script, racing obliquely, were addressed to me. The question they pose is so unlike all the usual queries that I want to devote a column to it, although it really has nothing to do with the concerns of fashion. But because we share all kinds of concerns, great and small, with one another, let us pause today over this one, which is certainly relevant to every woman.

The question is: what should a woman do when her husband is unfaithful?

Like all things in the world, this too cannot be seen in isolation. I do not believe in the morality of general, superficial codes. There are as many abilities, as many faults and as many injuries as there are hearts. Out of respect for the individual, I would never have the courage to say: this is what has to be done. Yet, all cases have much in common, all women have much in common.

First and foremost: I think one has to realise that the infidelity of a woman and the infidelity of a man are not faults of the same – let us say – *niveau*. They simply are not in a physiological sense; they are not because a woman has different responsibilities and different liabilities with respect to her sexual life than a man has. A woman can become a mother; motherhood is her mission and task. A woman's motherhood obliges her to be chaste and honest in her sexual life, even when it is difficult. A man is free. In a physiological sense, that is. For him, sexual life does not mean a mixture of delight, responsibility and privation; for him, sexual life is only a joy, and a need, in so far as it is a joy. I want to say only that: an act that for a woman is full of serious physiological consequences, has no such consequences for a man. That is a decisive difference.

I am far from defending infidelity in general. Marriage only has meaning when it is connected to fidelity; fidelity is more than chastity; fidelity is the keeping of a sexual secret, the greatest friendship, the closest bond. But we are people, incomplete and imperfect.

Anonymous, unhappy Madam, who wrote me that desperate letter: do not be unjust to your husband, whom you love and who is the father of your children. First of all, do some hard thinking about yourself and try to understand your husband. Remember everything that preceded the infidelity. Perhaps you were not attentive enough? Perhaps you were not patient or pleasant enough? Perhaps you were not interested enough in those ordinary wishes and worries of his that you had to listen to daily, for years? Perhaps you were tired of them? Perhaps you did not try hard enough to please him? Perhaps in your haste, worries and work, you forgot to be pretty, attractive? Perhaps, exhausted by worries, you did not try to be cheerful and patient? Men are big boys and it only seems like they understand life. In reality, they only understand themselves. But when you love, isn't that enough?

When you found out about your husband's infidelity, how did you respond? You see, perhaps it is a bitter truth: an ageing woman who has children must be able to extend a little of her motherliness to her biggest boy, her husband. Do you remember how, when we were children, our mothers kept quiet about all the childish struggles of our hearts and we thought that they did not know what was going on? And then how all of a sudden one word betrayed that they knew everything and were more afraid on our account than we were? And how we wondered: what am I seeking for out there in the world when my home is here? You see, that is perhaps what is necessary. A man who stands at a crossroads between two women always experiences conflicting feelings: love and kindness for the one, sexual desire for the other; a man, however, cannot bear conflicts; every conflict makes him selfish. His way simply turns in the direction that is more pleasant. The dearest, most beloved woman loses worth when she has eyes red from crying and a haggard face, when she spreads an atmosphere of pain around her and, mainly, when she can be compared to a cheerful, lively girl. If you want to hold on to your husband, be more pleasant than his lover. Truly, a very difficult role. A woman, familiar after so many years and ordinary on account of shared worries and a girl who drops by for an hour and disappears – what a difficult role for the former, what an easy one for the latter! But you care about him, Madam; you care about him and he is important to you; peace in the family and the children are important to you. Well then, be brave!

Men are, I repeat, big children. They need to test their strength, like schoolboys. They need confirmation of their existence. They need to hear now and then that they are handsome, strong and wonderful. They need to test whether or not they are still young. Sometimes that means an innocent longing for something unfamiliar; sometimes curiosity; at other times, a little infatuation. Believe me, usually it does not run deep. It often happens that a woman achieves the opposite of what she wants through her behaviour. An indulgent smile and patience would soon cure your husband of his romance. A tragic gesture, a scene, reproaches and threats often make a mountain out of a molehill. You make him feel resentful – and that – and only that – no man will forgive.

But didn't you once promise to be his friend? I believe that you were a friend to him through all his worries. Today, you both stand at a boundary, which is perhaps not that of old age, but it hints at old age. You have children and you are a woman: thus you certainly look forward to growing old without bitterness. You do not know how much turmoil is provoked in a man by the fear of growing old. I think that men experience crises twice in their lives, once over puberty and a second time before growing old. Home, wife, children, everything is forgotten. Fear alone possesses them. They throw themselves into passions, sometimes great and powerful passions. Well then, be a friend to him now; understand him; smile at him; and wait. He will certainly come back.

Do not berate, Madam; because you are suffering that does not mean that those who caused you pain are base. Because you are in the right that does not mean you gain anything by it. Believe me, sometimes being in the right brings a person terribly, miserably, mercilessly little. You will not buy anything with it. Those who hurt you are probably also in the right. Usually people are in the right and yet they are wretched and torment themselves. You must understand: it is not a matter of right or wrong. It is a matter of the heart. Truly, only of the heart. Well then, be magnanimous. Do not be afraid of a little pain or a little jealousy. Be kind. Think of him and not yourself.

All the laws about divorce, marital infidelity, adultery and so on are – forgive me for saying so – useless. What did they ever accomplish in the world? Look around you, all people are governed by mysterious sexual forces and they are all urged on by laws they do not understand. Either a woman is able to be the sort of person her husband wants to be faithful to. Or she must learn to tolerate his infidelity, if she does not want to lose him. But both share the blame: the one who wronged and the one who was wronged.

# A Beautiful Woman

## 29 November 1923, *Národní listy*

You claim that I favour the skinny; that I condemn the fat; that I only help the thin; that I am unjust to the obese. Well then, you do me wrong. I love only beautiful people and I do not love the ugly. But please, finish reading before you bombard me with reproaches for being unfair.

Just as one has to consider the individual before passing judgement, it is impossible to adopt a general aesthetic standard. It is not true that skinny women are beautiful and fat ones ugly; it is not true that tall ones are beautiful and short ones ugly. There is no division at all into this kind or that kind; there are beautiful women and there are ugly women; there are beautiful and ugly people.

Beauty is not something physical. Beauty is not a gift from God. Beauty is a personal merit. The harmonious face of a Madonna can be distinctly unpleasant; and the most unattractive face can be miraculous. There is no division between body and soul. A person is not physically ugly and spiritually beautiful or vice versa. A person is one, a person is whole. Her movements, expression, gait, the way she holds her head, offers her hand, her face and her heart, her deeds, everything is interconnected. One thing conditions another. A woman who has an alert, intelligently refined face, a direct gaze and the ability to transform her face into one that is sweet, quiet and gentle, a woman who has an agreeable smile and discreet movements and who shines with purity cannot be ugly. All this can be achieved through working on one's inner self.

For heaven's sake, don't talk to me about fashion. I have been writing about it for so long that I cannot help but know how secondary it is. Beautiful clothes, fashionable lines, all the social forms, injunctions and objections are important; they are infinitely important, just as every form in the world is important. But the form is only important when the content is in order.

First and foremost: be individuals; be consistent, open and honest; learn kindness and benevolence; do not lapse into pettiness through insignificant base acts or little dishonesties; love honourably; have straightforward relations; control yourselves, learn to deny yourselves and learn to take what belongs to you; be individuals; not this kind or that kind, but yourselves. Know your-selves and be yourselves without following any models; a woman who has her own personality, who has a profound, inner, radiating expression, whose spirit is in her every glance and movement, is a beautiful woman. A woman who is complete, with a profoundly refined individuality, is a beautiful woman. Everything else, jars of cosmetics, fashionable garments, corpulence, slenderness, height or lack of it, all that comes later. All that is an aid and a means to perfection. Beautiful clothes will always be beautiful; but clothes do not make the individual, the individual makes the clothes. Happy are the beautiful women who improve their appearance through elegant attire. But woe betide those who think that elegant attire will make them beautiful.

Of course, it is possible – when we build on the specific premise outlined above – to guard against ugliness and protect one's beauty. A shapeless fat person truly is not pretty, nor is a shapeless thin person. Of course, every era also has its firmly prescribed ideal and the ideal female body today is not the classical beauty of the Venus de Milo, or the voluptuous beauty of Rubens' women, or the petite, fragile beauty of Rococo dolls, but the slender (not skinny), sporty girl, sturdy, independent, bright, lithe and lively. Of course, fashion is always governed by the specific ideal of the era and it is up to you to adapt to the ideal, if you want and not up to fashion to adapt to you.

I do not know to what extent a person has power over herself and her appearance. Certainly this too is an individual matter. I do, however, know this much for sure: if a woman is shapelessly fat, it is too late to think about the ideals of beauty. Slimming cures hardly ever help; they are almost always harmful; and even when they are successful, you pay for the violence of the cure in that you soon return to your former state. Starvation destroys your skin and the youthful expression of your face; you attain the skinniness of the diseased, the grey complexion and ugly shapes of the malnour-ished. The only way to attain beauty is to avoid getting fat. Every woman over thirty is in danger of getting fat. Every woman after giving birth is exposed to the danger of growing ugly. Well then, do not let it come to that. Look after yourselves to avoid getting ugly; use this care not as a means to remove ugliness, but as a means to preserve beauty. What young, vigorous body is not pretty, if it is properly trained? From your youth on, devote as much care to it as you do to your soul, your stomach and your future security; exer-cise, move, do sports; walk, run, swim, bathe, jump!

Ninety percent of Czech women – between thirty and forty – would be outraged if I asked them to do a somersault on the floor, to run nimbly to catch the tram, to climb over a fence, to walk at a brisk pace down the road for two hours, to wash themselves with a scrubbing-brush and to sleep by open windows. And why? In themselves, these things are not at all difficult or crazy. But if the body does not exercise, it grows lazy, the spine stiffens, the muscles grow slack. Flab settles on the muscles; and flab is the enemy of youth and beauty, of mental and physical vitality. Try exercising just once. At first, you will be appalled to discover how little control you have over your body, how little you are able to bend. You will be appalled that you do not know how to walk, to jump, to turn. This is an unnecessary ugliness. A superfluous ugliness.

How modern is everything here! Not good, proper, elegant attire, but rather caricatures of fashion illustrations. Not loose, superbly sewn, hygienic clothes, following a line that is truly modern, but senseless exaggerations, painful monstrosities; heels too high, shoes too small, skirts too short or too narrow, hair frizzled; all conceptions of human naturalness are turned upside down.

So, chin up! All the ideals of the fashion dummies on the rubbish heap! All worries about the surface out the window. Begin on the inside, in the depths. From the core, from the centre, from the bottom.

# From One Person to Another
12 January 1924, *Národní listy*

In my first article in the New Year, I would like to wish you something nice and substantial, something that will not sound as hollow as 'health and luck and happiness'. When I think of the letters I have received over the course of the last year, of the small and great, the familiar and unfamiliar worries, the trifling and serious griefs that I have detected in them, it seems to me that luck and happiness are not nearly as important or worth wishing for as something else that we lack.

A person at a desk sometimes learns more than you would think from a strange letter, written in a strange script, sent from some strange place. A little word, a turn of phrase, the paper, some absent-minded detail of the script, the signature – they all speak volumes about the person who sent it. Tiny, trifling, but still, obvious lies, awkward civilities, simple cordiality, conceit, humility – what one finds in such a spontaneous letter, even when it is short and insignificant, no more than ten words! In the long ones, however, that complain and tell stories about people's lives, I almost always sense that there is something else in addition to the pain: that people do not speak directly to one another, but off in some other direction; that language is poor and powerless; and that people are woefully alone with their rigid words of wisdom, nailed to the wall. Sometimes I can almost see the blind alley of conviction and opinion where people bang their heads against the wall. I can see how they try to forge ahead with the weight of a thousand prejudices, a thousand rigidities of upbringing, environment, desire and ambition. Mainly, I can see how often life as it is shatters against the idea of how it should be.

If I could wish anything for you, the young and the old, the rich and the poor, it would be this: more inner sincerity and more magnanimity. There are two things in the world that are a sin against life and they are an inner lie and an intolerant heart. I do not want to say that they are faults or conscious sins. Usually life forces them on a person and, succumbing to them, a person forces them back on life. One could, however, respond to most people who talk about their lives: 'hold on, that's not the way it is. I do not know why, but I sense that it's not like that. Start over again and tell the truth. Relate everything bitter and ugly that you have done and everything beautiful that the other person has done. Do not speak about fault, there is none; do not speak about responsibilities, rights; do not criticise, simply tell the story.' It is rooted in this: each person arrives at a certain formulaic outlook, he swallows the formula and is in turn swallowed by the formula. From that moment on, from his perspective the whole world is governed by that formula. The one truth, however, the one unwavering truth, is that we do not know anything, that we are petty and wretched and forlorn and that there are as many truths as there are human hearts. The one truth is that life is tremendous, multifarious, incomprehensible, mysterious, inscrutable. That there are no ordinary, insignificant people; that there are no good or bad people. That things are not at all as they are written in the primers or as they are written in the primers of the hearts.

I so often see how people with a fixed idea about life try to avoid life and when life does not correspond to their fixed idea, they do not change their idea on the basis of life, but deny life on the basis of the idea. So two people live next to one another in a single apartment as if they lived in separate worlds. Children grow up thus next to their parents, sisters next to brothers. An agenda is made: now we will live, we will be faithful to one another, at Christmas time we will go to visit Auntie and in three years, on the fifth of December, we will buy the third mattress for the bed. Doesn't anxiety grip your heart at the thought that a person seems to be travelling alone in an empty locomotive without a driver, oblivious to the future obstacles? Yet every day brings new events. Every day, the heart evolves, the soul takes shape, the brain works, a person is base, a person is good, a person sins, a person is corrupted, a person is liberated.

In response to my article about a man's infidelity (was it really an article about infidelity?), I received many letters from frightened women. How could I excuse something like that? Why didn't I freeze in horror at such a crime? Well then, I did not excuse anyone, just as I did not condemn anyone. That is the thing: it is not a matter of criticism, but of reality. In truth and in reality, similar conflicts arise for every couple. The entire world, entire cities, all of history, all lives, have erotic conflicts between people as their central motif. Every marriage is shaken by them like a forest by a storm; every person is overwhelmed by them like the earth by a flood. How could I, in all sincerity, gloss over something so elemental, so desperately acute and so powerfully decisive with a phrase about responsibility and the comment, 'I won't put up with it'?

Because a gale uproots frail trees, can I say that there is no gale, or that I excuse the gale, or that I condemn the gale? Can I take a critical stance towards a flood, a lightning bolt or an earthquake? Certainly I cannot. I can do one thing, however. I can look at it straight on. I can struggle, exposed, against its danger. I can last it out or I can run away and hide. But I must know about it. Know about its essence and cause, appearance and potential.

This is true not only of infidelity, but of all human traits. A person stands before you like a tree in the woods. Conditioned by mysterious circumstances, shaped by mysterious influences, but unshakeably the sort of person that he is. Even the little that he has can help him; it depends on him, his talent, flexibility, perceptiveness. Even the little that he has can harm him or make him happy; it depends on what is in his heart. Well then, look carefully at his face, examine carefully his hands, movements, smile, gaze, the expression on his face, the stoop of his shoulders. Listen carefully to what he says and understand him. Recognise what he can and cannot do. Live beside him, not with curses for what he cannot do, but with praise for what he can do. There are people who can be faithful, honourable, strong, truthful and brave; there are people who cannot. To ask bravery of a coward is like asking a cat to bark. One can, however, love even a coward, with all one's soul, with all one's heart, love the path that led him to cowardice, the anxiety that caused it, one can love everything. That bravery is beautiful and cowardice ugly, that fidelity brings happiness and infidelity pain, are correct concepts, but not important, or at least, not of the first order of importance. We are not judges and let us not be moralists. We are human. It is necessary to help a coward. Necessary to help the evil, the deceitful, the odious. Not by saying 'he is not cowardly' (when he is), or by saying to him, 'you should not be cowardly any longer' (when he is). But with a profound recognition of the roots of cowardice, of the causes and events of the heart. Until I know and see the heart before me, I cannot go to it; it can only come to me. An intolerant heart is the other bane of the individual, the intolerance that eternally places itself in the foreground. It happens to me; I cannot; I am suffering; I am disappointed. My God, that trivial, comical 'I'! Have you ever lain on your backs on the ground on a July night and looked at the stars? If you shouted out with all your lungs, if you screamed like a wounded animal, if you cried, laughed, killed or were killed, not a sound would reach the sky. Try staying there for about an hour: then you will see what astonishing thoughts caress you. Everything you do, eat, dream about, strive for is insignificant, like the diligence of ants on a heap of pine needles. Everything – even you too are insignificant. You laugh calmly at your own pain and love and hate and fear of death, as if they did not belong to you. You stand outside yourself and reflect critically and all of a sudden, there is nothing you cannot bear.

Exaggerating the importance of your own feelings is like tying a blindfold over your eyes. You see only that you suffer from grief, without knowing why. If, however, you say to yourself just once, 'it doesn't matter', at a time when you can hardly breathe from the anxiety and oppression, the other person will appear to you in a different light. All of a sudden, you will see that he is powerless, wretched and lonely like you. All of a sudden you will see that he has a sleepy face, you will hear what he says. A pain completely different from your own will appear before your eyes. Without knowing how, you will say something that helps both of you. Something simple, truthful. Something that is perhaps painful in its own fateful gravity. Something, however, that is not blind, unjust, from another world. From one person to another, a direct, calm, sincere word.

Forgive me if this is a strange New Year's wish. I always wonder why people care so much about happiness and so little about much more important things. So I can only wish you what seems to me most important of all: the courage to be sincere and the courage to be magnanimous. Chin up, the world is large, the stars are up above and we are poor and insignificant. Amidst all the desolation in the world, however, there is consolation on every corner for the hardy and for those who are not afraid.

# The Curse of Outstanding Qualities

Just because someone manages to acquire a good quality does not mean that that person is pleasant. It is odd, but I have noticed countless times that people who are not exactly bad, but have some passion or fancy, some important shortcoming that troubles them considerably, are far more pleasant than people who are proper and perfect. This is natural: if I feel like I am carrying something inside me for which I should apologise, something, which is not, perhaps, entirely in order, I am far more tolerant of others and look on their faults and shortcomings from a totally different perspective. It might happen, for instance, that you have some awful experience and there is so much muttering about it that in the end you are not even sure what is right and what is wrong. Pain screens your eyes, like blinkers screen the eyes of horses; the longer it lasts, the stronger it is; it prevents you from making a reasonable judgement and torments you. Without wanting to, you do something that perhaps you would never have done if you hadn't been so deadly tired, if it weren't all the same to you by now, if you didn't feel the lacerating need to end it at any price, even more violently than might be necessary. From the outside, however, everything looks different and the people who observe you always have an easy time of it. Perhaps they condemn you and there is even much truth in their judgement. All of a sudden, however, you find a person who is kind to you for no reason at all. His fate is completely different from yours and he has never had a similar experience, but once he felt on his own skin how easy it is to condemn. Perhaps he experienced the sort of inexplicable misunderstandings that can sometimes come between two people, experienced how much it hurts to defend oneself powerlessly and fail to save oneself. So, for no reason at all, he is suddenly kind to you.

In this respect, it is almost a virtue to have some kind of shortcoming. With respect to human kindness, it definitely is a virtue. Perfect and proper people are the cruellest. I know of no crueller type of people than the Germans and they are perfection and propriety itself. Proper people often have a complicated psychological apparatus for tormenting others. It practically gives them pleasure to demonstrate their propriety and of course they can demonstrate it best in contrast with other people's lack of propriety. A perfect official is, for example, the most callous person in the world. You rush to the train station at the last minute, perhaps because you were parting with someone longer than was prescribed or permissible. You want someone to carry your luggage but somewhere it is specified that there has to be a label with your name and address written in ink on your luggage. 'Impossible,' the official tells you, 'and now go find some ink.' The more enraged your expression is, the more obstinate he becomes. It seems to me that only such perfect people sit at the train stations, post and other offices.[6]

It can also happen that you live with a landlady who loves cleanliness. That is terrible. In itself, it is not so terrible to love cleanliness, but it can be a purgatory on earth for others who love cleanliness in a rather moderate manner. Such things can be amusing, but they are sometimes quite serious, mainly when those good qualities become a source of conflict between parents and children. The father has never told a lie in his life and that is truly wonderful of him. But because the son tells a little lie, that is no reason to claim that the son is deceitful. The father, however, is so cruel and merciless in his proud awareness of his truthfulness, in just satisfaction with his own integrity, that perhaps it would have been much better from the point of view of parenting if he too had lied once in his life. Today he would not be so mercilessly hard on the boy.[7]

Perhaps you know just how detestable people can be when they have some good aesthetic habit. Not only do they imagine that by having clean hands they have achieved the height of perfection, but they also classify people only according to who has clean and who has less clean hands. 'I wash my hands every day,' they say snootily, at every opportunity. When they go to a cabin in the mountains where one cannot get water right away, they do not let the opportunity pass and insist: 'I can't enjoy anything here when I can't wash my hands. You see, that's just the way I am.' Perhaps

---

6 This recalls Kafka's description of the difficulties he encountered at the Czechoslovak-Austrian border after visiting Jesenská in Vienna because he did not have a transit visa for Austria. Date of letter: 5 July 1920. Franz Kafka, *Letters to Milena*, pp. 64–67.

7 This recalls what is known of Kafka's relation to his father and Jesenská's relation to her father. See Kafka's 'Letter to Father', written in November 1919 and published posthumously. All biographies of Jesenská treat her love-hate relationship to her father. He is usually described as an anti-Semite and a tyrant. In her study of Jesenská, Wagnerová presents a more complex portrait of the man. See: Wagnerová, *Milena Jesenská.*

there is talk of some talented person and everyone praises him. 'But he has such dirty hands!' your friend says and in doing so, he is only asserting that his own hands are clean.

I think the best person I ever came to know was a foreigner whom I often met on social occasions.[8] No one knew much about him and no one considered him in any way exceptional. It once happened, however, that someone accused him of something and he did not defend himself at all. Because he had an honest and manly face, however, and because the accusation was serious, I did not want to believe it. I was somehow terribly sorry to think that this fellow with an open face and quiet eyes that looked directly into your own was supposed to have done something so ugly and I inquired into what had actually happened. It became clear that he had not defended himself because the whole matter was completely different and if he had defended himself he would have had to betray something infinitely beautiful and noble about himself, something anyone else would certainly have boasted of, even without such a convenient opportunity. I had never seen anything like it before. Later I learned that he was altogether the strangest person I had ever encountered and nothing caused such a disturbance in my life as a little insight into his heart. He was remarkably noble, but I would say that he concealed this, like someone who was ashamed to have advantages over others. He was never able to do anything that would betray what he was like and he did the most beautiful things quietly and shyly and timidly, in secret, but truly in secret and not in such a way that it would only seem to be in secret. When he died – he was really too good for this world and I am not afraid of this platitude, it stands here truthfully – I read about a little incident from his childhood in one of his diaries and because it seemed to me the most beautiful thing I had ever heard, I will tell it to you in conclusion. When he was little, he received – he was very poor – a ten-kreutzer coin from his mother.[9] He had never had ten kreutzers all at once before and thus it was a momentous occasion for him. He had earned the coin and

---

8 Jesenská's daughter, Jana Černá, stated that Milena described Kafka as a foreigner. From Černá's commentary, it is clear that she understood 'foreigner' to mean 'Jew'. She wrote of those who used to frequent the Arco Café: 'They had been foreign to the country they lived in, foreign to their homes, foreign in the language they spoke and foreign to their own bodies. They had all been branded deep in their souls in such a way as to predestine them at least partly to homelessness: the eternal state of the Wandering Jew.' Jana Černá, *Kafka's Milena*, p. 99.

9 This coin was known as a *Sechserl*.

therefore the occasion was all the more momentous. When he walked down the street to buy something with it, he saw a beggar-woman who was so wretched that he was terribly shocked and immediately he felt a passionate longing to give her the ten-kreutzer coin. At that time, however, a ten-kreuzter piece was a small fortune for beggars and small, poor boys. He was so afraid of the praise and thanks that the beggar would shower on him and of the attention it would attract that he changed the coin, gave her one kreutzer, ran around the entire block of houses and, returning from the other direction, gave her a second kreutzer. He did this ten times and honourably gave her all ten kreutzers. He did not keep a single one for himself and then he collapsed in nervous tears, completely exhausted by the mental effort required for such a deed. I think that this is the loveliest fairytale I have ever heard and when I read it I decided never to forget it as long as I lived.[10]

---

10 It appears that this article was first published in the collection *Cesta k jednodu-chosti* (The Path to Simplicity, Prague, 1926), along with articles originally published in *Národní listy*.

# For Whom Do We Write About Fashion in the Newspapers?

14 April 1929, *Lidové noviny*

Everything we do, we should do as well as we can. Many very important things are included in this seemingly simple imperative: responsibility for one's work and admiration for well-made objects. The ability to distinguish good from bad and the subtle appreciation for good form, which is never innate. The relationship to one's own property and the property of other people and, in general, the ability to surround oneself with beautiful things, to select them, to love them without exaggerating their importance, which very few people are able to do. In short, nothing in the world is isolated; it is always people's situation that mediates their approach to the world and everything in it. It is just as senseless to think only of clothes as it is to scorn thoughts of clothes. The concept of clothing, however, is very complex. I would almost say that nothing in the world is so dependent on the most diverse living conditions, on character, outlook, inner and outer formation, as clothes. In recent years, it looked as if we were getting closer to a uniform and that women, like men, would be distinguished from one another only by their ability to wear their clothes well. (As if that were a trifle!) This winter has shown that this was not to be. Fashion is back, the same as ever – a frivolous, complicated and expensive thing that has not lost its importance for women. As always, since time immemorial, it has been the most reliable measure of a woman's personality because the way we wear clothes reveals more about us than do other qualities. The way a person dresses is a trait and this trait is subject to all the laws of heredity, intelligence, contamination, the impact of the environment and education, just like any other trait. Perhaps it is strange that, on the basis of the knot in the silk scarf that we wear (or do not wear, or do not know how to wear or know perfectly well how to wear), we could create a kind of graphology and appraise people. In the end, however, the heel of your shoe, dear ladies, is just as causally wedged into the chain of your character description and is just as important a sign of your personality as your gait, your handwriting, the lines on your palms and the modulation of your laughter.

For whom does fashion exist? For everyone? What is fashion? Is it only clothes? What do clothes have in common with fashion, or rather, what does fashion have in common with the necessity of being dressed? Relatively little. Fashion is a complex ceremony, a complicated, conditioned code. For example, to be fashionable we must be well-kept and being well-kept in terms of fashion does not mean either cleanliness or the toning of the body through sport, but rather pampering oneself with ointments, lotions, gallipots, pills and makeup, thorough massage, steaming, bathing in fragrant salts, polishing the nails with a pink varnish, trimming the bits of extra skin behind the nails, carefully removing little hairs, rubbing in fragrant ointments, something like what happened in the stories of *The Thousand and One Nights* to noble and cherished princesses on the eve of their wedding nights. Not only time and money are needed for that, but also a certain world outlook. We have to consider ourselves something very precious if we are to have the patience to pay so much attention to ourselves. Or we have to be very bored with the world and regard this self-love as a kind of spleen. In any case, only such an extravagantly tended body can provide the figure needed for a fashionable appearance. As I have already said: only rich people have this time, this spleen, this boredom. Rich people, however, are cut off from the world, as if they lived on a desert island. They never board any train except the express-D train, second or first class, or they drive in closed cars that are identical to one another. The hotels where they stay are very similar, as are the villas and apartments where they live. The salons for cultivating the beauty of young, rich and beautiful girls are identical. Fashionable salons and fashionable stores for rich women are identical. The entire complex apparatus of their lives is very similar. There is always a house filled with well-bred servants where there is a staircase for the owners and a staircase for suppliers and employees. No one has as many responsibilities with respect to money as a rich woman. It seems that it is very difficult and tiring to spend one's money. Now and then we see in fashion journals pictures of their bedrooms, automobiles, dogs and children, their expensive gowns, tennis courts and luggage for a trip to the south. Rich people of all countries are as alike as two peas in a pod and are the only people who have achieved true internationalism. Peculiar fabrics and peculiar styles are invented for them and thousands of people exist in order to dress them. Their attire is not a display of individuality; likewise, that which spices up our lives – adventure – never enters theirs. Few such people, of course, live in Czechoslovakia, but there are many who can, at least on a small scale, imitate them. While we do not have dollar kings, we have small-time rich people who journey abroad and dress according to the dictates of the large fashion enterprises and are thus justified in speaking about fashion, rather than about clothes. It would be ludicrous to suppose that one of these people consulted my weekend fashion column in order to dress well. All she has to do is telephone a few of the good seamstresses and in no time they will bring parcels of fabric, colour samples, designs and models to her house. Two tailors and designers will surround her and after a few days and a few thousand, she will be dressed in the latest fashion, without having to make the slightest decision or selection on her own.

Thus the fashion column in the newspaper is really for people for whom there is no fashion. Because all the rest is no longer fashion, but clothes. The average person with an average job and an average salary cannot dress fashionably. She can, however, have superb clothes. She has much more work assembling her one outfit than a rich person has assembling ten: because it is up to her to make clothes for herself according to fashion, adapting to it without aping it. In short, the less money she has, the more art it takes to look good. Not only in direct proportion, in that she cannot buy as many things as she needs, but also in indirect proportion, in that she is forced to decide on the best and consequently must know what is best. While many people think for a rich person, a poor person must think for herself. Thus, a salesgirl who is well dressed is a much more cultivated person than Mrs X because she has had to discover everything for herself: taste, good style and economy of form and line.

The fashion column in the newspaper is for people who love beautiful things and cannot afford them. Only these kinds of people make culture. Only these kinds of people have style; they are innovative, daring and modestly restrained. The desire for things cultivates taste, as the palm of the masseuse kneads muscles. In the world today there is a good percentage of people who care about how they live, how they eat and how they dress; who love the world and everything in it as a manifestation of the power of beauty. They know the value of money and they do not love money for the power it offers, but for the joy it facilitates. For them, having nice clothes is a need, like having clean hands and flowers in a vase: heartfelt and unimportant at the same time. They would never turn their desire to have pretty things into a law, a restriction or a convention, as has so often happened in the past. Whenever they buy something, however, they prefer to buy something pretty rather than something ugly. And here we are back at the beginning: everything we do, we should do as well as we can.

It would be senseless to write in the fashion column of the newspaper about things that we can never indulge in, things that we would not even want to indulge in if we could afford them. It is senseless to ape people whose outward appearance requires totally different living conditions than those that we have. The fashion column in the newspaper is there in order to select the best, to advise, to direct and to prescribe, to put its taste at the disposal of a wide readership, to advise rather than to review. It will not help you to learn what fur coats are worn in the summer. But it will probably interest you to know how to dress in the summer next to those people who have summer furs, so that you do not look the slightest bit worse and so that perhaps, according to the laws of the spirit, you might look even better or at least just as good as they do. It is a rare art to look like a good human specimen, without much money or expenditure, through one's own efforts and the proper organisation of one's life.

# Baby

## 21 April 1929, *Lidové noviny*

When mummy was carrying the baby under her heart, everyone treated her with care, gently and quietly, as if she were precious. Mummy, however, felt ugly and repulsive; she was afraid of people; she felt ashamed in their presence and preferred to sit in the park alone on a bench and study the children who played nearby. She compared them to her future baby and said to herself: will it have hair like that? Will it smile so sweetly? Will it also hold me around the neck and say something adorable?

When the baby was born, nothing of the sort happened. The baby did not smile at mummy, but screwed up its mouth in a strange way and uttered strange screeches. The fluffy layette of delightful little clothes for baby, tiny jackets and downy shirts that looked like painted candies, soft light-pink flannels – in a minute everything was crumpled in a lump when it came into contact with that unpoetic, peeing and pooping tiny tot. It came into the world with thick black hair, but after a while it lost even that and was nothing but a conical, spluttering, bawling tot lying in swaddling clothes.

The strangest thing of all is that the infant understands a certain kind of human language, but usually it is not mother's language, but that of the nanny, that wonderful pseudo-mother about whose heroism nothing has yet been written or said. This ordinary woman presses another person's child to her heart and loves and understands it from the first moment. Her hands have a golden touch. From baby's perspective, the world speaks to it for the first time through these hands and it is annoyed when it is bathed by someone else; it misses the familiar movements, the familiar sequence of events. And that language! That senseless and stupid language that no intelligent mother can master and that consists of innumerable 'koo-chee-koo-chee-koos' and 'tickee-tickee-ticks', during which the nanny laughs and baby laughs and mother only stands to the side, helpless and excluded because every little word that does not belong to this mysterious vocabulary estranges and frightens baby. The nanny's love is ardent, but also provocative and demonstrative: in her destitute life, the love of this foreign child is a miracle of which she is proud and by which she sets much store.

She does not let pass a single opportunity when she can show mother how baby depends on her, on the nanny and how it turns away from mother grumpily. 'Come here, darling, ba-ba-ba-boo, they're hurting you, hoopa-hoopa-hoop,' she says, in a sorrowful voice when she carries baby away from mother, in whose arms, of course, it immediately started to bellow, missing the familiar touch of its nanny. Behind the door one can still hear a few comments about how they would do better to leave the child alone and how it certainly does not bawl when it is with her – along with the plaintive gurgling of baby, which still feels sorry for itself and, after a moment, falls quiet. But mother remains in a corner of the room with preposterous tears in her eyes and reflects: what is it really, love for a child? They all say that it is something amazing. She too had imagined that from that moment on, life would be free of obstacles once and for all. Now she has the baby and it really is not amazing at all. It splutters and screams and she could not last two hours in its presence without making a great effort. What is it, a baby? A little person. In her mind, mummy can see Stromovka Park on a Sunday afternoon: a crowd of repulsive, ugly people. You have added yet another to that crowd. What else? What is a person? The world is not as it looks in fashion magazines and American films. That charming image just does not materialise. Mother sits for a long time in one spot in the corner and in the end she realises that her feelings do not resemble anything that has been written or said about such feelings. What she feels for the little one is not love and the fuss that the little one makes in the world every day is not happiness. Mummy is despairing. She has the impression that she is even more deformed and ugly than when she was laboriously dragging the unborn baby around with her. She studies the concepts from every angle, she tries to arrive at some conclusion, but in vain. In the end, she decides that she will leave this non-feeling as a deep secret at the bottom of some terribly deep place, that she will never reveal her disappointment or lack of love, that nonetheless she will be an excellent – or even better – mother for the baby; she faces the future, very unhappy and discouraged. The very same night, however, she wakes up and listens in the dark. Reflections from the street lamp quiver on the ceiling, long, trembling shadows. Otherwise it is quiet, lonesome; people and the world are far away; mummy is still on the edge of dreaming. In the basket nearby, baby sleeps and pants. All of a sudden, mummy remembers: once she found a little hedgehog in the forest. It was numb; its paws were frozen and it was terribly hungry. She carried it home, and the hedgehog thawed out, ate – how much it ate! –

and then fell asleep in the warmth. Back then it panted in the same way that baby does now. In mummy's heart, something breaks and pours forth, as if hot lava were flowing inside her. The next day, when they bring baby to mummy in bed, she forgets her embarrassment, her intelligence and says: 'hoopa-hoopa-hoopa-hoop!' Baby's smile spreads from ear to ear and it replies, 'ooboo, ooboo, ooboo ...' very gratefully and sociably. The ice has been broken.

Every time baby puts its paws in mother's mouth, or twines mother's hair in its fingers, when a victorious cry of joy issues from its toothless mouth in mother's direction, that stream of hot lava flows again, like it did that first night. Mummy joins the ranks of endless regiments of mummies, ordinary, nameless, motherly and foolish, those who knit little clothes and booties. When baby is a quarter of an hour late returning from its walk, she pictures it killed by an automobile, buried under a demolished building, stolen, scalded or lost, according to all the laws of maternal horror. Mummy's 'happiness' is just beginning. The question is, is it 'happiness' to have something in the world, the loss of which one could not endure?

# A Cry for Independence
## 27 October 1929, *Lidové noviny*

Our recent survey, 'New Modes of Life', about independent and wage-earning women, had an interesting outcome: it did not shed the slightest bit of light on the problem, although hundreds of letters from the most diverse correspondents of both sexes were received.[11] The outcome revealed a contradiction; likewise the problem itself, which is today a vexing question for every young woman, has many contradictions within it. Yes, it is natural that we marry and have children. That is what we want, that is what we long for. We also want, however, to be independent. Above all: we feel a very pressing need to earn our own money. How to combine these things? What to choose?

This need to earn one's own money, which every average woman feels today, is definitely new. Our mothers did not feel it. Our mothers had a completely clear conscience when they accepted money from their husbands. Since that time, however, something has changed. I would say that there has been a mistake in that only women have changed. If women's emancipation has not sunk in in the minds of all women, all women have at least appropriated the benefits, even those who are not emancipated. I would say that the woman of today takes many things for granted that would never even have occurred to the woman of yesterday. Customs have changed and demands have changed. A good marriage of yesterday was founded on the assumption that at home the man was the master, the commander, the god and the provider. All the woman's time, all her freedom, all her will and being, belonged to him. The woman's task was rather simple: she was supposed to make sure that the man was happy. She tended to him, she cared for him, she arranged everything for him, she submitted to him. She took care lest a little frown of indignation spoil his good mood. His good mood was her reward, his bad mood was her punishment. For buttons not sewn, for a burnt lunch, a delayed

---

11 She refers to the survey published in two parts: 'Anketa: O nové formy života' (Survey: New Modes of Life), *Lidové noviny*, 15 September 1929, p. 21, and 22 September 1929, p. 21. Jesenská regularly organised and edited reader surveys for the newspapers *Národní listy* and *Lidové noviny*.

lunch, a different opinion, there were storms and rows in the household. If the man did not like something, he simply made a row. The entire household shook during such a row: the wife, the children, the servants. Doors and cruel words flew. Everyone went about feeling panicky, cowed, unhappy. Everything possible was done to conciliate the god of the household. Only then did the woman sigh with relief.

I do not think that men are very different today. Women, however, are different. One does not have to be a very intellectual or emancipated woman to discover the truth that there can never be a meeting of minds when one person is the property of another. The moment someone can command us, he cannot ask us to be sincere, open, ingenuous and trustworthy. If we cannot be sincere, we cannot love. It is a very simple computation, but few men understand it. Men like to rule and dominate. They like to make a fuss; they are crude and nasty; they cause pain and they are pleased when they see that they have succeeded in doing so. They love situations in which they can forgive a tearful woman and make her happy with their kind, forgiving smile. In such situations, they feel their power and so they provoke them too often. They get angry on account of an overturned plate, dirty clothes, ten minutes of waiting. The more a woman is dependent on them, the less they try to control their bad traits. They have not yet learned to regard a woman as a free person with her own will, with a need for solitude, with a desire for her own intellectual life. In looking after the household and her husband, a woman works for her money and should stand next to her husband, free and independent. Perhaps there are ten such cases out of a hundred. The other ninety are identical to the old established marriages of years past. How could you tear the blouse I paid so much money for? How come you want to go to the theatre when I want to sit at home after work? How come you're going to eat at your girlfriend's when I'm coming home for lunch? In every word one can hear: I am the master! I pay, therefore I am the master! Ask every second married woman around you what she longs for most: to earn at least six hundred a month so that she can buy a few nice things, some flowers, a book, clothes, a purse – and not have to depend on the good or bad mood of her husband for her every wish. The proletarian marriage has been like that for a long time. The husband and wife both work all day long. In their case, of course, it is for the most pressing existential reasons. There are thousands of wives and mothers in the factories who earn as much as men and who take care of the household and the children only after work.[12] In the middle class, there is hardly a woman from a so-called good family who has not bitterly experienced now and then the lack of money earned by her own labour and the wonderful benefits that it brings: complete self-confidence, freedom and independence. Fundamentally, however, it is not a longing for independence that lies behind this longing for independence. Every natural woman in her prime longs for love, a home and a child. The longing for independence is nothing but fear of being dependent. Dependence spoils our marriages. When one person is worth less than the other, the quiet contentment of friendship cannot flourish. Yet we have silently resolved that this quiet contentment of friendship is the gift that our generation will give to its children, so that they will grow up to be reasonable, upright, sincere and honourable people. For this we need an equality far more profound than the bluestocking equality of men and women on the basis of laws. For this we need a real equality, developed on the basis of women's skills, abilities and strengths. Girls today enter upon life equipped with an ability to earn their own money. This signifies such a tremendous revolution in the lives of women that only now can we speak of emancipation. Only now, when we gain complete freedom in our erotic life and when marriage ceases to be a financial contract.

The independence of women is a healthy, good, bright thing and – as the last letter in our survey stated – it is through this condition that we will finally leave the Middle Ages behind.[13] Through it we gain so much that is worthwhile, so much that is needed for a healthy mental life, that it has become an indispensable need we can never relinquish. Now, how do we arrange things so that we can do both well: so that we can keep the independence, the job and at the same time marry and have children? This is a purely superficial problem of labour organisation and in the next column we will see how it is managed elsewhere.

---

12 A similar point had been made by the Czech feminist Pavla Buzková (1885–1949) much earlier. She argued that equality between men and women already existed in practice in the working class. According to her, middle-class women had a position inferior to men because they had no economic – that is, wage-earning – worth. See: Pavla Buzková, *Pokrokový názor na ženskou otázku* (A Progressive View on the Woman Question), Prague, 1909, p. 34.

13 The last letter printed in the survey is signed M. F. One wonders if Jesenská did not write the letter herself. It includes English words, which also regularly appear in Jesenská's articles. The letter writer states that a man should look for a partner who has her own distinct style, her own inner richness; this is a theme that recurs in Jesenská's writing. See: 'Anketa: O nové formy života', *Lidové noviny*, 22 September 1929, p. 21.

# Civilised Woman?
## 1 December 1929, *Lidové noviny*

*Die neue Sachlichkeit* is not only the slogan of the modern era.[14] It is also the creed of a generation and the magic formula that liberated – or at least, should liberate – us from the humbug of the nineties, from stucco ornaments, from plaster statues, from real and symbolic braids.[15] New objectivity is the cry of thousands and millions of young people who heard the rhythm of the era and turned to it for guidance. In its symbolic meaning, this ordinary and sober ideal, for which no one has died and or heaved a hysterical sigh, but on the basis of which young people have decided to live and to live happily and optimistically, brought delivery from bad taste. It also brought liberation from the small-minded convention and petty prejudice of the times when a young girl had to walk on the streets with a chaperone in order to protect her reputation. This era has also introduced the greatest achievement of all the centuries following one another up to the present; that is, the independent, thinking and working woman – in a word, the civilised woman. Should I repeat everything that we have asserted ad nauseam about the modern woman? She is sporty, thrifty, clever and astute. She is educated and resourceful; she knows how to manage a weapon, a machine, her job, her own life, freely, on the basis of her own independent decisions. She is straightforward and simple, she is bright and brave and, above all, she is independent. I am not sure if we have properly understood the significance of this fact. Independent, that is, able to support herself. Literally, that

---

14 The new objectivity, or functionalism.

15 Braided hair was a symbol of an out-dated conception of femininity. In the play *Cop* (The Braid, 1905), for example, by the Czech writer and feminist Božena Viková Kunětická (1862–1934), liberation from nineteenth-century hairstyles represented emancipation for women. The cover of the book *Civilisovaná žena, Zivilisierte Frau* (The Civilised Woman, 1929, B. Horneková , Zdeněk Rossman and Jan Vaněk, eds), designed by Zdeněk Rossman, depicts a man's hand cutting a woman's braid with a pair of scissors. For a treatment of this book and the question of the relation between reform in fashion and reform in architecture, see: Martina Pachmanová, 'Collective Desires: Czech Avant-garde Architecture and the Production of Degendered Space', *Umění*, 2000, no. 4, pp. 265–276.

means that the twilight has fallen on the era when we pitied prostitutes and sympathised with the suffering of misunderstood women living in degrading marriages.[16] Although it is still very difficult, it is nonetheless possible to support oneself. People expected that this reality would manifest itself in some external form, just as every internal revolution has manifested itself in a changed inner form. For three years it looked as if woman had also changed her outward appearance: her attire ceased to be bait and became simply clothing. A new life began for young girls and they adapted to it. In the day, they worked, studied and trained. For this they needed simple and durable clothes. They got them. Never before had a young girl had so many joys to choose from, never before could she spend her free time so happily. Thousands of amusements awaited her when she finished work: gymnastics, weekends, scouting, dance, motoring, winter swimming pools, winter tennis courts, kayaks, tents under the open sky, skis, mountains, water, snow. The whole world was opened wide to healthy people. Never before had the world offered so many miracles to sweethearts, never before had such feasts of physical joy been celebrated, never before had life included so many beautiful things. For all the beauties of movement, for all the pleasures of sport, a woman needed sports clothes and she got them. Our new homes are full of light and sun. Our new relationships are full of sincerity and trust. Our new era is teeming with exuberance for the very reason that we have discarded the ballast binding us like shackles. For three years, woman kept pace with this progress. Then came the baneful blow: the fashion of today. Paris has prescribed for us senseless trains, an ugly line, a skirt short in the front and long in the back. These new clothes, adorned with pretty and useless trinkets, are expensive, useless and ugly. They restrict our stride; they change us back into sedate matrons; they cost a ghastly sum of money if they are made by a good seamstress and they look ridiculous if they are sewn badly. Beautiful fabrics are cut to pieces for them, fabrics that cannot be altered when Paris prescribes for us a fashion completely different from that of the present-day. Our hair is once again full of combs, decorative pins and headbands and we let it grow out even though that is ugly, unhygienic and uncomfortable. Not even morning dresses have a simple line anymore. They are, at the very least, full of buttons that do not fasten anything and seams that do not join anything. The long afternoon gowns hang down

---

16 Jesenská sometimes wrote about prostitutes. See, for example: A. X. Nessey, 'Tři šestnáctileté', *Tribuna*, 3 November 1921, pp. 3–4.

below our coats and we wear disgusting, useless half-veils on our hats. The city is full of clever, astute, independent women: these women work in factories, in shops and in workshops; they sit behind the steering wheel and the typewriter; they are wonderful at telemarking and Christiania turns; they swim underwater and they read modern books; they look at modern photographs. And among them there is not a single one who would reject the torrent of tastelessness that crashes upon us, not a single one who would listen to her well-trained brain instead of Mr Poiret.[17] Thus we will walk about in our liberated homes with trains on our dresses, lipstick on our lips and a permanent wave in our hair. On the weekends we will go for a drive in clothes that have – just for a lark – one hundred and fifty buttons. We will sit behind the steering wheels wearing hats with little veils. Not because we like it. But because it is modern. Because for fashion and finery we give up, instantly and without deliberation, all the achievements of real worth that we have won for ourselves. Today, when we stand in a salon and look at the silhouettes of the young women whom we know to be clever and when we see how they are dressed, we have to admit that the three years of freedom and simplicity, the beautiful, simple, elegant line of our dresses, the love of good-quality fabrics and objects, were not progress, as we had wrongly supposed – they too were only a fashion.

---

17 She refers to the designer Paul Poiret, who was the first to hold a fashion show of French designs in Prague in 1923. See: Uchalová, *Česká móda 1918–1939. Elegance první republiky*, p. 23.

# III. Articles from *Přítomnost,* 1938–1939

# Judge Lynch in Europe
## 30 March 1938, *Přítomnost*

Perhaps a foreigner, driving through an unfamiliar city and looking out over the sea of houses, might think he had a great metropolis in front of him. But a person who lives in a city so large that not once in his life does he see how it empties into the fields knows that really there are no big cities in the world. There are only streets running into one another and houses pressed close together with no gardens or fields; there are square stone cages in five storeys on top of one another. In a big city, the individual lives as he would in a village. Among neighbours, with the tobacconist's shop across the road and the grocer on the corner. The concierge, the mailman, the tax collector, the telephone, work, a few friends and that is all. In the morning, the shop-assistant leaves milk and a bag of rolls in front of the door; the man who lives next door goes off to work; the girl who lives across the way and has a night shift at some bar comes home from work. The day begins with an indifferent greeting of good morning. All fates are noted in the tobacconist's across the road. The walls have ears; women and children are talkative. So the whole building knows what debts and worries you have, what clothes you wear and what political convictions you hold. The man from the first floor greets you a little carelessly on account of those political convictions and the man from the second floor is particularly polite on account of them. If you belong to the same camp as the landlord, you can get away with paying the rent a little late. If your membership card is different from that of the concierge, your son has to wipe his shoes with particular care so as not to dirty the stairs. If the woman from the third floor passes by, the building grimaces quietly, today a little maliciously: that woman is a Jew. And if the student in the white knee-socks from the fourth floor makes a ruckus on the stairs, he walks through an icy calm on the scowling streets of today.

That is how the political life of the ordinary man looks in private. His political life is so blatantly private and so intertwined with his personal situation that it is closer to his skin than his own sense of honour. The radius of his political activities usually does not extend beyond the radius of his daily movements: across the square and three streets down, the way to work, the way home, the pub on the corner, the tobacconist's across the road and the eight square metres that are called home. From this reality there arises what is known as a pogrom. A pogrom is, among other things, the ordinary man taking revenge on the ordinary man, a battle across a gallery railing, from one storey to another. Long suppressed anger – whipped up and exploited by some propaganda – concentrates on a certain concept, crystallises and explodes.

## Blacks in Europe

In more peaceful – and peaceful – eras all different kinds of people probably lived next to one another and did not bother much about politics. It did not trouble them; it did not seem to touch them but was played out in some distant place. Today politics has entered the dwellings of ordinary people, the two-room flats with kitchen, bathroom and lavatory; it has sat down at the tables with crocheted covers and it jangles from the radios, which used to play nothing but songs. Today Mr Novotný is above all a Czech and a good neighbour, Mr Kohn is a Jew and the son of the tenant Keller is a very square-shouldered, very athletic youth in white Bavarian knee-socks – in the middle of tranquil Smíchov, where there are no mountains far and wide – and Mr Svoboda, the tailor in the basement, is a social democrat.[1] There are also two émigrés living in the basement, German socialists; they survive on a registration card, without work or documents and all the tenants in the building – Czech, German, Jewish – are a little uncomfortably offended by their presence.[2] Because an émigré is a black man and what's more, a black man among whites, living where he does not belong, damn nigger![3] In four years, Europe has changed so that it is full of blacks. Black men, as is well known, are not allowed to touch white women; they must live in quarters that are assigned to them and they are second-class citizens. Blacks in Vienna today – those

1 Smíchov is a district in Prague.

2 The socialists would have been refugees from Germany. The registration cards were issued by the charitable organisations that supported the German refugees. The cards functioned as a form of identification for people who did not have valid passports. Černý lists seven organisations of this sort. Bohumil Černý, *Most k novému životu. Německá emigrace v ČSR v letech 1933–1939* (Bridge to a New Life. The German Emigrés in Czechoslovakia 1933–1939), Prague, 1967, p. 24.

3 The phrase 'damn nigger' is used in English in the original Czech article.

are the Jews, the socialists, the former Austrian nationalists, the monarchists, Czechs here and there and often Catholics as well. In America it sometimes happens that a crowd, maddened by racial pride, hangs a black youth from the nearest tree – because he is black. Some time ago, the whole world stirred with a justified compassion for three black youths from Scottsborough, who were sentenced to death on the basis of the false testimony of a white prostitute.[4] Europe welcomed their mother with open arms; Europe, through the voices of its best people, asked for freedom for the three innocent, sentenced youths. Europe spoke with the centuries-old traditions of its culture to the rather young and rather noisy America. In Vienna they do not hang anyone from trees. In Vienna today there are a good half-million blacks. For the moment, no one has done them any great harm. They have 'only' been forbidden to work. Doctors are not allowed to treat patients; lawyers are not allowed to conduct their practice; no one is allowed to listen to writers or musicians. In addition, 'only' their property has been confiscated and they have been given to understand that they should leave – needlessly, because those who could leave have already gone. *Otherwise*, however, they can live. Strange, terrible, *lawful* Judge Lynch!

For four years those people lived in Vienna hardly daring to breathe. Over four years they learned all sorts of ways to deny themselves and to keep quiet. They took pains to be inconspicuous and to avoid giving cause for offence – because they wanted to live. In his last attempt to maintain Austrian independence, however, the former Chancellor Schuschnigg made an appeal to these very people.[5] To the very people who had defended Austrian independence in February 1934. These people came out of hiding, out of the silence that was so difficult to learn and they spoke: in the streets, at meetings, at home, on the stairway, on the gallery, in the pub, at the tobacconist's. They made themselves known once again. They cast off the four years of quiet denial like a mask and prepared to

---

4 She refers to the Scottsboro Case, in the city of Scottsboro, Alabama, USA. In this case, nine black youths were charged with the rape of two white women. They were brought to trial in April 1931. The doctors who examined the women testified that no rape had occurred. Nonetheless, the all-white jury convicted the nine and all but the youngest (12 years old) were sentenced to death. The cause of the 'Scottsboro Boys' was taken up by liberal and radical groups – in particular the Communist Party of the USA – in the north. In 1932, the US Supreme Court overturned the convictions. There followed further retrials of the accused by the state of Alabama, more re-convictions and successful appeals. The state finally freed the four youngest and paroled all but one. *The New Encyclopaedia Britannica*, vol. 10, 15th edn, Chicago, 1992, p. 568.

say 'yes' to Schuschnigg's question. When Schuschnigg resigned on 12 March 1938, these people stood revealed for *a second time* and defenceless before their enemies, this time with faces completely black.[6] Four years of silence and humility were in vain. A third of the white people in Austria lost their rights, work and civic existence among white people in Austria. In Europe today people do not have to have skin of colour in order to become blacks.

No one really knows exactly how many of these white blacks there are in Europe today. In the League of Nations they have statistics on post-war emigration, but these were outdated long ago and give only an approximate picture of the political migration of nations. Numbers also do not say *why* ordinary citizens have suddenly become blacks in some countries. Jews have almost always and everywhere been in a distinct position and in Eastern Europe they were essentially blacks even in the era considered to be the golden age of blossoming European culture and civilisation. How many Jewish blacks are there today? In the Third Reich about half a million. In Vienna and in Austria about 300,000. In Hungary there

5 Kurt von Schuschnigg (1897–1977), a Catholic lawyer and Christian social from Tyrol, was named Federal Chancellor of Austria after Engelbert Dollfuss's (1892–1934) assassination by Austrian Nazis in July 1934. Dollfuss was killed shortly after suppressing the outbreak of civil war. Fighting broke out in Vienna in February 1934 between the private army supporting the Social Democratic Party, the Republican *Schutzbund*, and the government forces. In addition to the police and the army, the government had the support of a para-military, anti-Marxist, anti-parliamentarian, pro-fascist organisation, the *Heimwehr* (Home Defence Unit). The fighting in Vienna lasted for a week and was limited mainly to the outer proletarian districts. The aims of the *Schutzbund* members were mainly defensive: to resist seizure of their weapons and defend themselves against the army. The government forces lost 105 dead and 300 wounded; the *Schutzbund* lost 137 dead and 400 wounded. As a result of the fighting, the Social Democratic Party and its associated organisations were outlawed. Jesenská refers to the plebiscite that Schuschnigg intended to hold, in 1938, on the question of Austrian independence. He hoped that the plebiscite would put a stop to Nazi pressure on Austria. The former social democrats would have supported Schuschnigg in the plebiscite against Hitler. The latter, however, demanded on 11 March that Schuschnigg cancel the plebiscite, which he did. Schuschnigg was compelled to resign and the German army marched into Austria on 12 March 1938. See: Elisabeth Barker, *Austria 1918-1972*, Basingstoke and London, 1973, pp. 84–112; and F. L. Carsten, *The Rise of Fascism*, London, 1967, pp. 223–229.

6 After the German army occupied Austria, there was a wave of arrests of government leaders, Christian socials, social democrats, Jews and others. The number arrested has been estimated at 70,000. The Nazis had at their disposal the police records of the Schuschnigg regime. See: Barker, *Austria 1918–1972*, pp. 114, 128.

are Jewish mulattos, who are allowed to live and work and thus far also have civil rights, but all the same are bound by the laws of *numerus clausus.*[7] Only a certain percentage of Jews are permitted to study and it is almost impossible for Jews to become state employees or officials. Almost half a million Hungarian Jews are living in this kind of lifelong quarantine, although they have been distinguished by their great patriotism. In Poland, where the number of Jews is several times greater, the restrictions are even more severe and thus you meet in Prague, in Paris and in London poor and undernourished Polish Jewish students, who study medicine passionately and with amazing diligence, only to find, once they receive their doctorates, that they are not permitted to pursue their profession anywhere in the world. The situation is similar in Romania. There are about fifteen million Jews in the world, but a third of them live outside the law.

Nonetheless, there are far fewer Jewish blacks in the world than there are other, literally Aryan, blacks. For five years, many thousands of German émigrés have been wandering over all countries and continents; now the outcasts from former Austria have multiplied their ranks. How many of them are there? About 300,000, according to reliable estimates. Thousands and thousands are in prisons and concentration camps. Does that account for all of them? Not by a long shot. Today even a full-blooded Aryan can easily become a black in his own country if he is a socialist or a democrat, or if he considers the Gospel, for example, to be a higher law than various decrees. The number of such blacks, who have remained at home, who have not left and cannot leave, is boundless. Over their lives, thoughts and dreams, over their every day and every step, house patrols are watching, as well as neighbours, co-workers at the factory, the office, school or sports club. Social and political *activity* has always had certain consequences, but it is only today that a part of Europe is in such a state that millions of people are blacks only because they are, because they *exist* and have opinions and have the sort of parents they have. They do not have to do anything forbidden; indeed, they are not even permitted to conform (Jews in Vienna are not allowed to

---

7 The first *numerus clausus* law, limiting attendance at universities, was introduced in Hungary in 1920, but was not strictly applied. On 29 May 1938, the First Jewish Law was passed restricting the percentage of Jews to be employed in business, banks, the professions, journalism and the entertainment industry. Ezra Mendelsohn, *East Central Europe between the Wars*, Bloomington, 1987, pp. 105, 116.

hang flags with the swastika); they suffer only because they are in the world.

## Events Flare up Over the Border

The press and radio bring news of events that are flaring up close at hand. There are people among us who have gained much self-confidence from these events abroad. Vigorous youthful calves in white knee-socks march over the Prague pavement with unusual energy. Then there are people among us who are under the impression that even here the development of events might produce blacks overnight. There are accounts of émigrés who go from one border to the next and are always turned away. Every country now harbours more of these people of colour than it can afford economically. The states have closed their borders; the flood of foreigners threatens their internal balance. But people come anyway, without documents, on foot, with empty hands. Wandering among us is the reflection of many hundreds of appalling human fates, hundreds and thousands of painful partings, suicides and injustices. Many people have grown nervous. The ceaseless flurry of classification of people has descended on us as well. In the Vinohrady, Smíchov, Karlín, Holešovice, Libeň and other suburban streets, a quiet breeze of mutual tension is blowing from person to person. A dangerous breeze from a distant, German, alien country. In the small pubs, people sit debating. What will England do, how will France act, what will Hitler undertake? In truth, these are very urgent and important questions; for all of us, they stick to our skin like a shirt; it is impossible not to think of them. But above all we have to know something else: and that is, what we will do ourselves. Not on that great, international scale, but on our private scale, the radius of which is three and a half streets, the way home and a two-room apartment with a kitchen. We have to know what we will do on this very piece of earth where we are standing and in this very sphere of ordinary work that we are carrying out. Perhaps the outlines of this will become clear in our thoughts if we recall the dead engineer Weissl and the eleven living *Schutzbund* members.

## Eleven Schutzbund Members

The last year truly was not stingy when it came to terrible news. We heard so many terrible tidings from the world that we almost grew numb to them. Bombarded cities and dead people were practically part of the daily routine. Before the feature film we used to

see regularly photographs of women searching for their children
and husbands in the wreckage, wringing their hands over the ruins
of buildings or something lying in the street – it looked like a
grotesque rag, but it was a dead man. I do not know if the world
can offer us even greater horrors. But three days ago, a little piece
of news in tiny brevier type went through the papers and stopped
the hearts of those who read it. An account of eleven Austrian
*Schutzbund* members – firemen.[8]

These *Schutzbund* men fought with guns in February 1934 against
Austrian fascism. They fought, they fell, they lost and – they were
put on trial. Weissl had led those eleven arrested people. He was
not a political leader or a political functionary; no one really knew
him; he had never done anything political. He was a private individual like you or me, an individual who was, by conviction, an
anti-fascist and a socialist. For many years his convictions were a
purely private matter, falling in between his private life and work.
But then there came a time when in Austria people took up guns
on behalf of such convictions and Weissl stood at their head. Not
because he had any rank, or because anyone commanded him to –
only because of that inner human command that proclaims that
there are things we love more than our lives. He was wounded, he
was arrested, he was dragged from the hospital on a stretcher and,
straight from the hospital stretcher, he was hanged. He died without
saying much, very peaceful and matter-of-fact, with a salutation to
freedom on his lips. The world had only just learned about Weissl
– and the world soon forgot him. Beside him, however, there stood
eleven fellow fighters, eleven *Schutzbund* members, who could not
and should not forget. The Nazis put a question to these eleven
people: do you want to swear the *same loyalty* to your new leader
as you once showed for your ideals? *And those eleven people said: yes.*

The last month in the world perhaps did not provide a more
oppressive or cautionary testimony. It would be good to consider
these eleven people as a great warning for all of us who are not

---

8 According to the account in the newspaper *Lidové noviny*, the Nazis promised
that those who had lost their jobs because of their participation in the civil
war in February 1934 would be returned to their former positions. The account
also mentioned that eleven former members of the Social Democratic Republican *Schutzbund*, who had fought in the Am Spitz fire station in the 21st district
in Vienna on 12 February 1934, had recently been ceremoniously accepted
back into the firemen's force. Their leader, the head officer of the firemen,
Weisel [*sic*], had taken all the responsibility for the fighting upon himself and
had been hanged. See: nč, 'Nacisté získávají rakouské dělníky' (Nazis Win the
Austrian Workers), *Lidové noviny*, 23 March 1938, p. 1.

politicians, who do not have an impact on events except through the personal weight of our fundamental beliefs. It is not true that we do not matter. Today all of us matter – but also each one of us matters. If some day someone requires of us a complete reversal of convictions and we are willing to answer 'yes', there is no salvation for us. Because first and foremost a person must save himself and only then can one help him. We do not know those eleven *Schutzbund* members by name. Nor does anyone know us by name. But the greatest illness of the European individual is the easy willingness to retreat, to offer no resistance, to surrender and to conform 'because one has to live, after all!' It is more urgent that we know *how* we want to live and that we consider this *how* to be as important as life itself. A difficult task faces each of us today – to find the precise boundary between prudence and cowardice, between daring and an outburst of passion. Today, not only the leading people of this state must find this boundary, but also every ordinary person, even the most ordinary. We can think with respect of the brave-hearted people in Barcelona and Madrid who work, sell, teach, go to the cinema and live right under the rain of bombs. And we must remember without sympathy the eleven *Schutzbund* members who raised their right arms to greet the new leader.

These two reminders delineate for us the course needed to create a quiet courage in the people of this country. If I were not ashamed of quotations and big words, I would dig out from the awestruck memories of my childhood the saying to the effect that people who are as hard as flint create a nation made of ashlars.[9]

---

9 She quotes from Canto XXVI of Jan Neruda's (1834–1891) *Písně kosmické* (Cosmic Ballads): 'if each one of us is as hard as flint,/ the whole nation will be made of ashlars'. Jan Neruda, *Písně kosmické*, Prague, 1878, p. 47.

# There will be no *Anschluss*
25 May 1938, *Přítomnost*

## *The Strongholds of the SdP*

When you drive over the length and breadth of North Bohemia, two things strike you at first glance: first of all, the lovely, magical countryside, everywhere in bloom today, full of gentle hills and panoramic views. The entire region is submerged in the fresh green of spring and although it is an industrial countryside, nowhere is the usual gloom or greyness in evidence. Then you notice the large isolated brick buildings, which loom up from the blossoming countryside near every city, every town, every village. They are two to three storeys high; they are not factories; they are not apartment buildings; they are not schools; this is a shape of building entirely unfamiliar to us, with high windows and expansive spaces: *die deutsche Turnhalle*.

Czech schools, of course, also have excellently equipped gymnasiums – but these are attached to the schools. The German gymnasiums are almost never attached to schools. Because of this seemingly minor circumstance, German children march from the schools to the gymnasiums in closed ranks, singing German – that is, Nazi – songs. German youth belong in a German gymnasium, you read and hear everywhere. You see girls and boys striding in file down the road, singing and raising their arms in the German – that is, the Nazi – salute. The march, the songs, the military gait, the gatherings in gymnasiums and the spirit in which the youth is raised there: this is all a powerful support for the Henlein movement. Henlein himself comes from such a gymnasium.[10] There, instructions and commands are issued; there, guards are selected

---

10 Konrad Henlein (1898-1945) was a gym instructor at a Sudeten German club. In 1931 he became leader of the German Gymnastics Union in Czechoslovakia. When the NSDAP was banned, he founded the Sudeten German *Heimatfront* (Patriotic Front) in 1933. In 1935 this was transformed into the *Sudetendeutsche Partei* (SdP, Sudeten German Party), which won 66 percent of the German vote in Czechoslovakia in the elections on 19 May 1935. From 1935 on, the SdP received financial support from the Third Reich. During the Second World War, Henlein was Reich Governor and *Gauleiter* of the occupied Sudetenland. Robert S. Wistrich, *Who's Who in Nazi Germany*, London and New York, 1995, pp. 104–105.

and orders are given. There, the core of the movement is consolidated.

When the government banned the German National and German National Socialist Parties, it did not forbid the Germans to train their youth. In their gymnasiums the Germans trained young people to raise their right arms, to hate Germans who were not Nazis, to hate all Czechs indiscriminately and to despise Jews. They taught them that there was one great man in the world to whom every German owed love and fidelity and this man would come and liberate the Sudetenland: without a struggle, without violence, he would simply come and they would salute him with their raised right arms; they would follow him and bring him all this beautiful countryside as a gift.

First it was whispered that he would come in March. Then it was whispered that he would come in April. The SdP exhorted all Germans to join; the notices on the posters declared: *Komme zu uns, ehe es zu spät ist.*[11] First they announced that 30 April was the last day new members would be accepted into the party before the *Anschluss*. Then they extended it a little – to 15 May. Then – perhaps for technical reasons – to 30 May.

[Five lines censored.]

And the army came. At night, in long sober ranks, in a supremely quiet and calm manner; long lines of vehicles rumbled over the square in Liberec.[12] The army came – but it was the Czechoslovak army.[13] From the centre of the country, the swell of the army surged towards the border in an indescribably ordered, calm and quiet manner. Small crowds of people stood on the square, speaking excitedly. By Saturday afternoon not a single white knee-sock was visible in Liberec and people who on Friday evening had raised their arms in salute were wearing tri-colour rosettes in the buttonholes of their coats. The Czechs came and I tell you, they came just in time. With their arrival, they showed all the German and Czech heroes who had fought against fascism for years in the border regions that they had not fought in vain, that they were not in a vacuum, as it might have seemed to them sometimes.

11 Join us before it is too late.

12 Reichenberg. In 1890, according to the census carried out that year, it had a predominantly German-speaking population.

13 On 20 May 1938, there was a rumour that German troops were moving towards the Czechoslovak border. As a result, Czechoslovak troops were partially mobilised. The crisis was over by 23 May. Keith Eubank, 'Munich', *A History of the Czechoslovak Republic 1918–1948*, eds Victor S. Mamatey and Radomír Luža, Princeton, 1973, pp. 239–252, see p. 244.

## Behind the Scenes: the First of May

In capital cities, the May Day demonstration is a political and national manifestation of a great many people. There are also many, however, who stay at home, go on outings or observe from the windows. In capital cities, it is a symbolic manifestation of the will and freedom of the people only for part of the population. The smaller the city, the more earnest are its holidays and the more important is the May Day procession. In the Czech-German border regions, May Day was a most important manifestation for every individual. It was not only a manifestation of his opinions and convictions about political matters, but also an open declaration of his world outlook. Conditions are such in our border regions that there a person's convictions can cost him his livelihood. For democratic Germans in the border regions, the decision not to march in the SdP procession meant that they would be blacklisted, but above all, that they would lose their jobs, without notice, at one stroke. And not only lose their jobs, but never find another.

In large cities, one person can perhaps hide. Or at least imagine that he is hiding. In small towns – and in the north, most of the towns are small – not even a mouse can slip away. Everyone knows about everyone else. In any case, Henlein's supporters saw to it that they had absolute certainty. The factory personnel received an order to gather on the first of May at the factories and the workers were taken straight from the factories to the processions by party activists. Whoever did not work at a factory was picked up at home, at the store or at the workshop. These activists – they were mostly youths and children, twelve- to eighteen-year-old boys, exactly like those who 'took over' the Vienna enterprises, editorial offices and train stations on 13 March. Boys from the German gymnasiums, boys in white knee-socks, boys making the Nazi salute. These boys – in groups of two or three – led grown men from the factories – their fathers, uncles, brothers, neighbours and friends – to the procession. These children noted down the names of everyone who participated in the democratic procession on a 'blacklist'. On 30 April – on a Saturday – the representatives of the SdP approached the workers in the factories and said to them: if you don't come with us tomorrow, don't bother showing up for work on Monday. These people had wives, not always brave and resolute ones and they had children, distressed and for the most part abnormally disturbed and hungry children. They had years of unemployment around their necks and they succumbed to the fear that was spread artificially:

[One line censored.]

Nonetheless, many of them refused and went on the first of May to proclaim their democratic outlook.

But at that time – unfortunately – those calm, silent, resolute soldiers, fully armed and in round helmets, were not yet in the border regions. At that time, many people had the feeling that their cause was lost and that they would never get help. Many people – very many people – changed sides and fell in line to chant *Sieg Heil!* and raise their right arms. In Česká Kamenice, a forty-eight-year-old worker who was a member of the Christian Social Party was given an ultimatum: either join the SdP, or don't go to work.[14] He did not join. On 3 May, he was fired from his job and on 4 May, he hanged himself.

The psychological impact of these processions was considerable. The democratic procession was a typical May Day demonstration, with chants, slogans, shouting, songs and flags – something very powerful, bright and promising. Then the SdP processions marched: mostly in uniform (in April, in a community of 4,500 residents, a shoemaker received orders for five hundred pairs of black high boots), performing a military goose step, in unison, rows of people with raised right arms, chanting to the rhythm of a military march – *Sieg Heil!* – *Sieg Heil!* The little communities trembled under the impact of those marching steps because this was not a demonstration for progress or social justice; this was not even a military parade; soldiers would not frighten anyone here –

[Six lines censored.]

## Not Elections but a Plebiscite

Some communities in the border regions voted on Sunday.[15] The last communities in the border regions will vote on 12 June. '11 June is the day of our *Anschluss*,' it was whispered from person to person in the border regions. '*Zum letztenmal wird zum Appel geblasen*,' wrote *Der Aufbruch* on 19 May and it was not even confiscated.[16] On 11 June, the German army will come, occupy the country and at one stroke we will become part of the German Reich. The election slogan of Henlein's supporters is not: vote for the SdP! Vote for Konrad Henlein! But rather: are you a German, or aren't

---

14 Česká Kamenice (Böhmisch-Kamnitz), a town in the mountainous landscape of North Bohemia.

15 She refers to the local elections of 1938, in which the SdP won 86 percent of the German vote. Sayer, *The Coasts of Bohemia. A Czech History*, p. 221.

16 The call-up is sounded for the last time.

you? Make yourself heard, if you are a German! *Bist du ein Deutscher oder nur ein Deutschsprechender?* Are you a German, or only a person who speaks German? If you do not join the SdP, you will voluntarily exclude yourself from the German nation! So: yes, or no?

After the first of May, several SdP members of parliament went to one of the largest factories, which lies right on the border and employs more than 3,000 workers. They had the entire factory and all of the machines decorated with the emblems of the SdP; they held a banquet and even the roast meat and geese were decorated with the emblems of the SdP. Lord in heaven, when do the local people ever get to eat goose? After the banquet, they walked through the enterprise, seeking out the German social democrats. They approached them and offered to shake hands – following the example of Mr Bürckel in Vienna – very affably and full of concern.[17] Do you know how difficult it is to refuse the grip of a proffered hand? When you are, in addition, almost certain that the rejected handshake will cost you your own subsistence, as well as that of the people dependent on you? Despite that onslaught, more than six hundred people remained firm. There were many who defected to the other side. The next day, they went, some of them in tears, to their organisations. They recounted what had happened. They said: I can't go on anymore. How were the organisations supposed to respond? They consoled them: we know that in your hearts you support us. Is that consolation? Does any kind of consolation help? Do these people ask for consolation? Not at all, they ask for help! Lasting help can only come when the economic pressure crushing them is lifted.

The border regions have always been industrial, sensitive to every economic fluctuation. When there was a crisis elsewhere, here it was much worse. When people inside the country were without work for three years, here it was six years. Unemployed workers get ten crowns a week and one bowl of soup a day – and they let that soup cool so that a dirty grey layer of grease settles on top, which they greedily scrape off and carry home to their children on bread. Today, the economic misery in the border regions has several other peculiar features: sales have dropped for the textile factories because they are mostly outfitted for retail drapery and those who have

---

17 Josef Bürckel (1894–1944), Nazi Governor of Austria. Wistrich notes: 'A talented organizer and shrewd politician, Bürckel sought to bring to a halt the orgy of violence and indiscriminate robbery against Jews, which accompanied the Anschluss, by issuing decrees requiring all Nazi commissars who had taken control of Jewish businesses to report their actions. In some cases he even instituted criminal proceedings against those who had stolen assets for themselves.' Wistrich, *Who's Who in Nazi Germany*, p. 27.

retail drapery businesses are Jews. The Jews, however, are not order-
ing goods because their shops are empty of customers and supplies
lie untouched on the shelves. Henlein guards stand in front of the
doors – Nazi youths – and they note down or photograph everyone
who enters. I have observed these nasty fourteen-year-old fellows
myself for about three hours. When the buyer is someone over
whom they have power, he can be certain that a threat will await
him the next day: one more time and you will lose your job; you
are a traitor to the nation. This practice, of course, cripples the
factories directly and the workers who are dismissed bear the consequences. Obviously *only* those who do not support Henlein are
dismissed.

Other factories, for example, glass works, have lost a great deal
on exports to Germany. Goods are no longer sent there on account
of the strict German foreign exchange provisions and this decrease
amounts to 25 percent, sometimes 75 percent and, on average, to
about half of production. Henlein's propaganda, however, does not
say: Germany abandons the people who declare allegiance to it and
intensifies their difficult predicament with an artificially imposed
hunger. On the contrary, Henlein's propaganda says: after the
*Anschluss*, there will be no foreign exchange provisions.

After the events in Vienna, capital was moved *en masse* from the
region. It was withdrawn from the small Czech savings banks and
transferred either to central institutions in Prague or to the *Credi-
tanstalt der deutschen Sparkassen*. Mortgages that had already been
negotiated were cancelled all over the region with the blatant justification: the political conditions are unstable. Half-finished houses
were left without roofs, new homes were no longer built, the building trade collapsed and many construction workers – the local
German and Czech social democrats and communists – were left
without work.

In some cases it happened that orders from America, England and
France were cancelled in the factories in the border regions with
the beautiful and lucid justification: we do not place orders with
industrialists who work against their own state. A superb and well-
intended, but double-edged, gesture. Superb because we can
truthfully say to the Henlein industrialists: now you see where you
are leading the country. Double-edged because it results in more
dismissals and once again it is only the social democrats who lose
their jobs. With a sneer to boot: there you see – that is how your
protectors look after you!

On such an economically explosive soil, of course, it is easy to
practice terror *as long as the association of German industrialists is*

*permitted to use it!* The members of the association of German industrialists are – except for rare and, of course, wonderful exceptions –
*all* SdP members. They all submit to the orders of the SdP and they
all participate in the Nazi economic oppression. Without them, the
membership of Henlein's party would be reduced to a third of its
size because they alone provide Nazi ideology with a genuine
weapon. The terror depends on them; they alone carry out this
terror.

[Seven lines censored.]

The work committees at the Henlein factories can no longer
promote the interests of the labourers. The work committees belong
to DAG – *Deutsche Arbeiter Gewerkschaft* – and these unions are
supported and controlled by the employer.[18] It is exactly the same
method of liquidating social institutions as in Germany: the institution remains, but the content is deleted. The members of the
work committee are German and the employers are also German;
they all raise their right arms; they all shout *Sieg Heil!* and walk
together on May Day in the Nazi procession. That is all they have
in common, but on the soil of this state social institutions have
ceased to be an instrument of social progress and are permitted to
operate as an instrument of Nazi oppression. Because you must,
please, finally understand one thing: if anyone in these parts, on
this volcano, the eruption of which would shake Europe, if anyone
supports the right to democratic thought, it is the Czechs, the
*German* and Czech social democrats and today also the communists.
To put it in ordinary and non-partisan language: working people
and poor people, the very poorest. With sacrifices greater than you
can imagine, with a strength greater than you can understand. They
are the front-line soldiers taking the first hit. That procession in
Czechoslovak uniform is marching today for their sake. On the
whole, they have held up well under the first hit. Let us thank them
for it.

Labour offices do not have an easy job in this region. That is,
there is no regulation specifying that a factory owner must accept
unemployed workers *in the order in which they apply*. The clerks at
the labour office are members of the labour parties, but the bosses
are often Henlein's people – or at least people frightened by
Henlein. If a factory owner is hiring new workers at all, he first
makes the selection *on his own* and then gives the labour office a
list of the workers to be supplied. Those selected are, of course,
Henlein's men. I spoke with a communist who is in his seventh

---

18 German Workers' Union.

year without a job, while Henlein's workers find jobs even when
they have only been unemployed for half a year. Can you imagine
what it means to be without an income for seven years? He has not
defected. And he is not the only one.

## The Sources of Terror Outside the Factory: How Will We Fight Them?

Until we manage to alleviate this enormous pressure to which
people are exposed, we can do nothing but shrug our shoulders
regretfully when they say that they cannot go on any longer. Why,
however, do people go over to the SdP when they are not even
exposed to this pressure? How can one explain, for example, that
all of the teachers at the *state* schools all over the border regions
were in the SdP processions? (I was in twenty-seven communities
and did not discover a single exception.)

This can be explained by three psychological factors:
1. The mood that developed after the events in Austria.
2. The remarkably well organised whisper campaign that creeps
   over the entire region like a plague and says: hurry! hurry! Or
   tomorrow you will be cast aside! I am even beginning to believe
   that the feared chancellor of the Third Reich is an amiable and
   innocent child in comparison with the German minister of propaganda.
3. Our utter inability to produce democratic propaganda to counter
   the Nazi propaganda. The first two factors are altogether obvious
   and clear. It is understandable that Henlein's men, after Austria,
   imagined that they would have a peaceful stroll into the Third
   Reich. We know all sorts of things about the whisper campaign
   and I still have all sorts of things to say about it. The third factor,
   of course, is something that is hard to fathom.

Germans live up here in the north, as everyone knows. Staunch
Germans, they do not speak Czech; they are at home here and they
speak German. Yet before 1933, both Czech and German gendarmes
and the excisemen lived here in complete harmony and peace. The
Germans came to Bohemia for a beer and the Czechs went to
Germany. They knew one another and behaved politely. After
Hitler's victory in Germany, that changed overnight. Different
people came from Germany. The old ones disappeared without a
trace. The passable relations grew taut as a string and remained taut.
Neither the Czechs nor the Germans felt like trying to communicate any longer. The last five years, truly, have not improved

relations. For those five long years, people in the region went home from work exhausted and run-down and the only entertainment they had was the radio. The radio is today what print was in the age of the Reformation. In the age of the Reformation, print made it possible for people to have their own Bibles. In our age, the radio makes it possible for all people to have concerts, entertainment, sports reports and, of course, news reports, in their kitchens at home. For five years, all they had to do was turn the dial and Nazi ideology from German stations rushed right into the flats of people in the border regions – of course, they tuned in a station they understood!

[Two lines censored.]

and as a counterbalance, we broadcast half an hour, usually dull and indigestible, of German radio. Well, by now they are perfectly trained, persuaded and shouted down; they parrot the phrases about space for the nation and all those things that you can read about every day in the *Zeit*. Today – they have finally acquired a German transmitter. But in the German Henlein journal *Der Sudetenfunk* there is not a single word, not even today, about the existence of the German transmitter; it goes without saying that its programme is not listed there.

Or: in one border town I found six large cinemas. Five were running German films that were remarkably sub-standard, clearly shot for the Sudeten region, including weekly newsreels. The sixth was showing: *The Dragoons of Klatovy*.[19]

[Eight lines censored.]

Or: in Czechoslovakia there are, I suspect, various regulations about the import of Reich German newspapers. Completely pointless, believe me. Because in Czechoslovakia so many Nazi newspapers are published that other countries are flooded with them. Illustrated weeklies where there is Mr Henlein, nothing but Mr Henlein and a forest of raised right arms, a car festooned with Nazis, formations in uniform, youth, the changing of flags, the changing of the guard, the salute to the Nazi banner, the parade of Nazi workers on May Day – the same images of enthusiasm that we saw in Vienna, in Linz and in Graz, except that there they appeared in the days when Germany occupied Austria. Here, we can see them even today. *Der Aufbruch, Rundschau, Der Kamerad* (a campaign

---

19 *Klatovští dragouni* (1937), a film of sub-standard quality directed by Karel
　　Špelina, was a romantic comedy set against a backdrop of military exercises.
　　Václav Březina, *Lexikon českého filmu. 2000 filmů 1930–1997* (Encyclopaedia of
　　Czech Film. 2,000 Films from 1930–1997), Prague, 1997, p. 176.

drawing on the front page from 20 May: a German stands with his legs spread, watching two wretched figures; the caption reads: send them back to the red paradise!), *B. Kamnitzer Zeitung, Illustrierte Presse* (published by Mr Lischka, Prague), *Zeitspiegel*. There is not a single German democratic newspaper to counter the flood of these publications. They do exist here – *Volksbote*, for example – but the subscribers mostly – in the smaller communities all – receive them by post or from their distributor because to receive them publicly would mean losing their jobs. In the smaller towns the Henlein youth has divided the community into individual blocks and the boys watch over the houses; they note down who visits whom and, above all, who subscribes to what newspapers. For the five years that this atmosphere has lasted, we have done almost nothing to support those people in the German camp who resisted fascism. In those five years not one of us – not even in the last few months – has been able to recognise one of the most important truths of our time, a truth that will shape the fate of Europe: that one German is not like another.

# Hundreds of Thousands Looking for No-Man's-Land

27 July 1938, *Přítomnost*

## *Ahasuerus on Vinohradská Street*

On quiet and calm Vinohradská Street, a man stopped me.[20] He was tattered and wretched, but he was not begging. Perhaps a Jew needs courage even to make a request if he has lived through the liberation of Austria. 'Do you speak German?' 'Yes.' 'Are you a Jew?' 'I'm not.' It was certainly that strange form of address that compelled me to turn around and watch his disappointed back because I realised that this man did not dare to ask for help from someone who was not Jewish – in the middle of Prague, in the middle of Europe, on a calm, sunny afternoon in 1938. In recent years we have heard many stories like his. He had broken teeth and bloody gums; he had rags instead of clothes; he did not have a single heller and had not eaten for many hours.[21] He did not spend the nights in any one place – for fear that they would send him back. He only walked and walked and walked. How long can an exhausted and humiliated man without money walk before a patrol stops him? Maybe they will stop him tomorrow or the day after tomorrow. They will not have any choice but to send him back because caravans of wretched people would come if the border opened up somewhere. Send him back – but to where? He does not have documents and does not know anything about his relatives. The Czechoslovak authorities will send him to the border of the former Austria and at the border of his state they will not accept him. A postal package must be delivered to the owner's hands, but a human package is set down at the border and told: run! The human package runs a few steps on his own before the nearest patrol catches him. In Prague there was a man who held the record for such desperate wanderings: he had been driven away from the various borders of various states sixty times.

---

20 Ahasuerus is one of the names given to the Wandering Jew who is, according to legend, condemned to wander over the earth until the Second Coming of Christ. Vinohradská is the main street in the Vinohrady district in Prague.

21 The heller is an old Austrian coin of low value.

The subheading of the social democratic newspaper *Arbeiter-zeitung* – while it was still being published – was a very beautiful sentence: '*So lange es Stärkere gibt, immer auf der Seite der Schwächeren.*'[22] More than anything else, I would like to know how those wonderful, brave, manly and politically conscious Viennese *workers* are behaving towards the weakest of the weak, the persecuted Viennese Jews. Why is there no news about it? I am stricken with horror when I hear that many Austrian workers look on the torture of the Jews with relative calm. If this is true, it is further proof that hatred of Jews slumbers even in the best of people and there is nothing easier than to waken it.

## The Jews as a Nation?

There are many Jews in the world today who believe in the Jews as a nation, although science does not recognise them as such, considering them rather a caste, which, although scattered for a thousand years, has preserved many characteristic qualities, without having a common language, a common culture or a continuous territory of its own. In some countries, Jews were maintained as a caste by force and thus, of course, many features of their nationality were preserved very distinctly, although this did not suffice to give Jews what we would call a national character. On the contrary, Jews have become rooted in the most diverse nations, educating themselves in the diverse cultures – often also creating those cultures to a large extent – and accepting the legal basis of this or that state. Wherever the moral and legal supports of the social order collapsed after thousands of years, however, the first blow always fell on the Jews. I spoke with two Jews as different from one another as two worlds. One was Hungarian, a writer, a cultivated man, alert, with that charming, melancholy sense of humour, resigned to the true essence of things, which distinguishes the best representatives of this remarkable element. He shrugged his shoulders and told me: 'I would like to write the handbook: *How to Emigrate*. I know what it's like: I've already emigrated five times.' The other man was a peasant in Slovakia, an alien from somewhere in Poland who had no trace of the Jewish intellectual qualities as we know them: a man employed by the land and focused on the land. When I asked if he was renting the field and the house, or if they were his, he too shrugged his shoulders and said: 'What good is a house to a Jew? One day he will flee anyway.'

---

22 'As long as there are stronger ones, always [be] on the side of the weaker ones.'

You see – *that* is what they all have in common. The Jewish worker and peasant in the East like the Jewish lawyer, businessman, doctor and writer in the West – the knowledge that they will one day flee. The knowledge that the social and legal order they abide by – the culture they love, the language that has become their mother tongue – all of this can falter after the first blow and there will be no help anywhere.

## The Retraining of Jewish Youth

It is no wonder that a longing for power, which is a kind of security of one's own making, is more developed among the Jews than among other people. One can gain power all sorts of ways: with money, for instance, or education. Because the Jews lacked land a great many of them were forced into economic enterprise and for this reason modern capitalism is, at first sight, 'a creation of the Jews'. At least, it is very easy to make this assertion and exploit it according to the circumstances. Education gives a person an opportunity to pursue one of the so-called free professions: therefore many Jews are lawyers, journalists, doctors, scholars and so on. 'I treated sixty-thousand German children,' wrote the Viennese paediatrician Dr Knöpflmacher, before he shot himself – 'and this is what I have brought upon myself.' A tenacious vitality and unsentimental understanding of reality characterise this remarkable, dispersed element. Do you know what Jews in Germany have been doing for the past five hellish years? They are feverishly working on the retraining of their youth. Just as previously Jewish boys used to go and study, today they are learning the locksmith's trade, mechanics, plumbing, joinery, gardening and other manual occupations. In Austria, thousands of Jews are learning skills that they can use for colonisation – irrigation, the cultivation of heavy soil, bricklaying, road construction. They are people who count on exceptional good luck, hoping that they will be permitted to move to southern Australia or South America, to some wilderness or steppe. The old game of Fate will repeat itself: these tenacious people will prevail against all obstacles, they will settle the country, establish themselves there, build their homes, cultivate the earth literally 'by the sweat of their brow', only to hear, three generations later, that they are foreigners and exploiters. I spoke with a woman through whose hands all Jewish émigrés who come to Prague pass. She demonstrated to me that, based on the experiences to date, all attempts by Jews to colonise had come to ruin in the third generation – except for Palestine. But Palestine is a special case and has not yet been resolved by far.

As trained and qualified *tradesmen*, thousands of Jews are now trying to find a secure place in the world. As soon as one of them gets a foothold somewhere at the other end of the globe, you can be sure that before long he will help his near and distant relations. After a while, two or three are working and they become a ladder over which cousins, uncles, brothers-in-law, grandfathers and fathers-in-law will climb, with their wives and children, because a thousand years' experience of emigration has taught them a beautiful and admirable solidarity. About a year ago a young Jew left Prague with his wife to go all the way to the Philippines. He left empty-handed, after many hardships. There, however, they welcomed him with open arms and a touching hospitality and soon he found work. There was a little Jewish colony, Polish émigrés who had gone there during the last wave of anti-Semitism that passed over Europe: before the World War. 'They still hadn't forgotten,' the young man wrote. 'I'm not surprised. I won't forget either.'

## *Ahasuerus, Who Can No Longer Even Wander*

Recently, I spoke with two Germans. With a businessman from North Bohemia, a supporter of Henlein who was an activist until not too long ago, an educated, well-read man with the kind of business prudence that precludes total blindness.[23] In response to my question about what should be done, in his opinion, with the half a million Jews who were supposed to emigrate from former Austria by the end of four years, he shrugged his shoulders and said with a slightly ironical smile: 'That is, to be sure, a troublesome matter. Perhaps the states that moan so much on their behalf will take them in?'

'Why should they take them in? Those Jews are citizens of the German state, after all. Perhaps in a year it will occur to the German Reich to expel all the socialists and then perhaps all the safe-crackers, tuberculosis sufferers and black-eyed people? What would happen if every state acted like that?'

'Of course, of course, it's bad, it's very bad. I myself wonder where those people will go,' he said politely, without conviction.

---

23 The word 'activist' here refers to Bohemian Germans who demonstrated support for the Czechoslovak state through their participation in parliamentary politics.

I travelled in a train with an Austrian who was going to visit relatives in Česká Lípa.[24] A young man, apparently an industrialist
from 'Štájrn', tanned, healthy, narrow-minded.[25] He began to talk
very aggressively, without being invited to do so: 'Things are good
in Austria now. We don't have unemployment like you do here and
everyone is doing well.'

'It would be nice if that were actually true, but I'm afraid you are
mistaken,' I answered.

He rose to his feet and straightened up; the entire carriage froze
because the Austrian looked like he wanted to attack me.

'What can you know about that? Where did you learn that?'

'Partly from the newspapers, partly from the stories of people
who come from Austria. Jews, for example, certainly aren't doing
well in Austria and almost all of them are unemployed.'

Then something happened to the man that is difficult for me to
describe. He broke into proud, warbling laughter and slapped his
thighs, stuffed into short trousers; he began to bounce about on the
bench and sputter with enthusiasm. 'Hohoho, hehehe, you're right
about that, upon my soul, the Jews aren't doing well, you guessed
it. No, the Jews aren't doing well at all, on the contrary ... hehehe,
they're doing very badly.'

In a strange fit of choking, saliva and sadistic delight, the words
died out in the total silence of the astounded carriage. We all stared
as if spellbound. The man beside me, clearly a farmer, spat and
moved away. The rest of us followed. The Austrian remained alone
in the compartment.

There you have plainly the first and the last degree on the scale
of how the Germans regard the fate of the German Jews. Truly, they
are doing badly.

What is happening to Jews in Austria is worse than anything they
have experienced thus far. Not even what they lived through in
Germany in 1933 was so terrible. There it was a horrible, cruel and
bloody pogrom. Jewish history is full of pogroms – in the most
diverse ages and countries people were murdered, stripped of their
possessions, expelled from the land. In Austria there is, in addition
to this sort of pogrom, something entirely new. Something purely
German and unique in history in its flagrancy, its thorough inhu-
manity and legal brutality: *a cold pogrom.*

---

24 Česká Lípa (Böhmisch Leipa) is a city in North Bohemia. At the turn of the
century, the population was almost entirely Bohemian German. The encyclopaedia *Ottův slovník naučný* (published in Prague, 1888–1908), lists the
population as 10,406, including 305 Czechs and 560 Jews.

25 Štájrn refers to Styria, an alpine province of Austria, annexed by Hitler in 1938.

A cold pogrom involves programmatic, calm regulations introduced by the state that do not deprive the Jews of life, but deprive
them of any kind of possibility of living. Jews in Vienna sit in terror
in their apartments, trembling when someone rings at the door.
Nazi patrols are constantly going around. An old and ailing Jew
draws the curtains shut after lunch so that he can fall asleep. A
short while later, a patrol rings: why are the curtains shut? Does the
Jew perhaps have an Aryan girl with him? Don't let it happen again!
Sometimes the patrol rings to take the wife, the children and the
husband away to labour groups. It drives them to the SS or SA
barracks and orders them to clean the toilets, scrub the corridors,
wash the dishes. Sometimes it assigns them to hard labour outside
the city: road building, ditch digging, expanding the concentration
camps. Lawyers, doctors, writers and businessmen work until they
collapse with a spade and a hoe that they do not know how to use.
Even women and girls work, even pregnant women. Sometimes
they return home from this labour; sometimes they never return.
In all of Vienna there is hardly a single family that is not missing
someone. Jews get up at two o'clock at night and leave for the
woods outside Vienna because the Nazi patrols go around in the
early morning. Or they move from one apartment to another and
sit up all night long in the homes of friends, afraid to be alone at
night.

The city of Vienna began to shut its public gardens to Jews – the
other Austrian cities, of course, immediately followed suit. First the
Lainzer Tiergarten was closed, then the Türkenschanzpark, the
Schönbrunn, the Stadtpark. The benches in the small gardens of the
Vienna suburbs were provided with two kinds of notices: *Nicht für
Juden* – and *Nur für Juden.*[26] It is interesting that Prince Liechten-
stein refused to close his magnificent garden to the Jews; on the
contrary, he put it completely at their disposal. It is full from
morning to evening. Otherwise the Jewish women go with their
infants, carriages and children – to the cemetery. A sad, strange
garden for small children.

On 21 June, however, the international congress for the protection of children, organised by the *Association Internationale pour la
protection de l'enfance*, was opened in Frankfurt, *under the patronage
of Josef Goebbels.*[27] The Third Reich arranged a research trip for the

---

26 'Not for Jews – For Jews only.'

27 Paul Josef Goebbels (1897–1945), the German Nazi leader who became minister
of propaganda in 1933.

participants at the congress through northern and southern Germany, in order to show them how the Third Reich cares for its children. I do not know if the Third Reich also showed them how it cares for the children of Jewish citizens of the German state: whether or not it said that Jewish children either are not allowed to go to school at all, or must sit there on special benches, holding in their hands textbooks that teem with slurs against the Jews. They definitely are not allowed to study at universities. They are excluded from all aid and support programmes. They are not allowed to go to any playgrounds, spas or summer resorts. I do not even know for sure what they are allowed to do. Colonel Locker-Lampson, a conservative English member of parliament, sent a telegraph to Hitler: 'All of us Englishmen, who have in mind the good of Germany, observe with regret that your attacks are directed only against the powerless minorities. Why do you only fall upon the weak and defenceless? If you have to attack someone, why don't you choose someone as strong as yourselves?'

Well, that is the way the Third Reich behaves towards its citizens, the same Third Reich that, for months now, has been thundering from all loudspeakers about how oppressed the Czechoslovak Germans are.

One woman – she was not Jewish – witnessed an incident in the Prater, which seems more terrible to me than the accounts of torture: a group of SA 'men' (soon we will have to put this word in quotation marks because it differs so much from our conception of what a man is) led a crowd of Jews to a tree and forced them to climb into the branches and 'act like birds'.[28] Down below stood armed men; up above in the branches, adults, bearded Jews, young women and boys squatted and at the cry 'what do birds do?', they answered: peep, peep, peep, tweet, tweet! The woman fled as if hounded, afraid she would lose her mind.

Landlords in whose buildings a few Jews live have received an order to evict their Jewish tenants. By contrast, landlords in whose buildings many Jews live must give notice to their Aryan tenants and accept evicted Jews into the vacated apartments. Thus 'Jewish' buildings and 'Aryan' buildings are created. (The Aryan owner of a building, of course, can throw Jewish tenants out on the street immediately, without bothering to arrange alternative accommodation.) *Gauleiter* Bürckel has made no secret of the view that this provision is the beginning of a new ghetto.

---

28 The Prater is a large amusement park in Vienna, on an island in the Danube. Gilbert describes the same incident. See: Martin Gilbert, *The Holocaust. The Jewish Tragedy*, London, 1987, p. 60.

Where would you go if you were afraid that someone would ring at the door and drag you off to a concentration camp? – Into the street? But the policeman at the crossroads will stop you and ask: are you a Jew? If he receives a reply in the affirmative, he will stop the nearest patrol and hand you over. – To the café? But in the cafés there are frequent raids hunting for Jews. Some they lead away, some they leave. Those who are spared this time will get a stamp on their hands, like pigs or cattle; during the next raid all they will be able to do is hold out their hands. – To the cinema? But almost every screening in the cinema is interrupted, the lights are turned on and Jews must leave. Jews are not allowed to go to the theatre. So where then? Over the border? But that is closed. A Jew, a Czechoslovak citizen, wants to go to Prague. He picks up the telephone in order to inquire if he is permitted to leave Vienna. When he calls the relevant office, the following conversation takes place:

'Could you please give me some information ...'

'Aryan or non-Aryan?' the voice on the telephone interrupts him. 'Non-Aryan ...'

'No information.' The phone goes down with a click.

If a Jew has property, he may one day receive a notification: in the interest of the state it is necessary that you sell your property. The Jew, of course, immediately complies and writes down how much the property is probably worth, declares that he is willing to sell it 'in the interest of the state', signs it and sends it off. He receives a reply by return mail that a court assessor will come to his house. He actually does appear and appraises the villa and the garden – at two marks. The document receives an official stamp, everything has been done according to law and on the Austrian streets there is one more beggar.

The 'Aryanisation' of shops and businesses is another net through which no one slips. Jewish shopkeepers have been forced to lay off their employees. The *Gerngross* firm, for example, a draper's shop like many others in Vienna, laid off 180 Jewish employees in a single day. The Reich German commissar appears at the store and from that moment on it is entirely under his control, submits to his orders and his management. Only Jews, of course, buy from a Jewish shopkeeper – if they are still able to buy anything at all. Entire businesses thus fall into state hands without compensation or into the hands of Reich German private persons. In two days, for example, twenty-five large enterprises were 'Aryanised' in Austria in this way (sanatoriums, a brewery, factories, department stores and so on). Mischitz, the Secretary of the Vienna Commission 'for Aryanisation', has stated that first it is necessary to

Aryanise those businesses that compete with Aryan concerns. That means: those that the state still needs have to be left alone. But even those businesses that remain in the hands of Jews are exposed to boycotts, the withdrawal of credit and merciless tax burdens. The bank accounts of Jews are frozen; confidentiality is violated. Taxes are assessed arbitrarily and a 'tax offence' is almost always a pretext for an arrest. But there are other methods as well. For example, Vienna wine merchants were compelled by a decree to pay the current market price for wine bought before 14 March or else the wine would be confiscated. As the price of wine rose considerably after the *Anschluss*, the price difference amounts to almost 50 percent – and the merchant is ruined at one stroke.[29]

Jews who had cash tried to do the most obvious thing: buy jewels. A ring does not lose its value, it is easy to hide and carry away. Goldsmiths did sell the jewels, but they reported the purchases immediately – or rather the commissars assigned to their shops did. The next day a patrol would turn up at the apartment and take the jewel away.

Thus the beggars and the unemployed increase in number every day. Foreign states – America, in particular – have set up relief kitchens in Vienna and give Jews something to eat at least. The American relief organisation, however, is not allowed to bring in supplies. It is only permitted to use foreign currency to buy goods in Austria. The Third Reich manages to make money even on the soup that a foreign state gives to Austrian citizens. Several times SS men came to the soup kitchens and poured the vat of soup out on the ground before the eyes of the hungry crowd. But this did not pay off. The American consulate reacted immediately; it demonstrated that the soup was its property and insisted on immediate compensation. The next day the Jews received a double portion.

Crowds of Jews trying to get visas stand all night long in front of the foreign consulates. Usually in vain. Most of them do not have passports and if even they did, they could have no hope that the state would open the border. Transit visas are only issued if the owner of the passport has an entry permit for a particular state. Only by chance, every now and then, does someone manage to leave. Is it any wonder that everyone does everything he can to get help from abroad? One Viennese Jew, whose name was, let's say, Goldstein, went to the main post office, requested the New York telephone book and wrote down the addresses of all the Goldsteins

---

29 *Anschluss* (union). German troops entered Austria on 12 March 1938 and Hitler proclaimed the union of Austria with Germany on the next day.

living in New York. There were quite a few of them. A Jew can only
get to America if he has a guarantee from some relative living there
who pledges his entire property as security that the immigrant will
not become a burden on public funds; this guarantee is called an
affidavit and is the coveted dream of all German Jews today. So our
Goldstein wrote a letter to all the American Goldsteins in New York
in which he described his situation in detail and asked for help –
for this affidavit. There were many, many identical letters – and sure
enough there was some Goldstein in New York who sent the affidavit to a total stranger whom he had never seen. This is not an
anecdote. It is the truth. This little truth indicates that a Jewish solidarity watches over a Jewish fate because there is no Jew in the
world who does not carry deep in his soul the thought: tomorrow
it could happen to me. This solidarity is sometimes touching,
delightful and naïve. A Jewish grandmother lives here in Prague, an
Orthodox Jew who has grandsons in Germany. Because there was
so much talk about how Jews in Germany needed Aryan grand-
mothers, this old woman decided to sacrifice what was most sacred
to her: in order to help her young grandchildren, she had herself
baptised.

Ahasuerus has come to a stop. There are people who are already
too tired and simply do not want to go any further. I think that
there are many Jews who are more afraid of humiliation than of
blows – and this humiliation cannot even be described. They are
dying voluntarily. Perhaps even a little proudly, silently and
disdainfully. In Vienna alone eight thousand souls have already left
the world in this way. Only at night is one permitted to bury and
there are so many burials that they continue even on Saturdays. A
Jewish shopkeeper in the Praterstrasse killed himself along with his
wife, son, daughter-in-law and five-year-old grandson. The next
day, SS men hung a notice on the closed shop: *Zur Nachahmung
dringend empfohlen! (Recommended emphatically as an example!)* Yes,
that is how a proud and brave German SS man behaves.

It seems that there is only one route left for Viennese Jews: from
the Westbahnhof to Dachau.[30] Every week in the early hours of the
morning a train stands on the rails, carrying Viennese Jews to a
concentration camp. Eight carriages, one man beside the next. They
sit next to one another, shoulder to shoulder, heads resting against
the seats, hands motionless in their laps, faces as if they had been

---

30 The Westbahnhof is a railway station in Vienna. Dachau was the first Nazi
concentration camp in Germany, created in March 1933 and located on the
outskirts of the town of Dachau, twelve miles north of Munich. It was notori-
ous for the medical experiments performed on the inmates there.

carved. They sit thus in numb despair for five, six hours, until the train moves. Police cars take the captives right to the platform, so that the crowds thronging at the train station cannot learn if a father, brother, husband or son is among those brought in.

Of course: it is not only Jews who suffer this fate but also Aryan Germans who are troublesome for the regime. Not even the fate of Aryan Germans is enviable. In the past few days, Viennese Czechs have also been arrested.

## Will the World Find a Solution?

It seems to me that for the moment this is out of sight for the majority, although many Jews still find some kind of salvation. There are Jews who believe in Palestine, in the revival of the Jewish nation, in a Jewish upbringing, Jewish culture and Jewish home. We can see, however, what kind of solution Palestine is. Although the work there is admirable and the achievements immense, it can never accept even a third of those who are seeking a home. It cannot, therefore, become the territorial base for the fifteen million Jews dispersed over the world. It is because the Jewish Diaspora is world-wide that the fate of the Jews is connected to and depends on whether or not the world takes the next step towards barbarism or towards freedom. It is no coincidence that there are relatively so many Jews in the socialist movement. More than anyone else, Jews are in need of social justice and *true* civic equality. There are a few fortunate countries in the world where it is impossible to stir up anti-Semitism. When you seek an explanation for this, you will find that the main reason is the absolute integration of the Jews with the nation in the midst of which they have lived for centuries. I believe that the physical and psychological integration of the Jews with the other nations is the only humane, reasonable and dignified solution – if the world gives them the chance.

# Beyond Our Strength
## 12 October 1938, *Přítomnost*

I am not one of those people who are enthralled by beautiful words like rights, justice and morality. Not that I wouldn't defend passionately their *real* and *true* meaning and sound, which have always seemed to me like the ringing of the one true coin in the world. But whoever has ears to hear and eyes to see has always caught these words on the lips of the powerful at times when they were laying a burden on the powerless. In recent years, too much injustice has been committed to the sound of marching music in the name of rights and humanity. Too many people have fallen for peace, to the jubilation of the world. Hard blows falling on the rights of the people have always been wrapped in the veils of moral and noble phrases. No one in the world is so hungry for nobility and rights as the poor because they need them like their daily bread. People were told many beautiful falsehoods whenever it was necessary to compel them to act cruelly, without understanding what they were doing. I say this because I can only write the following lines if I am allowed to write them *truly* clearly, honestly and bluntly.

On these pages I advocated support and protection for the Sudeten democrats with all my strength, *as long as the Czechoslovak state was in a position to give them support and protection*. I think it is beyond doubt that I wish this for them as ardently today as I did yesterday. The situation is such, however, that today the Czechoslovak state *cannot give* them this support and protection. This is a bitter predicament; I do not know if it is more painful for us or for them. It is necessary, however, *to state this clearly* instead of making allusions and vague statements and hushing things up. Not only that: it is necessary to realise clearly that although we can no longer do very much, *something must happen soon*.

This is how things stand: whether the boundaries of the occupied fifth zone remain as harsh as they are today, or whether they change a little bit, many Czechs who naturally belong here will be left on the other side of the border.[31] Thus far, no one knows how the complex option and property questions facing each individual will be resolved. Naturally, the Czechs in the Third Reich who want to return to the Czech Lands have first priority. A lot of Czech intellectuals will most likely return here from Slovakia and Sub-Carpathian Ruthenia; for a while, at least, they will certainly be out of work. This alone will result in the enormous overpopulation of the fragment of the Czech Lands that remains. We have, however, become very impoverished. There is no doubt that we will continue to exist, but it is clear that we will be worse off than before and that is true for each one of us. It will be a while before we begin to build new highways, new factories and train lines, as the newspapers write.

Above all it is necessary to liquidate yesterday. Unless we are able, in a peaceful and orderly manner, to liquidate economically what was ours yesterday and at the same time to master all the consequences of the enormous transfer of hundreds of thousands of people, we will resemble a life-raft that, bearing passengers to safety from a sinking ship, takes on more people than it can carry.

Democratic Germans are coming from the Sudetenland, occupied by the German army. I will not describe to you at length what they are living through, what they have experienced in their homes and what awaits them if they are forced to return. Many have been dragged off to the Third Reich, as were Czech inhabitants of the borderlands, gendarmes and excisemen. Those who want to flee now are no longer permitted to do so. Those who fled in time are here without a home, without food, without money, without work and without the prospect of work. There are women here who have no idea where their husbands are and do not know how or if they will meet them again. There are even children here on their own. All over Prague there is hardly a single building that doesn't house several cowering refugees. They are the lucky ones who have some acquaintance here. Thousands of people, however, have fled into the unknown. I do not want to describe their misery, anxiety and privation. Over the last five years we have seen many times how Germans live when they are fleeing from German national solidarity. The refugees here are living exactly like that.

31 The Munich Agreement of 30 September 1938 delineated four zones to be occupied by German troops in the first week of October. A fifth zone of territory to be ceded to Germany was to be decided upon by an international commission including representatives from Czechoslovakia and the countries that had signed the Munich Agreement. Theodor Prochazka, 'The Second Republic, 1938–1939', *A History of the Czechoslovak Republic 1918–1948*, pp. 255–270, see p. 256.

I am a Czech witness to the fact that, for five years, those people in the north stood up for the Czechoslovak Republic, each separately and all of them together, with unbelievable courage and fortitude. They have been fighting for five years. Neither the Czechoslovak Republic nor anyone of us can or should forget that. Those people, however, cannot survive on ardent gratitude or pained respect. If there had been a war, we would most likely have several hundred thousand dead today. Instead, in this time of peace, we have several hundred thousand fallen – but those fallen are still alive. A living person wants to eat and survive. We probably cannot continue to provide for them, although they have fallen in our front lines for peace. Even in the horrors of war there is something like a faint reflection of justice: we were all armed and in our places and we would have fallen depending on where the bullet hit. In the horrors of peace, however, there is a truly cruel and distinct injustice: all those who were for us fell.

Well then, we did not make this peace. It was forced on us. Please allow us to note that 'forced' is a mild word. When we open the newspapers, we read about the great recognition that Czechoslovakia has won for the sacrifice it has made for world peace. Wrong. We did no such thing because sacrifices are only made voluntarily. The truth is different: we were sacrificed and we have here among us several hundred thousand of the living fallen, together with several thousand German and Austrian refugees to whom we have granted the right of asylum. The responsibility for these fallen does not rest with us but with the French and English governments who wanted this peace.

Those several hundred thousand refugees and fleeing German democrats represent more than a humanitarian concern. They represent, above all, a troubling internal political problem. If it is not resolved immediately and in a planned manner, the problem could grow into a serious crisis. Czech people are, it is true, patient, kind and good, with a profound sense of right and wrong. But they are, at present, profoundly dejected, harassed and distressed. It is a small, a dangerously small, step from pain and exhaustion, from a great burden and disappointment, to a longing for revenge. Revenge has always been an expression of tormented injustice and it has never been vented in the right direction, but rather in the direction open to it. Revenge is an act of the weak against the weaker. If we are forced to place too heavy a burden on our people, we can be sure against whom their anger will turn. If we – or rather, if the Western great powers – allow people who must scramble for work to start throwing the innocent overboard as well – or over the border (and in that case not only the innocent, but also our fellow fighters) – the Czech people will suffer a profound moral blow, from which they will not easily recover.

We read in the newspapers that in France and England collections are being organised for the benefit of the democratic German refugees. Two million crowns have already arrived in Prague. Perhaps we should say: thank you. I am sorry that I am not able to do so. I imagine that not one of us who has lived through these days, nights and weeks is able to do so. We were silent when our billions were taken away from us – our mountains, forests, mines and train lines, the work of twenty years. Hardly anyone of our generation can feel humble gratitude. We were hard on ourselves – how hard, you can scarcely imagine. We must speak the hard truth to you as well. Because it is not over yet between you, our allies and us. You stood at the cradle of our new state and became its Fates.

Well then: two million is not enough. *It is not enough to make collections.* As much as we respect the private initiatives of people *who are not involved* in our fate – for example, the Swedish appeal to all nations 'in support of starving Czechoslovakia' – what we need is *a plan on the part of the Western great powers* to save the people we can no longer provide for because our hands have been tied. I am very familiar with such collections – bowls of soup and threadbare coats for homeless people. That is immediate aid, but immediate aid is not the issue. For the moment, no one is starving in Czechoslovakia. We too will serve out bowls of soup. We are already serving them. What is at stake is not aid for starving Czechoslovakia – but rather how and where to move people who are standing between two torments: the torment of concentration camps in the Third Reich and the torment of unemployment in an impoverished country that is exerting all its strength to secure its future and provide work for its people. For these people, Czechoslovakia can be a transfer station. But how can one create a transfer station when the borders of all states are hermetically sealed, admitting only a few dozen people after endless capital guarantees, while hundreds of thousands without a single heller cannot go anywhere? The division of Czechoslovakia not only prevented a war, it also spared the French and most likely also the English government great financial losses. A fraction of those losses would be enough to help the German refugees in Czechoslovakia find a new existence.

It is necessary above all:

1. To open the borders of one of the French or English dominions to a million German émigrés.
2. To use the money that is scraped together not for the endless boiling of futile bowls of soup for the hungry – a living person is hungry today, tomorrow, the day after tomorrow, in a year's time, in ten years' time, until his death – but for the planned and orderly emigration of these people and for their colonisation opportunities.
3. To inform the Czechoslovak government how long it can safely count on this aid. You were able to act very quickly – even with lightning speed – when the 'poor, oppressed supporters of Henlein' were at stake.[32] It is necessary to act just as quickly when what is at stake is a real injustice perpetrated against people who were guardians of the principle of democracy – and hence guardians of *your* principle – and who fell for it and yet remained alive.
4. If the Czechoslovak government knows the exact and binding date when these people can depart with your help, it will certainly find temporary aid for them, even in these days. For a short time, we all want to help, we can and we must help.

I believe that this is the minimum degree of responsibility you should bear for the peace that cost you so little.

---

32 The British had listened sympathetically to the grievances of the Sudeten Germans represented by Konrad Henlein and had pressured the Czechoslovak government to make concessions to the German minority. Cornwall comments: 'the pro-Sudeten reports of the British minister in Prague had been crucial both in making the British policy-makers sympathetic to the German minority and suspicious of Czech behaviour, and in enabling them to justify appeasement over this issue and its complete internationalisation in 1938.' Mark Cornwall, 'Dr Edvard Beneš and Czechoslovakia's German Minority, 1918-1943', *The Czech and Slovak Experience*, ed. John Morison, Houndmills, 1992, pp. 167–202, see p. 185.

# What Remains of the Communist Party?

## 26 October 1938, *Přítomnost*

Whatever happened in years past with the Communist Party [CPC], it never happened quietly. This party was always known for its strong and loud words. Strong words were one of the weapons it used to proclaim its intentions to the world. Communist resolutions, protests and goals accompanied the communist demonstrations, processions and manifestations. It is characteristic of these times of ours that the greatest event in the history of the Communist Party – that is, its suspension and exclusion from public political life – happened so quietly and as a matter of course.[33] Yet this was not a minor event, as the Czechoslovak Communist Party was the last legal section of the Comintern in Central Europe. To all those who reflect on the changed conditions in the new Czechoslovakia it seems that this event was an obvious consequence of the Munich Agreement. The silence that has accompanied the suspension of activities of the CPC is all the more strange as in recent years the Communist Party has in fact done nothing else but prepare for the defence of the Czechoslovak Republic. Now that it too has been struck by the new developments in Europe, the CPC stands powerless before this turn of events; perhaps it is not even surprised by the silence that has spread around it.

The news of the suspension of activity of the Communist Party raises the question of what good this party did for the people. These days, balance sheets do not bear much scrutiny. People, in so far as they were represented by the Communist Party, will probably ask what they gained from it. Being a member of the Communist Party was never easy. On account of the party card, people went without work longer than others did and many people found themselves in social and political conflict with their neighbours because of their party membership. The Communist Party, accepting the sacrifices of its members, had to be aware that these sacrifices were not made lightly. The workers and farmers, in joining the organisation of the

---

33 'The activities of the Communist party were prohibited in Slovakia on October 9 [1938], in the Czech provinces on October 20. On December 27, the party was dissolved.' Theodor Prochazka, 'The Second Republic', p. 262.

Communist Party, were firmly convinced that they were joining a party that wanted and was able to defend their political and material interests. Only because they were firmly convinced of this did they take upon themselves the risk of membership in the Communist Party – because it really did not mean anything else but risk. Most of the members of the Communist Party were not even motivated by the desire for immediate material improvement of their circumstances, but rather by the conviction that it was necessary to establish a political and economic state in the world that 'would be able to provide jobs, bread and freedom' for the workers and farmers. They expected that this would come about through the Communist Party and *only* through it. They put their faith in it, believing that it would have enough political foresight and enough political power to achieve this for them.

In earlier years, the CPC had been an indirect support for people in their wage battles. That is, 'indirect' because the CPC never had in Czechoslovakia – as it did, for example, in recent years in France or Spain – a direct influence on the social policies of the republic. In the past five years it did not even try to have this indirect influence. At the forefront of the social struggles of the people, one was much more likely to find the Social Democratic Party, which was also much more effective. The red unions were always in a precarious situation. Their members were, for the most part, unskilled or unemployed workers. The red unions were poor and could only offer their members the most meagre support. Yet for years the unemployed remained members of the red unions, with scant or no support at all, knowing that the red unions had less power than the other unions to place their members back into the work force. They remained because they believed very firmly and very honestly that they all had to lend their personal and political weight to these unions, which were striving together with the party for 'jobs, bread, and freedom for the workers'.

In 1933, the Communist Party changed its politics from an offensive to a defensive politics. The 'struggle *for* jobs, bread and freedom' was replaced by the 'struggle *against* fascism'. The CPC decided on this turn-about practically overnight. Looking around for something to lean on, it saw that it had nothing but the pillars it had smashed up until then: 'rotten democracy', 'the bourgeois army', 'the imperialist Czechoslovak government' and the Social Democratic Party, which only yesterday was 'the social bastion of fascism in the ranks of the workers'. It realised that the only way to counter fascism was to support the 'small threatened states against the expansionist lusts of fascism' and to create rapidly a popular front with whoever was willing. This was no small revolution. Literally, it meant changing from the foundation up all the concepts that the members of the CPC had mastered over the course of their long political training. The minds of the workers were not fickle. The life of the Czechoslovak worker was such that he could not keep up with the complex political consciousness acquired through study. His political consciousness had always been expressed in short slogans that could encompass the entire individual and that were often a matter of *faith*, rather than of *consciousness*. When a person has made many sacrifices for the world outlook that fills his entire being, he relinquishes it only with great difficulty. The CPC paid a high price for the turmoil that set in in the ranks of the party after that political turn-about. First and foremost, with the loss of any kind of inner party democracy. As it had no justification for the political change other than the changed foreign politics of the Soviet Union – and it did not openly admit to this justification – the CPC could do nothing but demand blind faith, iron discipline and complete obedience from its members. These qualities are not usually combined with strong opinions or independent political thinking. It was natural that the CPC lost many people who were politically trained, educated and experienced. It lost them in various ways: either they went on their own, or they were expelled, or they remained – absent in heart and spirit – in the hope that the political leadership of the CPC would at least allow them to engage in honest discussion. The old people were replaced by obedient people; obedience was something that the CPC had to demand of its members first and foremost if it was going to persuade a cadre to defend what he had previously been required to destroy. It had to introduce a tough regime and, as is well known, tough regimes are always 'in the interest of the people'. 'In the interest of the people', the CPC insisted that all its members begin to think about things in a different way than they had before. People experienced serious conflicts of conscience and character – and it was these very conflicts that the CPC designated as treasonous, 'Trotskyist', despicable and mendacious.

In organisational terms and within the party this reversal was carried off, although with a certain change in membership and voters. In reality, however, it failed miserably. The Communist Party was never able to convince anyone but its own members that it was *no longer* communist – members who had matured to such an extent in their obedience that the word 'convince' was a mockery of free human judgement. The tragedy of the Communist Party is that when it truly gave up 'revolutionary politics' for good and put itself and its membership completely at the disposal of the foreign policies of the Soviet Union, when it abandoned its original programme and original ideas – at that moment, no one took it seriously any longer. No one knew if it was a wolf in sheep's clothing, or a wolf that had truly changed into a sheep. As it was generally known that the CPC did not have an independent political life, the other parties did not consider it a reliable ally, even when it was 'more opportunistic' – to use the communist terminology – than the social democrats and 'more national' than the national socials. The alliance that was offered a hundred times to the social democrats did not come about; the merging of the unions was only partial and at the cost of the complete capitulation of the red unions; the CPC lost its cultural clout along with its moral clout because art does not flourish where there is an absolute lack of freedom and poems do not blossom where ideas do not blossom. It was probably as a result of this distrust – among other things – that a popular front did not form in Czechoslovakia, nor was there a popular front government, like the one in France that so effectively 'guarded the Franco-Russian treaties'.

30 September caught off guard a Communist Party that was totally helpless. Then the proclamation by the eleven 'fraternal' sections condemning the Munich Agreement appeared on the front pages of the communist newspapers and on 20 October the activity of the Communist Party was prohibited by law. Only the organisational body, however, was affected. The party, as an expression of a definite and very extreme world and political outlook, had been undermined from the foundation up years before.

The Communist Party, however, has left the people a considerable heritage. I believe that it is an inauspicious one because it is distorted by propagandistic dimensions: blind trust in the Soviet Union. This trust is not founded on reflection or prudence, but on *faith*. For some strata of the working people, the Soviet Union is a legend, like the legend of Blaník.[34] When the Czech people are in greatest danger, the Red Army will come and save them. Faith in the Soviet Union has changed into this, or a similar dream. With no other political task than to praise Soviet Russia, the Communist Party described it to its members in different ways in different periods of its political development: at one time as the land of gigantic enterprise, *controlled by the workers*. Then as *the homeland*

---

34 Blaník was a famous hill near Louňovice. According to one national legend, the knights of Blaník, along with St Wenceslas, dozed under the hill. When the Czechs were faced with great adversity, the hill would open, the knights would wake up and attack the enemy, liberating the country.

*of all the workers* of the world, the true fatherland of all working people. Then as an invincible barrier against fascism. Finally, as the only ally we had, the only one that was willing to stand with us *even against the rest of Europe*, although there are no documents to prove this and although the *actual* behaviour of the Soviet Union does not suggest that it is determined to go alone or even to risk a preventative war. If the Soviet Union had wanted and had been able to act as 'the fatherland of all working people' in the world, it had ample opportunity to do so before 30 September. If it had been determined to go into a world war on its own, with only Czecho-slovakia at its side, it would certainly have found the voices to proclaim this. Nothing indicates that it considered anything else but its own *state interests*. Russia appeared to be a great power that was, up to the last minute, honourably willing to meet the obliga-tions incurred by the treaties signed.[35] To meet these obligations was, *under certain circumstances, truly in the state interests of the Soviet Union*. But it was these very circumstances that did not materialise.

My friend, there is only one thing that can be said to you, the Czechoslovak worker, about 30 September, the dissolution of the Communist Party and the messianic propaganda in support of the Soviet Union: *stop believing*. The Saviour will not come from anywhere else. There is no Blaník. You are alone – and you alone will help yourself. Communist parties grow up and disappear. The idea of rights and freedoms is old and eternal. It can never die out. It will re-emerge, as it always has in periods of darkness.

The second legacy of the Communist Party is its members. In the past few days, we have all come to know them well. Wherever it was necessary to combat fascism, they were there, with a tough and true determination. They are firm and fearless people. They are used to hardship and discipline and they scorn weakness. They have militant hearts and they do not falter. Not a hint of luxury has soft-ened them with an immoderate love of comfort. Wherever the nation will fight for its rightful existence, for its future – many of them will be needed. This is, of course, an involuntary legacy, a legacy for which the Communist Party is not responsible. But nonetheless, it is a positive legacy and the nation that needs men will know where to place them.

---

35 France and Czechoslovakia had signed a treaty of mutual assistance in 1924. According to the Soviet-Czechoslovak treaty signed in 1935, France had to come to the aid of Czechoslovakia before the Soviet Union was obliged to send military aid. As France did not honour its treaty obligation, the Soviet Union was under no compulsion to act.

# Married Women out of Work

## 9 November 1938, *Přítomnost*

Almost always, a lot of people have to groan under every decree, even when it is packaged in the most beautiful words. When married women are dismissed from work now, one suspects that even a decree that is perhaps essentially appropriate could harm thousands, if it is implemented without regard for specific personal circumstances. Perhaps that is why one hears: *woman is restored to her natural mission.* How noble it sounds! But what is the natural mission of woman? Her physiological function? Can a physiological function sometimes be a mission as well? Is the world such that the physiological function of a person is an end in itself? Can we really marry and give birth to children in the calm paradise of physiological mission? Are we not further removed from 'our natural mission' at the very moment when we give up work than at any other time?

There were times when there was talk of women's emancipation, equal rights for women and champions of women's rights. That was a long time ago. Since then, an entire army of women has entered the workforce, not for any of the ideas or ideals of emancipation, but out of simple existential necessity. Not only the workers, but also the intelligentsia and middle class were hit by the Depression. Middle-class families could no longer provide dowries for their daughters. Instead of a dowry, a girl received an education. Parents could provide their daughters with accommodation, food and money for schooling. This was paid out gradually – a kind of instalment system on a dowry – and it was easier. A girl did not take a job because she wanted to avoid marriage or shirk her natural mission. On the contrary. She presented her education, employment and ability to work to her husband as a dowry. It was, of course, a much more natural form of dowry because it guaranteed a woman's independence much more securely. Property can be forfeited one way or another. The ability to work cannot be forfeited. It was, above all, more pleasant for the woman because she no longer felt like a possession. If her marriage was unhappy, she was not forced to remain in it for financial reasons. Man ceased to be a creature to be hunted down so that he could provide for us for the rest of our lives. He started to be a companion, freely chosen.

Two young people who had decided to marry – that is, to devote themselves to their natural mission – sat down with a pencil in hand and calculated whether or not they had enough money to surrender to their natural mission. You make this much – and I this much. We will buy furniture on an instalment plan and we will get a small flat. In the absolute majority of cases, with this decision the woman took upon herself a double resolve: to work and earn money and to manage the entire household. That is, to hurry home after work, clean, cook, mend clothes and do what was 'naturally women's work' because, on the one hand, the combined incomes could not support a servant in the household and, on the other hand, the household was no bigger than a broom closet and a capable woman could easily manage it after work. It was no longer so easy 'to devote oneself to one's natural mission'. It was not easy for a working woman to get pregnant, endure nine difficult months at work, bring a child into the world and get it ready so that it could be entrusted to a stranger for eight hours a day. That is the truth. If it was difficult for working women, however, it will be impossible for most women who have lost their jobs because they are married. For women who do not marry so that they can keep their jobs, it will be likewise impossible. For women who do not marry because a wedding would be a tremendous risk and incredible burden for the man – it is well known that a man does not need a wedding in order 'to devote himself to his natural mission' – it will also be impossible. It seems that a child will become a great luxury in life. The only woman able to afford a child will be one whose husband has enough money and enough love to take upon himself the responsibility of sharing the proceeds of his labour with two or three other people.

## What are the Figures?

If only married women whose husbands have *high* wages left the workforce, it would perhaps in the present situation be truly helpful for many people and free up positions for those in greater need. A woman who supports herself gains something else in addition to wages: a feeling of independence that is more precious than gold for many women. Of course, today one cannot take feelings into consideration, not even those that are most understandable or beneficial to the individual. Today the hopes and feelings of many people will necessarily suffer a great deal. In addition, a young woman whose husband earns enough to support two or three people comfortably will truly be pleasantly occupied at home. To have a nice home and a child, to be free of the most pressing worries about sustenance – this opens up great possibilities for a woman, not only for household chores, but also for quiet evenings, study, books, careful scrutiny of the newspapers and the conscientious upbringing of the child.

These are, of course, exceptional cases. The 'emancipation' of women did not advance as an idea, but as a necessity. That means: no man is enthusiastic because his wife is employed and earning money. The hostility of men towards the independence of women is longstanding, explicit and entrenched in all classes. If a man permits his wife to work, it is usually because the contribution of her labour is a necessary component of the household. Conversely: few women long for the independence gained through work; the majority of them long for someone else to work and earn money. Thus, if a married woman chooses to be gainfully employed, it is usually also only because the contribution of her labour is a necessary component of the household. On this point, many men and women are in agreement; for many decades, the traditional upbringing fostered such ideas about honour, rights and demands. If something changed, it was not the idea of equal rights for women (in any case, an idea that was often ill-considered, distorted and senseless in its distortion), but economic necessity.

Today, these women are supposed to give up their jobs, but what do their families look like, families that are organised on the assumption that the wife earns money? The most common case: after nine years of work, the woman earns 1,300 crowns (school-leaving certificate, study, etc.), the man earns 800 crowns. Rent amounts to about 300 crowns, heating 100, lighting 75. Thus far, it was easy to manage. But what now?

Or: the woman 800, the man 900. They live with their parents. The woman 950, the man, a typographer, employed only three times a week, brings home about 140 crowns a week. Or: the woman 1,050, the man, a civil servant, 800. Both support a mother. They have furnished their home on an instalment plan; they are 9,000 crowns in debt, paying considerable interest. For these cases, one can add or subtract 50 crowns here and there. If it is decided – there is some hope of this – that only women whose husbands earn at least 1,000 crowns will be dismissed, that still means that two or three people – perhaps even four – will live off 1,000 crowns. *How?*

In many cases it will be a painful blow to the life of the family, the living standard of which was calculated on the basis of a second income. In many cases, people will be faced with an insoluble problem – for example, if they have to pay instalments on furniture, etc. These couples probably will not be able to afford the rent they have paid thus far. How will the question of moving and accommodation be settled? Where will all the necessary new flats be found? Will two families move into one flat? If so, will the rent be paid directly to the landlord, or will one family earn money off the other? In that case, how will the matter of lighting and gas be resolved? What about the kitchen? The laundry room? The attic? Nothing but questions, wherever one turns.

One thing is certain: it will result in a radical impoverishment and proletarianisation of the middle class, much more radical than during the world-wide Depression. Of course, it is impossible to foresee what kind of consequences this can and will have. We can only judge on the basis of what has happened abroad. When the working class is radical, it is radical for something that *it has not received*. When the middle class is radical, it is radical for something that it has lost. Psychologically – and psychological causes are, in their consequences, political causes – this is something completely different. We have already seen that the radicalised middle class can be even more aggressive than the working class. As there is an infinite antipathy towards impoverishment and proletarianisation in the nature and mentality of this class, however, its aggression almost always turns in a different direction. A worker and a middle-class man can both live off 1,000 crowns – but the former remains a worker and the latter remains a gentleman. That means different needs, different expenditures and different desires.

## *And Young Girls?*

This, of course, is just one more series of questions. Young girls will be faced with a decision: *either* to work independently *or* to get married. I would not want to be an eighteen-year-old girl today. Will a young girl who shares a flat with a young man while she is still single be shown the same respect as a married woman? Will illegitimate children be accepted into society with the same rights as legitimate children? Hardly. Thus, a woman will either work independently or she will get married. Even if they adjust all their endeavours – upbringing, will and opinions – to the new situation, it is still an open question whether or not young men will be willing to marry girls who have neither dowries nor jobs. Remember that a wedding is no small risk for a man. It means an obligation to support and clothe a woman (as the case may be, to pay alimony) for the rest of his life. For a man earning 1,000 crowns a month, a wife with two hardworking hands is not, *in economic terms*, as much of a boon as a wife with a job – because an employed woman would also have the same hardworking hands for the household. By contrast, there is a big difference between living off 1,000 crowns on one's own and supporting two people on that wage.

Of course, young single girls who earn a few hundred crowns at work can look on their gainful employment as a transitional stage before marriage. Women, however, who have trained for a particular job will have to give it up if they want a husband and children. This means, of course, that they will hardly prepare for employment. How does a person, however, prepare for a wedding? Up to a certain age: with a sweet temper, the charm of youth and good character traits. It is an old law that the less attractive a woman is, the more good traits she has to have. Later, when she is no longer young, probably not even good traits will help her. There will definitely be more pretty young girls than young men willing to found families. With the best will in the world, I cannot imagine that this state of affairs will benefit the general moral standard. Perhaps the time will come again when expectant mothers will say: dear God, let it be a boy!

# In No-Man's-Land
## 29 December 1938, *Přítomnost*

A few days ago, a meeting was held in Paris at the High Commission of the League of Nations for aid to refugees from Austria and Germany (including the German and Jewish refugees from the annexed territory of the former Czechoslovakia). Sir Herbert Emerson ran it and Mrs Marie Schmolková, Chair of the Central Committee for Refugees, spoke on behalf of Czecho-Slovakia.[36] She spoke very emphatically, openly and clearly. She said, among other things: 'When Czecho-Slovakia offered refugees the right of asylum, they were – relatively speaking, of course – better off than in other countries. Following the Munich Agreement, however, it is, in practical terms, absolutely impossible for Czecho-Slovakia to offer asylum any longer. If German refugees continue to reside in Czecho-Slovakia this will represent, on the one hand, considerable personal danger for the refugees and, on the other hand, a political threat to neighbourly relations between Czecho-Slovakia and Germany in general.'

These are very clear words, all the more remarkable considering that they were uttered by someone who has represented refugees and émigrés for many years. I should probably speak to you at length about who Marie Schmolková is. I met her when I was writing my first article about those hounded people, when I was searching for figures and details. She lives in the Old Town, in an alley that I, a native of Prague, did not know, in a crooked little house with wooden stairs. When you enter it, however, you find a

---

36 After the Munich Agreement, a Central Committee was created in the rump state to speed up the departure of émigrés to other countries. Marie Schmolková, who until that time had acted as Chair of the National Committee for German Refugees (*Comité national pour les refugiés provenants d'Allemagne*), helped people to obtain visas for Paris, London and Geneva. See: Bohumil Černý, *Most k novému životu. Německá emigrace v ČSR v letech 1933–1939*, p. 28; and Zdeněk Huňáček et al., *Český antifašismus a odboj* (Czech Anti-fascism and the Resistance), Prague, 1988, p. 240. Buber-Neumann also writes about Schmolková, who managed to leave the country after the occupation but died shortly thereafter. Buber-Neumann, *Milena. The Tragic Story of Kafka's Great Love*, pp. 118-119, 124–125. In November 1938, a law was passed granting Slovakia autonomy and a new spelling was introduced for the name of the state: Czecho-Slovakia.

remarkably elegant and civilised apartment, beautiful books, sculptures by Štursa, beautiful, dark furniture and a telephone that never stops ringing.[37] Perhaps at first sight you might say that she is not pretty. Women who work all day and long into the night, who have looked for years on the suffering of other people, are perhaps not pretty. If she is not pretty, however, she is very beautiful. It is something within that makes this face so distinctive, strong and sculpted. This woman is personally acquainted with everyone who has crossed the border in the last five years. She knows their fates, she knows the dangers to which they are exposed. It is as if her fate has disappeared under the flood of those other fates. She moves endlessly back and forth between disease, life and death, between the authorities in London, Paris and Prague; she has gone through no-man's-land and the refugee camps and seen the ship that was on the Danube near Bratislava for two months after the annexation of Austria.[38] She sees practically nothing but hopelessness and, after terrible exertion, she manages to extract only a little hope: but she is so remarkably calm, as believers usually are.

When I was at my lowest point in September, I used to visit her and sit for a while. She emanates such certainty and confidence, such objective compassion and authentic fearlessness, that the moments I spend in her easy-chair are among my favourite. There are many women who work for the public welfare – as it is so nicely put – and few of them are remarkable. This woman does not work for the public welfare. She wanders somehow with her nation, with that humble pride – or proud humility – of its best individuals. She is not a functionary, a society worker who could be described as 'self-sacrificing'. She calmly ferries her unhappy nation over an era that has hit it harder than other nations and other peoples. When I sat across from her today she was very happy. After prolonged exertion, she had managed to find hope not for one, two or ten refugees, but for many people. They would go either directly to work in a state that I am not supposed to name at present, or they would go to temporary camps in England, France and the northern countries, until their passport matters were arranged. All in all, it could be said that most of them would probably be spending their last Christmas here and that in a year's time all the inhabitants of no-man's-land would disappear.

---

37 She refers to the sculptor Jan Štursa (1880–1925).

38 Jewish refugees attempted to make their way to Palestine travelling by boat down the Danube and across the Black Sea. Martin Gilbert, *The Holocaust. The Jewish Tragedy*, p. 79.

Many years ago, we saw a film in Prague called *No-Man's-Land* – a German film.[39] We have not seen such a beautiful film since then and I am afraid that much water will flow by under the bridge before people are permitted to say and reveal the truth as they did at that time in Germany. In the World War, the zone of land between the two fronts, the strip of scorched earth between the two barbed wire fences, was called no-man's-land. The war – in the film – had hounded four people to that spot: an Englishman, a German, a black man and a Russian Jew. Four terrified human animals from the most diverse corners of the world, from different social classes, with different languages and fates. The Russian Jew was, even then, mute in the film – played by the most remarkable actor of contemporary Europe, Sokolov, a man with the face of a sad little monkey and the typical eyes of the Jews: dark, sad eyes, looking out from the ages into the ages.[40] Today, Sokolov is in America and plays small character roles, for the most part comic because America, for all its understanding of the European spirit, has not yet discovered anything else in the melancholy face of the European Jew but a slightly ridiculous figure. For me, however, his character will always be somehow prophetic: a small, crumpled Jew from no-man's-land, a mute man among those who speak, set apart even among exiles, with a smile and eyes in which there is the sorrow of the countless thousands who go from century to century. Although they have a mind, a heart and a soul, they do not have a country, they do not have a home, they do not have a language. They are, in fact, mute. I heard a story about a rabbi who lives in Palestine today and speaks only Hebrew; he does not permit anyone around him to speak any other language; he imparts to young people a love for the – rather artificial – mother tongue of the Jews. But sometimes, at home, in a corner, when it is growing dark, he croons to himself – Russian songs. Palestine is home and Hebrew is the mother tongue. But Russia – that is his native land and Russian songs are the songs of his native land; his mother used to sing them, as did the women in the village, the children at school and the men in the fields. Through a thousand sounds, customs, colours and shapes the native land formed the soul of the man. The man was grateful to it because with this native language he formed his ideas and words. Then someone came along and said: you do not belong here, go away. The Jew wandered and wandered, he wandered to the promised land and spoke only Hebrew from then on, labouring with all his strength,

---

39 *No-Man's-Land* (*Niemandsland*, 1931), an anti-war film by Victor Trivas (1894–1970).

40 The Russian actor Vladimir Sokolov (1889–1962).

will and proud humility on land that, once again, did not belong to him. But in the evening, in the corner of the room, when it grows dark – he quietly sings Russian songs. That is the muteness of the Jew of no-man's-land.

Years ago we saw no-man's-land in a film and because the film was set in 1918 we thought, foolishly, that it was the past. At that time, we went home with a sense of pride that people were walking hand-in-hand towards a free and radiant future. At that time, we had not yet experienced the strange loops and detours, switches and blind tracks that history creates.

Today, no-man's-land is near at hand, a stone's throw away. At the Czech and German border – my God, what a border it is, a piece of wire in a field, a pole across a path, a string from tree to tree, a child could kick it away, a lamentable border – there is still a strip of no-man's-land in several places. First, the Czechoslovak army left the strip, then German (Hungarian, Polish) youths arrived, bringing Jews from the occupied territory. Jews who had fled returned from the rump Czecho-Slovakia. Some in compliance with the decrees, some out of concern for their property, others out of fear for their loved ones who had remained in the annexed territory. They made it across the Czechoslovak barbed wire. They did not, however, get across the German barbed wire. Nor were they allowed back over the Czechoslovak barbed wire. The barbed wire of 1938 is firm and resistant. It also happened, for example, that Hungarian youths woke up an entire village in the night, led the Jews – women, men and children – in their night shirts out to trucks and drove them to this no-man's-land, unloaded them and drove away. In the beginning, there were several dozen on the bare field in the winter. Then a hundred. Then thousands. Little by little they received permission to join Jewish families in Czecho-Slovakia, after the English had provided a guarantee that they would not be a burden on public welfare and would move on. The whole time they were living in the woods and fields, in the frost and ditches, they were supported by Jews – sometimes even from distant regions – who had not lost their homes. They were also supported, however, by Czech farmers and Slovaks. Even German farmers and German workers brought them food. For the human being is such that he helps even an animal when it is dying of hunger, even if that animal is of an inferior species. The human heart is a remarkable thing, beautiful and eternal.

What is it like when a group of three hundred people stays – as it did near Bratislava – in a field in the night and in the winter? What is it like in a century of technical progress and high living standards? What is it like after the Munich peace? Like this: the father digs three holes in the hard earth with his bare hands; in each hole he places one child; he weaves a little roof of dry corn stalks and leaves over them and sits down on a clod of earth beside them. If people in the area did not help, they would probably die of hunger, cold and shame. But people help. They bring food, warm clothing, some canvas, a tent and an abandoned moving van. A little straw in the van. Those in greatest need move there: a man whose stomach is haemorrhaging; a woman who is expecting a child in a few days; a woman who has already given birth in the field here and has a baby wrapped in second-hand rags; a lame old man whom they carry far away from the van when he feels the need; and a blind old man who sits in the heap of straw in the corner. Among them, two invalids, one with a serious case of tuberculosis and a rattling cough and one with an unidentified illness and a high fever. The others remain in the dug-out holes, or under the shelter of shabby canvas. An Austrian Jewish doctor runs about among them; he was the first to receive permission to leave the camp. He only laughed: how could he leave? He was the last to go. All that time, he went about in a thin little jacket and never lost his poise or calm for a moment. When children came to him with fingers frozen to the bone, he said: 'Come, I'll put some ointment on it for you.' When people from the commission came and stood there looking in horror at the stark human misery, he said: 'But it's not so bad, it only looks that way. Come along. Believe me, a person gets used to it.'

They had to walk a kilometre to get water. People brought food in sacks from far and wide all over the region and still it was not enough; it is not easy to feed three hundred people. They even received washbasins, but a few disappeared. People racked their brains: how could they vanish with barbed wire all around? Then it was discovered that some people had offered them food in exchange for the tin washbasins. So you see, it is possible to make money even off people in no-man's-land.

Those people lived like that for weeks. Today they all have a roof over their heads. Along the Polish border there are still about six thousand of them. Some temporary barracks, however, have been made for them. Soon they will all leave. That is, to tell the truth, not all of them. The old and the sick cannot leave. They will die there in some corner. But children, men and women, people who are healthy and able to work, will all leave. Next year at Christmas time they will be somewhere else under their own roofs.

It is not our fault that they have experienced so much hardship among us. As long as our house was still standing, we were hospitable and kind. Today we can only wish them a new and good life somewhere far away. We wish it with all our hearts.

# Good Advice is Better than Gold

## 8 March 1939, *Přítomnost*

A lot has changed here since the Munich events. This is an obvious truth and little by little it becomes tedious. I rather look forward to a time when articles will not have to start with this obvious premise and when the reality will be clear to us all: we did not want it; it happened anyway and now we have it. Perhaps we will live to see the day when not only we, who have experienced it on our own skin, but also all those over the border who are watching us will understand that something fundamental has changed here. Not only has about a third of the land of the former Czechoslovakia fallen away; not only have thousands of Czechs remained on the other side of the border; not only will we have to drive on the right side of the road.[41] Consequences that we will all have to take upon ourselves follow from the necessity of good relations with the German Reich. The possibilities are probably as follows: either we take the consequences upon ourselves or more blows will fall on us. This is the situation and we have to live, write and proceed accordingly. In this situation we have to safeguard the national consciousness, the national independence and what we Czechs call the national character. Whoever thinks that this is a small task has not yet understood what has happened.

It seems, however, that this small country, which has experienced so many troubles in recent months, is still of interest to the world. We can only sigh in resignation: unfortunately – as the interest of the world hardly does us any good today. When the division of the country was at stake, there was not a friend to be found far and wide. Today, when it is a question of any kind of aid at all from abroad, it is tied to dozens of contradictory and mutually exclusive conditions. When it is a question of standing in front of a radio loudspeaker, however, and giving us advice (in the form of reprimands and reproaches), then all of a sudden many heroes can be found ...

---

41 According to the terms of the Munich Agreement, signed on 30 September 1938, Czechoslovakia had to cede territory to Germany. Bohemia and Moravia lost about 11,600 square miles, or 38 percent of their combined territory. They lost 3,869,000 inhabitants (34 percent of the entire population). Theodor Prochazka, 'The Second Republic, 1938–1939', pp. 256–257.

No people are braver – at the microphones and three thousand kilometres away – than the officials of the Comintern.[42] Several times a week, in various European languages, they inject optimism and courage into the veins of people in Europe who have been subjected to all sorts of things in various parts in recent years. Nothing is more noble than to utter a few slogans over blood that has just been shed. As long as we had *Rudé právo* the Czech people could remain calm; after every defeat they suffered they could read the banner headlines: the workers won't allow it! The workers won't give an inch! The working people protest![43] After Munich, after the first, second, third, fourth and finally fifth zone, after the flood of refugees, after the familiar image that stubbornly refuses to recede from the life of our generation – somewhere in the world there is always a road full of carts with canvas covers, an old woman, children, chickens, a goat, feather bedding – it was always immensely reassuring to hear the shouts of the news vendors on Wenceslas Square declaring that the working class would not allow it and that the Soviet Union would not permit it ... and so on.[44] I always used to wonder with a downcast heart: how is it possible? How can one explain that the communist press in the last six years has differed from reality, like a landscape described by someone who is colour-blind? One of the causes of this very complex process is surely the fact that the Comintern has established pseudo-revolutionary organisations in all states all over the world, manned them with officials and thus created a new type of person: Comintern officials with a monthly wage of 1,200 crowns. The task of these officials has been to fulfil their duty; that is, to undertake so-called revolutionary activities in the country where they happened to be located. As Comintern employers are very strict with their employees, these people incurred displeasure as soon as politics failed to develop according to their wishes, just as the Soviet worker incurs displeasure when he does not fulfil the prescribed quota of piece-work in the production of shoes.

---

42 'Comintern' is an abbreviation for the Communist International, founded in Moscow in March 1919 as a body uniting left-wing socialists and communists. It was disbanded in May 1943.

43 *Rudé právo* (Red Rights) was a daily newspaper founded in 1920 in Prague; from 1921 on it was the main daily of the Communist Party of Czechoslovakia. After 1991 it became an independent newspaper published under the title *Právo* (Rights). *Všeobecné encyklopedie ve čtyřech svazcích* (General Encyclopaedia in Four Volumes), vol. 3, Prague, 1997, p. 716.

44 Wenceslas Square is the main shopping street in the centre of Prague.

For this reason, the communist secretaries generated activity. 'To formulate the problem, develop a programme and generate activity', was the favourite motto of all the meetings, consultations, lectures, training sessions and reports in the cells. The more forceful and tragic was the disagreement between individual groups of workers and the more crushing were the blows that fell on their ideals, the more optimistic and uplifting were the headlines of the communist press, the more collectively was courage produced and the more damned was anyone who could not succumb to the hypnosis of propaganda and tried to see things the way they were.

*Rudé právo* has ceased to exist – therefore loud propaganda activity is generated from abroad. I must admit that I am filled with sorrow when I listen in my room to Moscow Radio speaking in Czech – sorrow that a man three thousand kilometres away is speaking to us in sentences so cardboard, words so unreal, phrases so bombastic; that he clearly lacks any idea of the real truth in Czecho-Slovakia, having been informed by someone who 'generates activity'; and that he tramples over the complex social developments like an elephant in a teashop. It is not a living *Czech person* who speaks to us, but a Comintern official. Our worries do not concern him, but rather *Moscow's* Comintern worries.

The 'generation of activity' by the Comintern transmitter includes the 'analysis and criticism of social conditions and the search for a solution'. The Comintern's analysis of social conditions has always staggered from one pitfall to another. Its criticism is black-and-white, passing over in silence all complex and seemingly inexplicable social phenomena that contradict its views. The search for a solution is thus nothing more than vilification and the production of optimism. The vilification is particularly interesting: it is like a person sitting in the middle of a puddle, hurling abuse with all his might at someone whom a passing car has splattered with mud.

The Soviet transmitter addresses us regularly twice a week and its sounds are very vexing. For about three weeks now the Moscow transmitter has been talking about the fascistic and pernicious cruelty we show towards refugees, political and economic émigrés and our own nationals of the Jewish faith. For this enviably located transmitter, nothing at all has happened. There was no Munich. It is not a reality that we must now reckon first and foremost with the German political and economic influence. It is not a fact that the First Republic generously offered asylum to everyone who asked for it – Hungarian, German, Austrian and Polish émigrés. It is irrelevant that the small surface of our country is overburdened with

Czech refugees, for whom we must care first and foremost. Finally, it is irrelevant that '*autorita, non veritas, facit legem*', although this is clearly the foundation of any kind of political activity whatsoever. Our behaviour provokes outbursts of Comintern contempt and vilification – and the Comintern is located in *Moscow*! A person whose heart stops in grief several times a day over the fate of people who cannot fit on this truncated raft, stands for a moment perhaps indecisively and listens, arrested by pity and sorrow for the afflicted. After the fulmination has gone on for twenty minutes, however, a strange thought surfaces: strange because the brain, exhausted by the thundering of propaganda on all sides, slowly and shyly discovers the simple truth in the tremendous flood of half-truths and requires a long while before it becomes fully aware of the real situation.

For example, Article 129 of the new Soviet constitution, which is called Stalin's: 'the USSR *offers the right of asylum* to nationals of other states who are persecuted because they have supported the interests of the working people, because of their scientific work, or because they have fought for national independence'!

That is what the Soviet Union says on an important piece of paper – on the constitutional charter, no less. How is it, however, in reality? In reality, the USSR has not accepted émigrés for the past five years. The *Schutzbund* members from the February barricades in Vienna were the last. It is said that the Soviet Union did not have good experiences with them. The *Schutzbund* members refused to leave the main industrial cities and live under the surveillance and absolute rule of remote provincial party men (today, even the Soviet newspapers are writing about what this absolute rule is like); they started at the factories in Leningrad, Moscow and Kharkov and began to work with intense enthusiasm.[45] After a few days it became clear that the work of a man from the West differed completely from the work of a Soviet citizen, both in terms of quality and pace. It also became clear that the Austrian social democratic worker from Vienna or Linz from 1934, having been subjected to fascism, had completely different ideas about freedom, about the activity of associations and about standards of living than did the worker in the Soviet Union. The conflicts that consequently arose persuaded the *Schutzbund* members that they should return to their homeland – but it became clear that they could not be permitted to do so because the USSR doubted that these people would make good propagandists at home.

---

45 Kharkov is a machinery centre in Ukraine, founded in the 1700s. It was capital of Ukraine until 1934, when Kiev became the capital.

Many, very many of them were locked up; many were sent beyond the Arctic Circle or to work on the great construction projects. That would be an interesting question – who actually built the giant Soviet structures, the canals, dams and canalisation – and who actually built all the giant structures over the course of world history, the 'witnesses of high culture' – from the pyramids to the roads in French Guinea to the *Volgastroj*.

After 1934, the Soviets closed the borders to émigrés, in spite of the fact that Article 129 of the Soviet constitution was formulated in 1936. The émigrés from Germany remained in the former Czechoslovakia; they were poorly maintained, but they were alive. I spoke with them in 1937.[46] I asked one of them: why don't you go to the Soviet Union? You're a communist, aren't you? You fought in Germany for the victory of communism, so why don't you go there? He told me: 'They won't let me in. Not even a mouse slips in there. And then – I wouldn't go. If I'm going to be locked up or perhaps even shot, I'll go straight back home. At least there I will know *why* they have locked me up.'

Those are, you know, the bitter words of a person who was a communist worker for twenty years, who lived through everything that a communist in Europe had to live through – from months of unemployment to imprisonment and emigration. Besides being bitter, they indicate that the communists – not the communist functionaries but the communist workers – expected little benevolence from the Soviet government, even if it did accept them.

When there were negotiations in the League of Nations concerning the continued maintenance and prolongation of the Nansen Office – that international association that looks after the fate of refugees on a world-wide scale – the *only one* to take a stand against the further activity of this organisation was Litvinov.[47] He spoke on behalf of the Soviet Union.

---

46 Jesenská wrote an article entitled 'Lidé na výspě (Z osudů německých emigrantů)' (People on a Promontory [The Fates of the German Emigrés]), *Přítomnost*, 27 October 1937, pp. 684–687.

47 She refers to the Nansen International Office for Refugees, created in Geneva in 1931 and named after Fridtjof Nansen (1861–1930), who had received the Nobel Prize for Peace in 1922 for his work on behalf of refugees and prisoners of war. The Nansen Office initially cared mainly for anti-communist ('White') Russians, Armenians from Turkey and, later, Jews from Nazi Germany. Maksim Maksimovich Litvinov (1876–1951) was a Soviet diplomat and commissar for foreign affairs (1930–1939). He supported world disarmament and security with the Western powers against Nazi Germany before the Second World War. See: *The New Encyclopaedia Britannica*, 15th edn, Chicago, 1998, vol. 8, pp. 502–503; and vol. 7, p. 407.

When four of Franco's columns neared Madrid in 1936, the International Brigade of volunteers saved the city.[48] The International Brigade of volunteers also provided the local Spanish army with military experience and military training. That International Brigade numbered many thousands of men and they were truly brave men. When Barcelona fell, there were still eight thousand of them in Spain! At that time, the Spanish government sent forms to all the consulates in Barcelona with a few questions: will you accept your citizen back? Will you cover his travel costs from the Spanish border? Will you guarantee him immunity? Well then: Czecho-Slovakia accepted its citizens back, although it could offer them only wretched conditions. And Czecho-Slovak citizens had set out for Spain to fight *without* the knowledge of their government, secretly and on their own initiative. The Soviet Union did not accept back the people it had sent – and the men from the Soviet Union had left for Spain at the *command* of the Soviet government. Of course, they were Germans, Austrians, Hungarians, Yugoslavs and Poles. *Formally*, most of them were not Soviet citizens. They were only – *communists*. After long deliberations, Mexico took half of them. The other half – remained in Spain.

By sending volunteers to the International Brigades the Soviet Union killed two birds with one stone. On the one hand, it got rid of almost all the émigrés it had accepted in previous years – only select functionaries remained in Moscow. On the other hand, it had reliable people in Spain. Try and find out what happened to the German émigrés who sought refuge in the Soviet Union and you will discover that the bones of the German communists lie mostly under Madrid. The Hungarian, Yugoslav and Polish communist émigrés met the same fate. Only a tenth of the 80,000 volunteers in Spain survived – but not even they were allowed to return to the Soviet Union. Not even the people whom Fate has driven from their homes are allowed to seek refuge there.

One cannot envy anybody who seeks refuge in Soviet Russia – but still! In Europe, the Soviet Union represents the country that could most easily accept and absorb socialist and other émigrés. How much land there is, waiting to be cultivated! How much the émigrés could contribute to Siberia, the Far East and the eastern republics of the Union! How often we hear about the shortage of qualified labour in industry, agriculture and science – and émigrés

---

48 The army of General Francisco Franco (1892–1975) approached Madrid in November 1936. Supported by the International Brigades, organised by the Communist International, the city resisted the nationalist forces until March 1939. *The New Encyclopaedia Britannica*, vol. 28, pp. 58–59.

from the West are certainly excellent workers. Even if the Soviet Union accepted a million or two million émigrés, what would it cost a country with such vast territory, with so many opportunities and a population of 170 million? What harm would it do considering that the majority of émigrés could play a truly pioneering role? So why does the Soviet Union not adhere to its *own constitution*, if it has so much advice and so many reproaches for little Czecho-Slovakia? Wouldn't Moscow Radio like to explain this mystery to us? Wouldn't it like to tell us what has happened to the many Czecho-Slovak communists and simple Czech workers who went to the Soviet Union years ago, fleeing punishment and looking for work? Wouldn't we find out, for example, that most of them are sitting in the prisons of the GPU?[49]

That is how the USSR behaves towards those people who foolishly imagine that being a communist is the same thing as being under the protection of the Soviet government.[50] That is how the USSR behaves towards the people it has trained and sent into the world to preach the communist doctrine. As soon as they become émigrés, they no longer have entry into the 'mother' country. Clearly it does not accept them because they are familiar with the West. Because they have some kind of conception of freedom, of work standards and human rights. And perhaps also because they do not have much understanding for the cult of a single personality. I add this so as not to create the misleading impression that I am sorry for the communists of the Western countries because they *are not able* to go to the USSR. There are people among them for whom I have profound respect and people for whom I have no respect at all. But my personal lack of respect for any person could not extend so far as to wish that he be accepted today into the 'homeland of all working people'.

---

49 GPU – the Soviet military intelligence.

50 Jesenská's views may have been influenced by the experiences of her ex-husband, Jaromír Krejcar, who spent several years in the USSR (1933–1936). He returned to Prague in 1936 with a new wife, Riva, whose fiancé had been executed by the Soviets. See: Alena Wagnerová, *Milena Jesenská*, p. 144. Marta Marková-Kotyková relates that Riva's former fiancé, a White Russian émigré from the Ukraine who had studied in Prague, was won over by the Soviets and offered work in USSR. Once there, he was executed. NKVD agents continued to correspond with Riva in her fiancé's name. She set out to join him, only to be apprehended by the NKVD herself. Marta Marková-Kotyková, *Mýtus Milena. Milena Jesenská jinak*, p. 60.

# Prague, the Morning of 15 March 1939

## 22 March 1939, *Přítomnost*

How do great events happen? Unexpectedly and all at once. But when they are upon us, we always find that *we are not* surprised. A person always has some apprehension and knowledge of things to come, only deafened by reason, will, desire, fear, haste and work. As soon as the soul of a person remains for a moment naked and stripped of everything else except its secret intuition, it is sure at once: I knew it. There is a reason why so many people go about today and say: I suspected as much; I said so. I believe them. We all suspected as much and if we had listened attentively to the voice of our hearts when we sat at home alone, for instance, or when we woke up tired at dawn, if we had been able to clothe in words the feelings, which are true and not only the thoughts, which are often distorted, we would have said: we are waiting for it. But the logic of things is, at the same time, illogical. Every person awaits some kind of remarkable event in life: good fortune, poverty, illness, hunger, death. When it comes, however, he does not recognise it. All he knows is that it has overwhelmed him completely, not leaving him the time or the opportunity to act.

When the telephone rang at four in the morning on Tuesday, when friends and acquaintances called, when Czech Radio began to broadcast, the city under our windows looked the same as it had on every other night. The lights under the windows made the same configuration, the crossroads made the same cross. From three o'clock on, however, lights began to flick on gradually: in the neighbouring apartments, across the way, down below, up above, then all over the street. We stood at the window and said to ourselves: they know by now. We woke people up with a telephone call: do you know? They answered: yes. That sullen daybreak over the roofs, the pale moon below the clouds, the sleepless faces, the mug of hot coffee and the regular reports on the radio.[51] That is how great events come to people: quietly and without warning.

---

51 News of the occupation was first announced on Radio Prague at 4.30 a.m. on 15 March. Repeated broadcasts warned the population not to resist the German army. See: Vojtech Mastny, *The Czechs Under Nazi Rule*, London and New York, 1971, p. 45.

In the German newspapers there was a story about the German soldiers who drove to Prague: a quiet city in a pre-spring dawn, a line of German vehicles and in them men with beating hearts: what will it be like inside the city? How will people behave in these foreign streets? In the suburbs, they stop the first pedestrian, a labourer on his way to work. They realise at first glance that he knows everything. He behaves calmly; quietly and peacefully he points the way.

As always when great events are taking place, Czechs behave wonderfully. Thanks are due to Czech Radio for its concise objectivity, reporting patiently every five minutes without fail: the German army is proceeding from the borders to Prague. Act calmly. Go to work. Send your children to school.

At half past seven in the morning, a crowd of children set out on the way to school, as usual. Workers and clerks drove off to work, as usual. The trams were full, as usual. Only the people were different. They stood and kept silent. I had never heard so many people keep silent before. There were no crowds in the streets at all. People did not discuss things at all. In the offices, they did not even raise their heads from their desks. I do not know where this unified and consistent behaviour of thousands came from, where this consonant rhythm of many souls, strangers to one another, sprang from all of a sudden: at twenty-five minutes to nine on 15 March 1939, the Reich German army rode up to National Avenue. Crowds of people flocked over the sidewalks, as usual. No one watched, no one turned around.[52] The German residents of Prague welcomed the Reich soldiers.

They likewise behaved politely towards us. It is altogether strange how things change when a unit breaks down into individuals and one person stands before another. In Wenceslas Square, a Czech girl came across a group of German soldiers – and because by then it was the second day, because by then all of us had nerves that were a little frayed and because only on the second day does a person come to understand better and think more – tears ran

---

52 See the description of the same day by George F. Kennan, who was assigned Secretary to the American Legation at Prague in 1938 and stayed on after the occupation to write political reports: 'About seven o'clock, I took a ride around town. A full blizzard was blowing, by this time, and the snow was staying on the streets. The downtown section was crowded, partly by the normal early-morning traffic of people going to work but partly by people running about and making last-minute preparations of all sorts. The news was widely spread by this time, and many of the women were weeping into their handkerchiefs, as they walked.' George F. Kennan, *From Prague After Munich: Diplomatic Papers 1938–1940*, Princeton, 1968, p. 86.

down her cheeks. Then something strange happened. A German soldier walked up to her, a simple, ordinary soldier and said: *Aber Fräulein, wir können doch nichts dafür...!*[53] He said it as if he were comforting a small child. He had a freckled German face, reddish hair and a German uniform; otherwise he was in no way different from a Czech private, a simple man, devoted to his homeland. So two people stood there, facing one another, *'und konnten nichts dafür....'*[54] In that simple, terribly ordinary sentence is the key to everything.

Something else happened in one of the trams. A Czech youth with some kind of armband on his sleeve was boasting: just wait and see what we'll do now and who we'll thrash now and how we'll finish things off now and how we'll show the world now. In addition to the armband on his sleeve, he also had a swastika badge on the lapel of his jacket. When these words had fallen into the great silence of the entire car, all of a sudden a German officer, who had been sitting in a corner, stood up and walked over to the boy, addressing him in *Czech*: 'Are you Czech?' This put the boy's back up and he said with enormous self-confidence: 'Yes, I'm Czech.' The officer removed the swastika badge from his jacket and said very calmly and very emphatically: 'Then you have no right to wear something like this.'

You see, there are moments when a person would like to walk up to a German officer and say to him: thank you, Sir.

A few days ago I was speaking with a German, a national socialist, of course. He spoke at length and very sensibly about the position of the Czechs and the advantages, which we had acquired, according to him and the disadvantages, which he himself acknowledged. All this is not very interesting because today everything is in a state of change and even well-informed people can give no more than an opinion. What is interesting, however, is his opinion of the Czechs. He asked me almost shyly: why is it that so many Czechs come to us and utter the greeting *'Heil Hitler'*?

Czechs? That must be a mistake.

It is not a mistake. They come to our office, raise their right arms and say *'Heil Hitler'*. Why? I could tell you about one writer who is doing all he can – already and in haste – to get his plays performed on a Berlin stage. I could tell you about a lot of people who are doing more than they have to, zealously, breathlessly. You know, every German understands national pride and national backbone.

---

53 But Miss, we can't help it.

54 They couldn't help it.

Servile behaviour provokes only an ironical smile in the German of today, believe me.

In two days' time, the image of the city has changed beyond recognition.[55] In the bars there are men wearing uniforms that we do not even recognise from pictures. They drive vehicles that we have never seen before through the streets. They drive here and they drive there; they always know what they are supposed to do; they act decisively and purposefully. In the bookstores they buy maps of Prague and French and English books. Crowds of soldiers walk through the streets; they stop in front of shop-windows, look about, chat. Meanwhile, not a single cog-wheel has stopped, not a single pen or a single machine.

The Tomb of the Unknown Soldier is in Old Town Square. Today, one cannot even see it for the enormous heap of snowdrops. A remarkable power mysteriously guiding people's steps draws crowds of Prague residents here. Each of them lays a small bunch of snowdrops on that small tomb representing a great memory. People stand around and tears run down their cheeks. Not only women and children, but men too, who are not used to crying. Somehow it is all distinctly *Czech*: it is not at all a lament; it is not even fear; it is not despair; it is not a convulsion of emotion at all. It is only sadness. This sadness must find an outlet; several hundred eyes must grow moist with it. This is perhaps how national customs originate; these are the first ashlars of long-standing traditions. On 15 March, Czech mothers will go with Czech children to lay a bunch of snowdrops on the Tomb of the Unknown Soldier. It will be inscribed in people's minds like a great sacrificial act.[56]

---

55 Kennan comments in a letter dated 14 April 1939: 'The outward signs of Nazism are now almost all represented in the Prague scene, from infinite varieties of uniforms to the "Aryan shop" placards on the stores. Perhaps the only phenomenon of Nazi life which Prague has happily been spared is the sight of brutality against Jews in public places.' Kennan, *From Prague After Munich: Diplomatic Papers 1938–1940*, p. 114.

56 Sayer writes: 'One October night that same year [1941], SS men removed the remains of the Unknown Czechoslovak Soldier that had been installed in the chapel of the Old Town Hall in 1922 and threw them into the Vltava downstream of the city at Troja.' Sayer, *The Coasts of Bohemia. A Czech History*, p. 233.

I saw a German soldier walk past behind the crowd, stop and salute.[57] He looked at the eyes red with crying, at the teardrops, at the snow-covered mountains of snowdrops; he saw people who were crying because *he* was there. And he saluted. Clearly he understood why we were sad. Watching him go, I thought about the *Grand Illusion*: will we ever actually live next to one another – German, Czech, French, Russian, English – without harming one another, without having to hate one another, without perpetrating injustices against one another?[58] Will empires one day really understand one another as individual people understand one another? Will the borders between countries one day fall as they do between people?

How beautiful it would be to live to see it!

---

57 The commanding *Wehrmacht* general in Bohemia, Johannes Blaskowitz (1883–1948), ordered his soldiers 'to give a military salute when passing by the Tomb of the Unknown Soldier in Prague.' Mastny, *The Czechs under Nazi Rule*, p. 55. Kennan notes in March 1939: 'The German soldiers have maintained good discipline and a correct attitude. Their higher officers have done everything in their power, apparently, to placate Czech sensibilities, even to laying wreaths on the tomb of the unknown soldier.' He comments: 'All this I attribute not to any excess altruism on the part of the Germans but to a real desire that there should be – for the moment – the maximum of peace, quiet, and good feeling in Bohemia and Moravia.' Kennan, *From Prague After Munich: Diplomatic Papers 1938-1940*, p. 103.

58 She refers to the film *La Grande Illusion* (1937), directed by Jean Renoir (1894–1979).

# The Art of Standing Still
## 5 April 1939, *Přítomnost*

When something very, very momentous happens that changes the course of life for all people and gives rise to uncertainty and at the same time, therefore, also to fear, people start to move. They start to run away. I do not mean run away physically, but rather mentally. One can see many such escapes everywhere one turns. People who believed in something for years and even inspired others with their faith are losing the ground beneath their feet, but at the same time they are also losing judgement and a healthy perspective. When they utter the word 'homeland', they are thinking: 'for God's sake, what is going to happen to me?' They succumb to the vague idea that it would be good to do something, to give the appearance of being this or that. They throw themselves into motion and run either recklessly forward or recklessly back. People possessed by fear, people possessed by grief or panic, uncertainty or solitude, begin to run away. Some run forward and others run back. Some pull off amazing feats and others play cowardly tricks. Some act like martyrs when no one tortures them and others flee when no one chases them. That, however, is probably the essence of fear, that it does not allow a person to stand still.

To stand still means to be calm, to look straight on at something unfamiliar and come to grips with it. The people who run forward later assert: I am a hero. The people who run back insist: I was forced. Both focus all that is happening in the world on themselves; they see themselves in the centre of activity and they are convinced that their deeds and behaviour are of the utmost importance. They forget the sole meaning that the term *nation* can have: that they are not alone. As soon as a person separates his own fate from the fate of the eight million, in his soul he loses the profound essence of what the nation is: a profound awareness of collective belonging to the eight million. As soon as he is left *alone* in his consciousness – then, of course, he seeks in his soul some gesture to set himself in motion. Solitude is probably the greatest curse in the world.

When I was a young girl – that was under Austrian rule when conditions were totally different from what they are today and I would not like to be reproached for running away to reminiscences.

Today the citizens of the Third Reich stand beside us and we Czechs wait – and certainly no one will hold it against us when I say that we sometimes wait in fear – to see how relations between us will develop. Back then it was an oppressive period of tension and hostility between Austrians and Czechs, a period that carried within itself the roots of many later lamentable events.

So when I was a young girl, I lived on the corner of the 28th of October Street and Na příkopě Street and Wenceslas Square lay right under our windows.[59] At that time, of course, neither Na příkopě Street nor Wenceslas Square looked like it does today. There were small, very beautiful, Late Baroque buildings and all in all it was really a small, provincial town with a pretty, tidy square. The tension between the Czechs and the Austrian Germans was manifest at that time in all sorts of ways, but on Sunday mornings it had the character of a demonstration: German students in coloured caps walked along the right side of Na příkopě Street and Czechs in civilian clothes walked along the left side.[60] Now and then the tension culminated in some scuffle, some singing and some unrest – I saw it repeatedly, but I did not really understand it. But then there was one Sunday I will probably never forget as long as I live: I see it only as a memory and I do not know what lay behind it. The Austrian students in their coloured caps were marching from the Powder Tower, not along the sidewalk, but in the middle of the street. They were singing; they walked in a body, with booming, well-disciplined steps. All of a sudden, a crowd of Czechs approached from Wenceslas Square – they too were walking in the middle of the street and not on the sidewalks. They walked silently. At the window, mother held me by the hand, a little more firmly than was necessary. My father was walking in the front row of Czechs. I recognised him from the window and I was very happy,

---

59 Alena Wagnerová treats this incident in her biography of Jesenská. She asserts that the clash between the students probably occurred on 3 November 1905. At the beginning of November, there were demonstrations in Prague in support of the universal franchise. On 3 November, the police fired into a crowd of demonstrators and a number of people were wounded. Jesenská lived at the house no. 17 on Ovocná Street, now 28th of October Street. Alena Wagnerová, *Milena Jesenská*, pp. 9–13.

60 The streets in the centre of the city were transformed into a kind of corso on Sundays where young people and families promenaded, met friends and acquaintances, exchanged news, gossip and small talk. The crowd milling about was divided, like the city itself, according to nationality: the Czechs walked along Wenceslas Square, Ovocná Street (now 28th of October Street) and Ferdinand Street (now National Avenue); the German (and Jewish) corso was on Na příkopě Street. Wagnerová, *Milena Jesenská*, p. 10.

but mother went white as a sheet and she clearly was not happy. Then one thing quickly followed another: a crowd of policemen ran out from Havířská Street and positioned itself between the two camps. Na příkopě Street was closed to both groups. But both continued to move forward without stopping. Then the Czechs reached the cordon of policemen and they were commanded to stop. They were told once more. And then a third time. Then I have no idea what happened next. I know that some shots were fired, that the Czechs were transformed from a quiet into a shrieking crowd, that Na příkopě Street was all of a sudden empty, but one person remained standing in front of the guns – my father. I remember clearly, absolutely clearly, how he stood. Calmly, with his hands at his sides. Next to him something terribly strange was lying on the ground – I do not know if you have seen what a person looks like when he is shot, when he falls to the ground. There is nothing human about him; he looks like a discarded rag. Father stood there for about a minute – to mother and me it seemed like years. Then he bent down and began to bandage the human wreck that lay beside him on the pavement. Mother's eyes were half-closed and two big tears ran down her cheeks. I remember that she took me in her arms as if she wanted to smother me. Back then I did not know what had happened. I only felt the great tension, the unbearable tension and mother's distress.

Later, when I saw several times Czech policemen firing into a crowd of Czech workers, when I read about Slovaks wounded by Czech gendarmes, when I realised how hard it is not to run away when the whole crowd is running away, how unbelievably hard it is to *stand still* when something happens – only then did I understand how rare it is: the art of standing still.

Then I saw something similar once again. In totally different circumstances, of course. It was in the theatre during the war. At that time, Czechs were not yet thinking about independence and nothing of the sort was developing. Only the Czech character was stuck in their hearts like the thorn of a mallow from a Czech garden. On the stage, Tyl's *Fidlovačka* was being performed, a naïve piece, old and dull. But then all of a sudden they started to sing 'Kde domov můj'.[61] You know, back then it was not the national

---

61 'Where is my home?' Josef Kajetán Tyl (1808-1856) wrote the libretto for František Škroup's (1801-1862) *Fidlovačka* (The Shoemakers' Fair, 1834). One of the arias is 'Kde domov můj?', which became the national anthem of Czechoslovakia. Derek Sayer, 'The Language of Nationality and the Nationality of Language: Prague 1780-1920', *Past and Present*, 1996, no. 153, pp. 164-210, see pp. 188-189.

anthem, but only a Czech song. All of a sudden, however, someone stood up in front of me. Some gentleman, quiet and calm, with his hands at his sides. I do not know exactly what he wanted to say, but it was a kind of tribute to the Czech song. A moment later another person stood up. Then several more. Then we were all standing and singing. That song was played several times, played with such enthusiasm and ardour, like a prayer. '*Kde domov můj*' was not a song *against* anyone, but rather *for* something. It did not wish anyone's ruin, but rather our survival. It was not a militant song, but the song of our Czech homeland, this land with a mild landscape, a land of hills and knolls, fields and meadows, birches, willows and branching lindens, a land of quiet streams and fragrant baulks between fields. A land where we are at home. It was beautiful to stand for it because it is always beautiful to love one's homeland. I realised then that to know how to stand is dignified, honourable and forthright.

We are not, nor have we ever been in a position to take a stand *against* someone. If we ever did do so in the past out of youthful arrogance, we saw clearly that it did not bear fruit. We are also not in a position to trust anyone in the world, in good conscience, with a calm heart. If we ever did do so out of youthful inexperience, we saw clearly how little it took for the large states to break their promises to a small state with a wave of the hand – the same states that today, full of indignation, speak about the 'injustice that has been perpetrated against the small states'. Neither in our hearts nor in our character is there hatred for anyone. But rather a great love for what is Czech.

The past year has taught us one thing: one must know how to stand still. To stand by everything that is Czech, with head bared and an ardent love in one's heart, with profound dignity, openness and integrity. No nation in the world ever remained unbroken if it did not have the courage to declare its love for the nation, righteously and honourably. No nation in the world ever had a future if it was not willing to stand by the idea of the nation.

# Am I, First and Foremost, Czech?

## 10 May 1939, *Přítomnost*

Not long ago a certain person – altogether an admirable man of action and a great patriot – said to me: 'Whatever your opinions may be, I know that you are, first and foremost, Czech. I can sense it when I read your articles and it makes me happy.'

It was, therefore, a compliment and a great one at that. I should have been happy, therefore, because every compliment from commendable lips gives encouragement and dispels the suspicion that you are working in vain and in a vacuum. Because the person who said this was someone whose world outlook I would have rejected only a year ago, it was therefore also a pleasure to be sitting next to one another, to agree completely on the nature of the work to be done today and to shake hands warmly upon parting.

Yet the pleasure was spoiled by the formulation of the praise; probably it could have been expressed roughly thus: whatever kind of person you might be, you are, first and foremost, Czech and that is enough.

A good fourteen days have passed since then and wherever I go I carry the phrase with me: *first and foremost*. In my spare time, in walks around Prague in the spring – these days, a person all of a sudden feels uneasy in her apartment and she runs out to look, for example, at the weir, or at Petřín Hill, or Strahov Garden, in order to grasp a bit of Prague with her eyes and return home reassured – on the nights when I cannot sleep, in broken conversations with friends, everywhere the phrase creeps behind me: *first and foremost*. Now that I have mulled everything over, turned it upside down and reflected on it, I must, Sir, turn down the compliment. I am, *of course*, Czech, but *first and foremost* I try to be a decent person.

Please allow me to explain: we are all Czechs. That, in itself, does not mean anything. Seen through sober eyes, it is membership in a small nation that has all sorts of troubles and all sorts of worries. If people manage to wrest some kind of visa for themselves, in five years' time they can have American passports in their pockets and go about the world as American citizens, who definitely have fewer problems in the world. As far as I know, many of us have chosen a similar route. No, the fact that we are Czechs does not mean anything in itself. If this fact is not *first and foremost* tied to specific qualities, it loses its value. It is certainly a beautiful and proud feeling to be French and it is certainly uplifting to call the most beautiful song in the world one's national anthem. Nonetheless, in one week the French lost the respect of the world and today it is probably not so glorious to be French. You may object that it was only the French government that acted on behalf of the French people and that therefore only the government has lost the respect of the world and not France. Well, that is not what happened. It was the French people who cheered in the streets. Besides, in September 1938 the state of France was such that it simply would have been impossible – technically impossible – for the government to take a decision against the will of the people, if those people had acted decisively, bravely and honourably. Those people, however, cried for joy that their government had broken its word and they showered the men who had done so with flowers.[62]

In spite of everything we have lived through, I am firmly convinced that no Czech anywhere in the world has lost respect. The whole world was watching us and saw that this little nation behaved in a remarkable way.[63] When the hour arrived to adhere to the treaties, the whole nation stood behind its word, although it knew the cost of doing so. When it was a matter of enduring the losses with a calm face, we did so admirably. No one in the world could say that the Czechs were not determined and brave, honest and reliable allies. Today, however, the situation is different. Today it is a matter of maintaining one's own nationality in the sea of a foreign nationality. One's own freedom in the flood of a foreign freedom and one's own national character in the torrent of a foreign national character. Today it is a matter, first and foremost, of being *good* Czechs. We will not be that, however, if we are not, *first and foremost*, resolute people. Only through the identification of these concepts will the nation maintain the high moral standard that it has always had and that has won it the respect of the world.

That is not an easy concept: to be a good Czech. Of course, it is very easy to say and likewise easy to brandish this concept. To know what it means, however, and to demand it of oneself and others is a little more difficult. It would be a fateful mistake to assume that people can be content if they are united by nothing but common

---

62 In October 1938 Czech newspapers carried accounts of crowds in Paris celebrating the peace negotiated in Munich.

63 See Vladimír Macura's essay, 'Svět se na nás dívá' (The World is Watching Us), in his study on Czech national identity, *Masarykovy boty* (Masaryk's Boots), Prague, 1993, pp. 44–46.

nationality. This formation of eight million that is being created must have its own special content if it is to have any positive meaning. It must take over the spiritual expression of its true essence. It must stand up for the rights it has won for itself. It cannot be afraid – and it must know how to speak the truth.

We do not want to return to the past, but we do want to maintain our traditional character. For the Germans, it is obvious that we would want this. It would be good, however, if in the new unity of the nation every Czech also wanted it. We have a right to our own culture; we have a right to love the people who created this culture; we have a right to our own concepts of freedom, honour and work. We have a right to the high social standard that our people have enjoyed and access for all Czechs to Czech schools. For centuries, the Czech nation has been struggling for precisely this. The events of the last year have shown us very vividly that it is – due to the geographical position of this country – futile to realise this dream without consulting the Germans. For better for worse, we live next to one another and any politics that shuts its eyes to this fact is an unrealistic politics. The Germans are people who have always been able to build up a strong and powerful state, again and again. Under conditions more difficult than anyone else experienced, they overcame obstacles more serious than anyone else faced. We must always reckon with this neighbour, whose will to power is greater than any other kind of sentiment. To remain *free and good* Czechs in this proud and self-confident state, that is our task.

Not a small task. Although I believe the Germans of today when they say that respect for foreign nationality is as natural to them as respect for their own nationality, things have a logic and weight of their own and are sometimes shaped by the law of gravity, rather than by human will. It is in the essence of a large thing to weigh down on a small thing. A large tree overshadows a small tree and a large mountain casts a shadow on hills. Without even wanting to, the Germans today cast a shadow on the little nation in their midst; it is not their fault; it is a geographical reality. It is not that easy to know and uphold one's rights, to cultivate a little tree with distinct foliage in a forest of mighty trunks, to illuminate the shadow of a large nation with the light of one's own character. For this, resolute, hardened people are needed, ready to relinquish all comforts. For this, thorough and politically conscious work is needed. *First and foremost*, solidarity with the Czech people, who deserve more than to be left alone, who deserve to have us all remain here with them. *First and foremost*, love for these people, in whose cottages one finds the expression of the Czech spiritual essence. *First and foremost,* a strong will to justice and ideals. *First and foremost,* the personal bravery to insist on one's rights rather than surrender them voluntarily, as so often happens here. *First and foremost,* personal integrity and decency, which means being ashamed to vilify and disgrace another person – and that also, unfortunately, happens often. All these things together define what it is to be a good Czech.

The creation of a single political party was a political necessity. To give this political necessity a positive role: that is what we all must do. 'To unite' is a beautiful phrase.[64] But it is not enough to unite because we are all Czechs. It is necessary to unite as *good* Czechs.

---

64 Jesenská here refers to the 'Národní souručenství' (National Union) the sole political organisation tolerated by the Nazis in the Protectorate of Bohemia and Moravia, created in the spring of 1939. *Souručenství*: union, partnership, community spirit.

# Soldaten wohnen auf den Kanonen ...
## 21 June 1939, Přítomnost

That is a German song and one of the prettiest.[65] As far as army songs are concerned, the German ones are always prettier – or more soldierly – than ours. We had 'Flower in the Cap', 'Come along, My Dear and Live a Little too', 'Rosemary' – a sort of lyrical, private singing along in time to the stride. The Germans have army songs that are manly, for marching. In general, if anyone asked me what at first sight was the most obvious difference between Germans and Czechs, I would say: their gait. Czech soldiers used to go by under the window, making a slapping sound on the pavement. Now a single German rookie walks through a café and the glasses tremble and plaster falls from the ceiling, but he thinks he is treading quietly and carefully. He does not want to hurt anyone; it is just the German character that moves him from the knees down.

In this gait one sees, above all, the relation of a soldier to an army and in the other gait, the relation of a citizen to an army: self-confidence and other soldierly virtues tread, one two, one two, through the world. For many hundreds of years, the entire German nation has been raised in the belief that the greatest virtue of a citizen is to be a solider. A German becomes a soldier even if it means that his private life recedes into the background, that he does not go to all the schools that he had, perhaps, dreamed of in his youth, that he does not learn a trade but goes soldiering with a resolute step in time to a marching song.

For Czechs, the army was something different. Private individuals put on a soldier's coat for a while and the rest of us hardly even noticed. They went about quietly, they behaved modestly and there were never enough of them to change the character of the streets of any particular city. They did not have time for cafés or pubs. The farmer, the shoemaker, the cottager, the teacher, the doctor and the worker went to learn their civic duty, without seeing it as any unusual service. I think that the shoemaker set more store by well-made shoes

---

65 Literally: the soldiers live on the cannons. The title is taken from the anti-war 'Cannon Song' in Act I, scene 2 of Bertolt Brecht's *Threepenny Opera* (1928). The line has been translated felicitously as: 'The troops live under/The cannon's thunder'. See Bertolt Brecht, *The Threepenny Opera* (*Die Dreigroschenoper*), trans. John Willett and Ralph Manheim, London, 1979.

and the worker by the smooth operation of the machine entrusted to him than by dexterity in using a hand grenade. The swing-plough, sledgehammer and chisel were more pleasing to the Czech palm than the trigger of a gun. Consequently, this difference was manifest in the relation between the citizens and the army. Let us admit: on the whole, we did not know anything about it. No propaganda informed us about it, nor did anyone explain to us the importance of the army. We knew vaguely: when things are bad, the soldiers will defend the country. We did not have a clear idea how this trade was learned – we did not even realise that, in the present era, it is the greatest of all trades. We knew that we had excellent people, that we all loved our country, that we were able to produce superb weapons because we did superb work in general. No one had any doubts, either at home or abroad, about the quality of the Czech soldier – but this was because no one could doubt the quality of our work in general. When a Czech did something, he did it well, dispassionately, modestly and quietly. Our army was the same. This was the basic difference: if Germans were good citizens because they were good soldiers, with us it was the opposite, we were good soldiers because we were good citizens.

## Twenty Thousand out on the Pavement

With the liquidation of the Czech army, twenty thousand of our professional soldiers – from non-commissioned officers to generals – ended up on the pavement.[66] If we lived through the recent days with anxious hearts, these men lived through them a hundred times more intensively. It was their trade, after all, to defend this country. They devoted themselves to this task, learned it and lived it. They prepared for it for twenty years – and then they were not permitted to carry it out.[67] They wear their civilian clothes a little uneasily; you can recognise a soldier and a commander at first sight by their stiff legs, even

---

66 Mastny comments: 'Hitler ordered the Czechoslovak army demobilized and the military service of Protectorate nationals abolished. [...] He thought it advisable to order good pensions for the officers who were forced to retire, hoping that this would be the safest way to curb their militancy. The Protectorate was allowed to maintain only a pathetic Government Force. It consisted of 7000 men armed with light weapons and intended for auxiliary police duties.' Mastny, *The Czechs under Nazi Rule*, p. 61.

67 On 29 September 1938, a number of Czechoslovak generals tried to convince President Beneš (1884–1948) to resist the pressure to cede land to Germany and make use of the army. Beneš refused. When the Germans occupied the country in March 1939, President Emil Hácha (1872–1945) ordered the Czech troops not to resist. Mastny, *The Czechs under Nazi Rule*, pp. 19, 41.

in civilian trousers. Now they start to go about in their own country with the aching hearts of pensioners. I know doctors who retired when we began to make a racket about 'youth to the fore'. They walk on tiptoe – in actual fact and in their thoughts – past their former clinics – and when you look in their faces you have the impression that to lose one's place of work is the worst thing that can happen to a person. And those are private individuals who had the opportunity to carry out their work. 'All his life a soldier learns that life has no value,' a colonel wearing a grey suit, a shirt and tie, told me. 'You see, life is only a banknote that a soldier changes into a better future for his people.' He expressed this better future with such a broad, hopeful curve of his arm, while he only squeezed the paper between his thumb and forefinger, like a coin that can be broken down into change. These twenty thousand troops stand among us; they have a college education, but above all, they have a high moral standard. They are people with an unusual training and outlook, an unusual moral discipline. And the nation? It is a shame that it pays as little attention to them and knows as little about them now as it did before.

## Men Who Do Not Complain

It is in the nature of a soldier that he does not know how to complain. If we are now compelled to look on people in terms of professions, well then, this is a profession and a guild the basic instrument of which is courage. Then discipline and self-discipline – which is the same thing – and then organisation. When you speak to them and learn about their twenty years' experience, you begin to understand that this enormous organisation was a school for the nation, a school that every healthy man from every class went through. That this organisation, the way it used to be, in its developed sense of statehood but absolutely apolitical character, came closest to what we strive for so laboriously today: unity. Soldiers have vast organisational experience. In terms of mentality, they are very close to the ruling system; it could not be otherwise. A person cannot help but ask why, for God's sake, when we were negotiating the matter of entrusting the affairs of state to a unified, non-party and non-political organisation, we did not make use of this trained apparatus, which can do other things besides soldier? At any rate, what we need at the moment is so similar to soldiering without weapons that it seems tragically grotesque that these very men, in this situation, in this state, are without work. The opportunity, of course, has passed and it is futile to reflect on it. Now another question arises: what will they do today and mainly, what will they do when the government stops paying them a salary, which is supposed to happen dangerously soon?

One thing is certain: they have not been idle. They have not stopped even for a moment. As soon as it was clear that their work was coming to an end, they began to train for other occupations. The officers' association took the last step and arranged several courses for these men. They all had an excellent preliminary education and a high level of knowledge. Many of them took a number of courses in order to escape from lethargy, thus today they have exceptional qualifications. I personally was interested in the course that trained officers to be farmers. How does a person 'who lived under the cannon's thunder' change if he is supposed to live by the plough? What happens to a man who was raised to kill and let himself be killed if he is supposed to sow potatoes and grow beets? Is it a painful rupture in his manner of thinking? I went from soldier to soldier with this question, looking for an answer.

## Does a Soldier Make a Good Farmer?

Sometimes I got an indulgent smile, sometimes a cheerful laugh, but always a look of amazement. Trained to kill? How's that? Trained to defend his homeland. Isn't that the same thing? But of course it is not the same thing. We did not want to kill anyone. We wanted to put up a defence, so that you, for example, would not be killed. You are very much mistaken when you look at it that way, a man in one of the highest-ranking uniforms with many decorations on his chest told me. Look here: on 1 October those boys would come to me from every nook and cranny and then we had to *raise* them. In some counties literally, believe me. Sometimes we taught them to read and write, to use a toothbrush and to wash. After a few months, a collective grew up under my hands, a collective in which the moral values needed to make a good army could be cultivated: camaraderie, bravery, truthfulness, courage and hardiness. You don't know how wonderful it was to see a group spirit, so to speak, emerge from this random and formless handful of people. In a year's time they were changed people. They returned home and took away with them what they had learned. Why, it was a great school for the nation; you can't even imagine how close we grew to those people and what kind of comradely and good bond existed between us. How many of them went through my hands! How I trained them! Ranked them! Taught them! How well I understood them .... Well, I did not learn anything else because tears began to run like little glass beads down the cheeks of this man, whose own life was indifferent to him, when he thought of his rookies, from the hearts of which he had struck the best sparks of human dignity.

One thing is clear from this: it was positive, creative work. This kind of collective unit cannot be pieced together without the work of individuals. *The question of struggle is a question of nerves*, one soldier told me. If people are to have good nerves, their character must be trained. We turn people inside out. We know how to do it. A soldier will make a better worker than anyone else. He has a greater sense of duty and will naturally try to carry out his task as best he can. He will want to apply his instinct for organisation, his abilities and experience to everyday life. He will build in the garden and in the field in the same way that he built in the barracks. Or even better. The course gave him mainly a theoretical knowledge, but nonetheless the best and the most modern. All over the Czech Lands, people work according to the old traditions and tradition is 'a beautiful thing, but sometimes it is a monster that binds the ankles with a ball and chain'. On Czech soil, our former soldier could be an educator for the entire village.

## What Did They Learn?

All sorts of things. Here is a random list of the lectures they attended under the understanding and enthusiastic direction of our best specialists: veterinary care. Agricultural economics. (This is a separate discipline about the break-down of agricultural capital, profit, interest, amortisation, taxes, insurance and so on.) Dairy farming. Plant hygiene. Vegetable and fruit growing. Fodder crops. Root crops. The cultivation of cereal crops, legumes and oleiferous plants. Fertilisation and fertilisers. Treatment of the soil. The breeding and raising of cattle and hogs. The raising of small farm animals. The organisation of an agricultural enterprise. Each of these things is a science in itself. A science that has progressed in modern times further than the layman would suspect. Knowledge of this science is a national asset because the raising of pigs, for example, is something highly patriotic, as is the proper exploitation of the soil. It is true that soldiers who have completed theoretical courses need experience. Now it is a matter of providing them with this experience.

Some of them who have access to the land – either enough money to buy a piece of land, but that is very rare, or relatives who own land – will soon be able to make use of their newly acquired experience. They will throw off their military coats and take charge of the management of some farm, croft, orchard or vegetable garden and I have no doubt that in a year's time they will be successful, as all assiduous people are. But there are also men here who do not have the slightest prospect of acquiring land or a position in agriculture.

Then there is, of course, the question – forgive me, men, that I speak about it – of how the nation will behave towards its army. Whether it will ask its former officers to stand on healthy legs on the street corners and beg, or whether it will give them work. There is a lot of talk here of patriotism. There is no shortage of noble words or of good sentiments either. Now, however, it is necessary to ask something of people. It will be the eternal shame of this nation that in these times the industrialists, landowners, manufacturers and rich people have not been able to provide their people with work. Everyone who employs five people should feel an obligation to employ six, even if he is not prospering. The trains that carry Czechs to work abroad are the most serious indictment against us. Work should and must be found here at home for the Czech clerk, worker and farmer. Why hasn't a commission been formed that could go from enterprise to enterprise – agricultural and industrial – and ascertain how many more people each enterprise could support? The regulated economy that is the rule all around us shines its lights on us and makes our shadows stand out more sharply. Because a regulated economy is, among other things, the sort that can command an entrepreneur to look after as many people as his enterprise can support, even if it means that this trouble will cost him the loss of his personal comfort.

Now we find ourselves in a situation in which we have to look after twenty thousand former active officers. The state has decided on certain measures. The rest is once again left up to personal initiative, individual ability and chance. The quality of these people is a national asset. But no one *commands* us to make use of this national asset.

I do not doubt that one way or another our soldiers will make the most of their lot. Now it is up to the nation to remember them and to correct the mistake it has made, to value its army, finally, although now it is no more than a peacetime army. If our path in the future is to be one of peace then this army will be just the kind that is needed.

And you, men without uniforms, I will not bid you farewell! You are here with us and you will work with us on the work that has to be done. Blue overalls for the fields will suit you just as well as the uniforms did. I cannot but believe that you will find beautiful and honourable work among us. The nation will need you now more than ever.

# Select Bibliography

## Primary Sources

### Newspapers
*Lidové noviny*
*Národní listy*
*Přítomnost*
*Tribuna*

*Works by Milena Jesenská*

Jesenská, Milena. *Cesta k jednoduchosti* (The Path to Simplicity). Prague, Topič, 1926.

Jesenská, Milena. *Člověk dělá šaty* (The Individual Makes the Clothes). Prague, Topič, 1927.

Jesenská, Milena. *Zvenčí a zevnitř. Antologie textů Mileny Jesenské* (Inside and Out. An Anthology of Texts by Milena Jesenská). Hegnerová, Ludmila, ed. Prague, Franz Kafka Publishing House, 1996.

Jesenská, Milena. *Nad naše síly. Češi, Židé a Němci 1937–1939* (Beyond Our Strength. Czechs, Jews and Germans 1937–1939). Selected by Václav Burian. Olomouc, Votobia, 1997.

Jesenská, Milena, Hoffmeister, A., Ma-Fa, Mollenda, Miloš, Eiselt, J. and Marot-Oumanský, J. *Šťastnou cestu* (Have a Good Trip!). Prague, Topič, 1927.

## Secondary Sources

### Biographies of Milena Jesenská

Buber-Neumann, Margarete. *Milena. The Tragic Story of Kafka's Great Love* (*Kafkas Freundin Milena*, 1977). Manheim, Ralph, trans. New York, Arcade Publishing, 1997.

Černá, Jana. *Kafka's Milena* (*Adresát Milena Jesenská*, 1969). Brain, A. G., trans. Evanston, Illinois, Northwestern University Press, 1993. Introduction and new translations by George Gibian, 1993.

Hockaday, Mary. *Kafka, Love and Courage. The Life of Milena Jesenská* (1995). Woodstock, New York, The Overlook Press, 1997.

Jirásková, Marie. *Stručná zpráva o trojí volbě. Milena Jesenská, Joachim von Zedtwitz a Jaroslav Nachtmann v roce 1939 a v čase následujícím* (A Brief Account of Three Kinds of Choices. Milena Jesenská, Joachim von Zedtwitz and Jaroslav Nachtmann in 1939 and later). Prague, Franz Kafka Publishing House, 1996.

Marková-Kotyková, Marta. *Mýtus Milena. Milena Jesenská jinak* (The Myth of Milena. Another Perspective on Milena Jesenská). Prague, Primus, 1993.

Wagnerová, Alena. *Milena Jesenská* (*Milena Jesenská. Biographie*, 1994). Bláhová, Alena, trans. Prague, Prostor, 1996.

Wagnerová, Alena, ed. *Dopisy Mileny Jesenské* (The Letters of Milena Jesenská). With translations by Josef Čermák and Marie Janů. Prague, Prostor, 1998.

226 Bibliography

## Background Sources

Anderson, Mark M. *Kafka's Clothes: Ornament and Aestheticism in the Habsburg Fin de Siècle.* Oxford, Clarendon Press, 1992.

Barker, Elisabeth. *Austria 1918-1972.* Basingstoke and London, Macmillan, 1973.

Blanický, O. G. *O antisemitismu v českém národě* (The Anti-Semitism of the Czech Nation). Prague, Obrození, 1919.

Brod, Max. *Franz Kafka. A Biography* (1960). Roberts, Humphreys G. and Winston, Richard, trans. Second enlarged edition. New York, Da Capo Press, 1995.

Carsten, F. L. *The Rise of Fascism.* London, B. T. Batsford, 1967.

Černý, Bohumil. *Most k novému životu. Německá emigrace v ČSR v letech 1933-1939* (Bridge to a New Life. The German Emigrés in Czechoslovakia 1933-1939). Prague, Lidová demokracie, 1967.

Cornwall, Mark. 'Dr Edvard Beneš and Czechoslovakia's German Minority, 1918-1943'. In Morison, John, ed. *The Czech and Slovak Experience.* Houndmills, St Martin's Press, 1992, pp. 167-202.

Eubank, Keith. 'Munich'. In Mamatey, Victor S. and Luža, Radomír, eds. *A History of the Czechoslovak Republic 1918-1948.* Princeton, Princeton University Press, 1973, pp. 239-252.

Gebhart, Jan and Kuklík, Jan. *Dramatické i všední dny protektorátu* (Dramatic and Ordinary Days in the Protectorate). Prague, Themis, 1996.

Gilbert, Martin. *The Holocaust. The Jewish Tragedy.* London, Fontana Press, 1987.

Gilman, Sander, *The Jew's Body.* London and New York, Routledge, 1991.

Gilman, Sander. *Franz Kafka, the Jewish Patient.* London and New York, Routledge, 1995.

Holy, Ladislav. *The Little Czech and the Great Czech Nation: national identity and the post-communist transformation of society.* Cambridge, Cambridge University Press, 1996.

Horneková, B., Rossmann, Zdeněk and Vaněk, Jan, eds. *Civilisovaná žena, Zivilisierte Frau* (The Civilised Woman). Brno, Jan Vaněk, 1929.

Iggers, Wilma Abeles. *Women of Prague. Ethnic Diversity and Social Change from the Eighteenth Century to the Present.* Oxford and Providence, Berghahn Books, 1995.

Janik, Allan and Toulmin, Stephen. *Wittgenstein's Vienna.* New York, Simon and Schuster, 1973.

Kafka, Franz. *Letters to Milena* (*Briefe an Milena*, 1952). Boehm, Philip, trans. New York, Schocken Books, 1990. This edition is based on the enlarged and revised German edition, edited by Jürgen Born and Michael Müller, published by Fischer Verlag GmbH, Frankfurt, 1983. It also includes translations of five articles by Jesenská.

Kafka, Franz. *The Complete Stories* (1971). Glatzer, Nahum N., ed. With foreword by John Updike. New York, Schocken Books, 1983.

Kennan, George F. *From Prague After Munich: Diplomatic Papers 1938-1940.* Princeton, Princeton University Press, 1968.

Lahoda, Vojtěch, Nešlehová, Mahulena, Platovská, Marie, Švácha, Rostislav and Bydžovská, Lenka, eds. *Dějiny českého výtvarného umění* (The History of Czech Art). 1890/1938, vol. IV/2. Prague, Academia, 1998.

Macura, Vladimír. *Masarykovy boty* (Masaryk's Boots). Prague, Pražská imaginace, 1993.

Mamatey, Victor S. and Luža, Radomír, eds. *A History of the Czechoslovak Republic 1918–1948*. Princeton, Princeton University Press, 1973.

Mastny, Vojtech. *The Czechs Under Nazi Rule*. London and New York, Columbia University Press, 1971.

Mendelsohn, Ezra. *East Central Europe between the Wars*. Bloomington, Indiana University Press, 1987.

Morison, John, ed. *The Czech and Slovak Experience*. Houndmills, St Martin's Press, 1992.

Pachmanová, Martina. 'Collective Desires: Czech Avant-garde Architecture and the Production of Degendered Space'. *Umění*, 2000, no. 4, pp. 265–276.

Pasák, Tomáš. 'Problematika protektorátního tisku a formování tzv. skupiny aktivistických novinářů na počátku okupace' (The Problems of the Protectorate Press and the Formation of the Group of So-called Activist Journalists at the Beginning of the Occupation). *Příspěvky k dějinám KSČ* (Contributions to the History of the CPC), 1967, vol. 7, pp. 52–80.

Pasák, Tomáš. *Pod ochranou říše* (Under the Protection of the Reich). Prague, Práh, 1998.

Péter, Lászlo and Pynsent, Robert B., eds. *Intellectuals and the Future in the Habsburg Monarchy 1890–1914*. Basingstoke and London, Macmillan, 1988.

Prochazka, Theodor. 'The Second Republic, 1938–1939'. In Mamatey, Victor S. and Luža, Radomír, eds. *A History of the Czechoslovak Republic 1918–1948*. Princeton, Princeton University Press, 1973, pp. 255–70.

Pynsent, Robert B. *Questions of Identity. Czech and Slovak Ideas of Nationality and Personality*. Budapest, London and New York, Central European University Press, 1994.

Pynsent, Robert B. 'The Decadent Nation: The Politics of Arnošt Procházka and Jiří Karásek ze Lvovic'. In Péter, Lászlo and Pynsent, Robert B., eds. *Intellectuals and the Future in the Habsburg Monarchy 1890–1914*. Basingstoke and London, Macmillan Press, 1988, pp. 63–91.

Sayer, Derek. 'The Language of Nationality and the Nationality of Language: Prague 1780–1920'. *Past and Present*, 1996, no. 153, pp. 164–210.

Sayer, Derek. *The Coasts of Bohemia. A Czech History*. Princeton, Princeton University Press, 1998.

Schorske, Carl E. *Fin-de-siècle Vienna. Politics and Culture*. New York, Vintage Books, 1981.

Švácha, Rostislav. *The Architecture of New Prague 1895–1945* (*Od moderny k funkcionalismu*, 1985). Büchler, Alexandra, trans. Cambridge MA and London, The MIT Press, 1995.

Švácha, Rostislav. 'Architektura dvacátých let v Čechách' (The Architecture of the 1920s in Bohemia). In Lahoda, Vojtěch, Nešlehová, Mahulena, Platovská, Marie, Švácha, Rostislav and Bydžovská, Lenka, eds. *Dějiny českého výtvarného umění* (The History of Czech Art). 1890/1938, vol. IV/2. Prague, Academia, 1998, pp. 11–35.

Uchalová, Eva. *Česká móda 1918–1939. Elegance první republiky* (Czech Fashion 1918–1939. The Elegance of the First Republic). Prague, Olympia and the Museum of Decorative Arts in Prague, 1996.

Unseld, Joachim. *Franz Kafka: A Writer's Life* (*Franz Kafka. Ein Schriftstellerleben*, 1982). Dvorak, Paul F., trans. Riverside CA, Ariadne Press, 1994.

## Reference Works

Huňáček, Zdeněk, Jožák, Jiří, Kroupa, Vlastislav and Stříbrny, Jan. *Český antifašismus a odboj* (Czech Anti-fascism and the Resistance). Prague, Naše vojsko, 1988.

*Ottův slovník naučný* (The Otto Encyclopaedia). Prague, J. Otto, 1888–1909.

*The New Encyclopaedia Britannica.* Fifteenth edition. Chicago, 1992.

*Všeobecné encyklopedie ve čtyřech svazcích* (General Encyclopaedia in Four Volumes). Prague, Diderot, 1996–1998.

Wistrich, Robert S. *Who's Who in Nazi Germany.* London and New York, Routledge, 1995.

# Index

Lightning Source UK Ltd.
Milton Keynes UK
UKOW041448110412

190295UK00002B/1/P